Emergence of the Caribbean Empire

Emergence of the Caribbean Empire

Politics and Labour in Trinidad and Tobago, 1918–1976

Jerome Teelucksingh

PETER LANG
Oxford - Berlin - Bruxelles - Chennai - Lausanne - New York

Bibliographic information published by the Deutsche Nationalbibliothek.
The German National Library lists this publication in the German National Bibliography; detailed bibliographic data is available on the Internet at http://dnb.d-nb.de.

A catalogue record for this book is available from the British Library.

Library of Congress Cataloging-in-Publication Data

Names: Teelucksingh, Jerome, author.
Title: Emergence of the Caribbean empire : politics and labour in Trinidad and Tobago, 1918-1976 / Jerome Teelucksingh.
Description: New York : Peter Lang, [2024] | Includes bibliographical references.
Identifiers: LCCN 2023057828 (print) | LCCN 2023057829 (ebook) | ISBN 9781803743721 (paperback) | ISBN 9781803743738 (ebook) | ISBN 9781803743745 (epub)
Subjects: LCSH: Trinidad Workingmen's Association. | Labor movement--Trinidad and Tobago--History. | Labor policy--Trinidad and Tobago--History. | Labor unions--Trinidad and Tobago--History. | Working class--Political activity--Trinidad and Tobago--History.
Classification: LCC HD6595.7.T43 2024 (print) | LCC HD6595.7.T43 2024 (ebook) | DDC 331.880972983--dc23/eng/20240116
LC record available at https://lccn.loc.gov/2023057828
LC ebook record available at https://lccn.loc.gov/2023057829

Cover image: The Parliament building, Port-of-Spain, Trinidad & Tobago.
Cover design by Peter Lang Group AG

ISBN 978-1-80374-372-1 (print)
ISBN 978-1-80374-373-8 (ePDF)
ISBN 978-1-80374-374-5 (ePub)
DOI 10.3726/b21491

Published by Peter Lang Ltd, Oxford, United Kingdom
info@peterlang.com - www.peterlang.com

This publication has been peer reviewed.

Dedicated to trade unionists involved in party politics

Contents

Foreword

This volume is crafted by Jerome Teelucksingh, a patriotic historian of Trinidad and Tobago and the wider Caribbean region, whose energy, integrity and insight resonate not only within the islands but also echo across oceans, captivating scholars and community activists alike, even reaching the shores of the United States. A vital resource for those looking towards the heritage of Trinidad and Tobago for vistas of freedom and democracy, this book, by illuminating what we can be and do in our own place and time, not only reminds us of the struggles and triumphs of a small Caribbean nation but also speaks to perennial matters of modern politics on a global scale, of which such imperial centres are but a small fraction.

This study on the origins of party politics in Trinidad and Tobago can be read as a precursor to the heroic mass social movements, wherein themes of labour's sovereignty and national purpose were championed by the middle classes of Trinidad and Tobago during the electoral campaigns of the 1920s and 1930s. However, this warrants further attention and debate. These earlier campaigns can be read as foreshadowing those launched by the People's National Movement (PNM), Workers and Farmers Party (WFP) of 1965–1966 and United Labour Front (ULF) of 1975–1977. Teelucksingh's lucid account of labour's involvement in party politics in Trinidad from 1925 to 1938 underscores the importance of recognizing the profound role played by ordinary people in revitalizing political processes. But here, a question of principle arises: how should this involvement be interpreted in the twenty-first-century context?

Democracy has two contradictory meanings: the justification of existing and aspiring states and ruling elites versus a tradition of revolutionary popular liberation or direct self-governance. Intrinsic to these conflicting notions of democracy is the meaning of working-class sovereignty or majority rule. Teelucksingh's book is constructed in such a creative manner that the reader can discern both meanings of labour in this narrative if one peruses carefully.

First, there is "labour" as a Fabian moral economy of the middle classes, where there is an aspiration to a progressive guardianship – a claim to be a defender of the ordinary people who are viewed as agents unfit for self-government. The socialist sentiment expressed by early and later Trinidad politicians primarily manifests as administrative rather than direct democratic content or a vision of popular self-management. This can be lost in a historical context, especially in the period the author discusses, where British colonialism did not view even the colonized middle classes as suited for such a task and condescendingly claimed to tutor the nation of Trinidad and Tobago as a whole. Labour Parties are means through which the middle classes co-opt the democratic significance of the working classes (as embodying majority rule) where subsequent to the election only a minority will directly rule.

This holds true in both imperial and peripheral nations. To not take this proposition seriously is to attribute political power and privileges to ordinary people in imperial nations that they do not, in fact, structurally have. Whatever the aristocracy of political economy, party politics is indeed more "backward" in imperial nations. There is rarely even the pretence of electoral politics being regarded as a social movement. Much like in the Caribbean, electoral politics appear to adopt a radical stance only when independent revolts among ordinary people are pervasive.

In imperial nations, economies can be planned more independently and with less corruption. However, this raises other problematic questions. Is our ultimate version of democracy the wish for an accountable middle class in a bureaucratic office? Is the gravest insult of colonialism that it would not allow the Trinidad and Tobago middle classes to govern themselves as equals in the world and manage and exploit its very own nation's labour from on high? Which class leads the national liberation struggle? In fact, it is the very notion of Caribbean as well as American populist lamentations that those who govern from on high are not in charge. These politicians, without stepping down, bemoan that they are structurally obstructed from doing their job. Politicians in both the Caribbean and America complain of multinational capital's insensitivity to the man on the street. And then rejecting real popular self-management, attacks on other ethnic groups and immigrants commence (subtly or overtly). It is a universal feature of capitalist electoral politics that, even at its best, such scapegoating lurks just below the surface.

Second, in Teelucksingh's account, there is a crowd politics where masses gather to hear what politicians have to say at rallies around and below a platform or podium. Politics for everyday people becomes an "activity" where, only for a time, they can be heard in conversation with those who aspire to represent them. At times, the masses fight through the authority of those on the microphone or with the bullhorn by making some damning and humorous criticism. Although they can judge speeches and programmes, and those who may make policies in the future, as members of a crowd, they cannot, through this format, directly craft and execute politics and govern themselves. This can become obscure if Labour Parties are allowed to be seen as liberators. Further, if involvement of ordinary citizens in mass meetings is viewed as an enhancement of the electoral process, is facilitating such activities a major sign of a "masses-oriented" political party? Or is it a mode of co-opting and bewildering their direct democratic potential?

In Chapter 3, Teelucksingh focuses on the crowds that attended the aspiring middle-class Labour campaigns in Trinidad and Tobago. These parties function as vehicles of ethnic patronage and tend to be owned by families with business interests, however small in the world economy. These parties are erected and dissolved to comment on national purpose, taxation, infrastructure-building for industry, utilities and roads as a means to rally the masses around themselves as paternalistic guardians, which serves their business interests well even if state power is not achieved.

But this does not explain the most heroic moments of electoral campaigns as expressed by the early PNM, WFP and ULF. They were perceived as heroic precisely for their aspirations for multiracial unity, and their business interests did not appear to be a major preoccupation of its leadership. Certainly, these campaigns too raised the banner of labour as merely a theme of working-class sovereignty fomenting no more autonomy than the crowd politics of this earlier period discussed in this volume. The personal integrity of the leading individual politicians and organizers cannot be the standard of understanding. One must look at their political thoughts and practices that reflect on labour's relationship to national purpose for demystification.

Undoubtedly, C. L. R. James' *Party Politics in the West Indies* (1962) is the gold standard for critical political thought on electoral parties in the Caribbean. It is conventional wisdom that this text documents James' rift with the first Premier and Prime Minister, Eric Williams. The book has a certain reputation as a radical document because previously the author had a long career as a revolutionary socialist (not a Stalinist, Social Democrat or Fabian) in Britain and the United States. Williams refused to implement his prescriptions for making the PNM a mass party after independence. Such a party would, through a cultural apparatus, legislate the popular will of a people with a dual character.

James attests that it is people's self-mobilization, not that of their leaders who embody it briefly, which has contributed significantly to the history of freedom struggles in Trinidad. However, these ordinary people do not know exactly what they want and hence must be encouraged to build their independent organizations where they can develop unique programmes and perspectives. This implies the dual nature of middle-class bureaucracy in James' politics for peripheral nations.

This mass orientation, James says, would enhance what the government can do and is not a threat to Williams' party. In the same breath, he concludes that politics merely imagined as an election is a form of degradation. But, in fact, while Williams did not take up James' suggestions, James merely sees the working masses as an appendage to an aspiring progressive developmental state and its leader if they are smart enough to orchestrate their popular self-activity instead of calling for the army and police to smash them from time to time.

Franklyn Harvey's classic *The Rise and Fall of Party Politics in Trinidad and Tobago* (1974) critiques his mentor James and his concept of the mass party. If independent popular committees and assemblies of the working class are not organized independently of the middle classes, Harvey concludes, their sovereignty will be perennially stolen. Thus, electoral politics, even at its best, is an inherently compromised medium.

The New Beginning Movement, of which Harvey was a co-leader with Bukka Rennie and Wally Look Lai, lent critical support to the ULF to educate the Trinidad and Tobago public in another fashion. The ULF, like the early PNM and the WFP, was an opaque coalition of the middle and working classes, despite suggesting labour could hold the reins of society.

At their best, the ULF would have allowed workers' sovereignty indirectly. If the ULF had achieved state power, any independent organizations of the working classes would likely have been viewed as a threat. Thus, in any Labour Party campaign where there was significant mass "involvement," the urgent task was for everyday people to defend their autonomy in popular committees within that movement from the middle classes as well as to be prepared to break away from those who aspire to enter the rules of hierarchy despite their claims of being labour's champion.

From ancient Greeks to the Soviets in the Russian Revolution in 1917, from the Indo-Caribbean heritage of the panchayat to the Afro-Caribbean tradition of maroonage, in addition to the general strikes of the turbulent 1930s, there has always been more to the Jamesian adage that "every cook can govern" in popular councils and committees. The limitations of direct democratic forms (not the ideal), including mass assemblies and popular committees, need further study. They can have a populist and indirect hierarchical character of their own, even independent of electoral politics and representative government, when distinguished by professional politicians who rule as a class above society.

Darcus Howe, a radical activist based in England, has posited that James' ideal was "every cook can govern" not must or ought to govern. This interpretation shouldn't be read as sophistry on Howe's part; rather, it can be seen as a profound insight into James' most radical inclinations. This reminder should broaden the significance of Teelucksingh's work which critically examines early electoral campaigns that captivated the masses for a time in Trinidad and Tobago's history. The vibrancy and objectivity of the author's account allow readers to go back in time, become immersed in these campaigns and crowds as well as decide for themselves whether labour can truly hold the reins through electoral politics.

Matthew Quest*
United States

* Dr Matthew Quest has taught history and political thought at the Empire State College in New York City and Lewis University in Illinois, United States. He was a visiting lecturer in the Department of History at Georgia State University. He is a member of the editorial board of the *CLR James Journal* and has published articles on C. L. R. James, George Padmore, Frantz Fanon and Tim Hector.

Preface

In earlier publications, I have justified the existence of a Caribbean Empire. This book reinforced the argument that the Caribbean Empire had been formulated, though flawed, during the occupation of the Americans and Europeans in the region. The creation and propagation of rifts among the population, denial of voting rights and suppression of labour voices have been part of the tragedies of colonialism and imperialism. Those from the United States and Europe sought to abort the birth of the Caribbean Empire. However, the working-class leaders and trade unions remained steadfast in their demands for justice, equality and representation.

Many citizens in the Caribbean would view trade unions as irrelevant. Often there is a perception that the activities of unions were limited to protests and efforts to "shut down" the country. Many unions were seen as performing the limited role of obtaining higher wages and better working conditions for their members. Much of the public is not aware that, prior to 1962, trade unions were the most powerful opponents of colonialism and imperialism. Caribbean citizens owe their independence to the long struggle of labour leaders and members who undermined European colonialism.

Labour made an invaluable contribution to the political evolution of Trinidad and Tobago during the turbulent and formative period between 1925 and 1938. There is a need for a greater appreciation of the work of the pioneers and nation-builders who led a new wave of emancipation from the political enslavement of colonial rule and accelerated the process of decolonization, self-determination and independence. Colonial rule was the matrix for the emergence of labour-inspired leadership, which confronted metropolitan oppression and challenged its dominance in factories, ports and plantations.

In 1925, a new Constitution was implemented which allowed seven elected members in the Legislative Council. The Trinidad Workingmen's Association (TWA), formed in 1894, and emerging trade unions optimistically and eagerly participated in the elections during the 1920s and 1930s.

This study will demonstrate that the TWA, transformed into the Trinidad Labour Party (TLP) in August 1934, along with independent candidates representing labour laid the foundation for twentieth-century party politics. Interestingly, the TWA/TLP functioned as both a trade union (even though it was not registered) and a political party. The work will attempt to prove that the comprehensive organizational skills of the TWA/TLP in organizing meetings, selecting candidates, campaigning for votes and debating issues on the electoral platform were determining factors which resulted in creditable performances in the municipal elections and ensured limited electoral victories in four elections: 1925, 1928, 1933 and 1938.

Instances of heckling, rhetoric and mudslinging as reported in the *Labour Leader*, *The People*, *Trinidad Guardian* and *Port-of-Spain Gazette* have been included. Such reports are pivotal in understanding the composition, behaviour and responses of the crowd at meetings. Furthermore, these newspaper articles allowed for a partial reconstruction of the political scenario to better evaluate the speakers, their support among the masses and their interest in the concerns of the disenfranchised masses. The responses of speakers to occasional heckling (or picong) from the crowd illustrate the informal nature of these meetings. An overview of the speeches and allegations of independent labour and non-labour candidates who opposed candidates from the TWA/TLP reveals a battle to convince the electorate who were the bona fide representatives of the working class. Undoubtedly, the nature and conduct of electioneering campaigns would serve as a blueprint for future national and municipal elections.

From the 1920s to 1940, labour had a strong presence in the Port-of-Spain Borough Council. Among these, members who served as Mayor included Tito Achong (1941–1942, 1942–1943), Alfred Richards (1936–1937, 1940–1941), Arthur Cipriani (1929–1930, 1930–1931, 1931–1932, 1933–1934, 1934–1935, 1935–1936, 1938–1939, 1939–1940) and C. H. Pierre (1924–1925). Furthermore, Richards, Pierre, Cipriani, Achong and L. A. Pujadas also served as Deputy Mayor during the 1920s and 1930s. Undoubtedly, the involvement of these persons in municipal politics boosted the publicity and credibility of labour candidates in the national electoral campaigns.

It was an attempt by labour to deal with the marginalization of the masses. The emphasis on these issues did not constitute a real and substantial threat to the social fabric of local colonial governance. One of the important contributions to the development of party politics during this era was the high quality of debate on issues such as citizenship, taxes, social services, trade, agriculture and self-government.

The differences of opinions between labour and non-labour candidates reflect class, ideological and racial divisions. For instance, the divisive issue of race increased mutual fears and suspicion among whites, Africans and Indians in the colony. The existence of an Indian middle class in politics was a noteworthy phenomenon during this political transition.

Labour's endeavours in heightening the political consciousness contributed to an ongoing quest for liberation from the yoke of colonial rule. The role of labour and similar voices of protest served to considerably weaken British colonialism and eventually materialized in the granting of universal adult suffrage in 1946. It cannot be denied that labour laid the foundation for self-government upon which others built their legacies. One illustration is the first Premier and Prime Minister Eric Williams, who would gain power in 1956 and receive accolades for seeking Independence in 1962 and Republic status in 1976 for Trinidad and Tobago.

Some political scientists and scholars have posited the year 1956 as a watershed moment in the history of the emergence of party politics in Trinidad and Tobago. Others preferred to concentrate on labour's participation in party politics in the era of the WFP formed in 1965 and the ULF in 1975. The contribution of labour to party politics was a double-edged sword: it had both positive and negative effects. Indeed, social concerns, political discontent and economic ills of the citizens were publicly highlighted. It was an attempt by labour to deal with the marginalization of the masses.

Acknowledgements

I am grateful to the National Archives of Trinidad and Tobago and also West Indiana and Special Collections at the Alma Jordan Library, University of the West Indies, St Augustine. Institutions in England were also helpful, and these included the Public Records Office, the TUC Library at the University of North London and the Modern Records Centre at the University of Warwick. I am grateful for financial assistance from the Campus Research and Publication Fund Committee at The University of the West Indies, St. Augustine. The staff at Peter Lang must be commended for their assistance in ensuring the manuscript was published.

Introduction

Extant primary and secondary literature, inclusive of dissertations and research papers on twentieth-century labour history, constitute valuable resources for an understanding of working-class struggles and the evolution of labour organizations in Trinidad and Tobago. Some of the historical data can be located in correspondence and official despatches between governors and administrators in the Colonial Office. Similarly, the reports of commissions appointed by the Colonial Office assist in appreciating the political, economic and social conditions in the Caribbean.

In his doctoral dissertation on the achievements of labour in the larger West Indian colonies, Francis X. Mark adopted a comparative approach in his analysis of early working-class organizations and the subsequent evolution of mass movements from 1896 to the early 1950s.[1] Overand Padmore's thesis on the trade union movement dissected a growing demand for labour's services and its subsequent effect on the evolution of trade unionism from the 1930s to the 1950s. He made a brief reference to the TWA and its role in the growth of trade unionism in the colony.[2]

Basil Ince analysed the colony's political development from 1925 to 1956 and included an examination of the socio-economic factors contributing to the early successes of labour representatives in the general elections.[3] Brinsley Samaroo's doctoral dissertation, "The Constitutional and Political Development of Trinidad 1898–1925," sought to highlight the role of the TWA and the reform movement of the late 1890s and the early twentieth century. He assessed the rise of political radicalism and its contribution to the semi-representative government.[4]

Complementing these academic endeavours were studies by Wendy Charles and Susan Campbell. Charles' thesis focused on the early period of the TWA, its activities during the 1920s and Butler's involvement in the 1937 riots. Campbell's doctoral dissertation provided an account of the responses of Britain's Colonial Office during four decades of working-class activity in Trinidad.[5] Her work also takes into account the influence of the international Communist movement on the British West Indies.

During the 1930s, there were two noteworthy studies, of which the first featured one of the outstanding labour leaders of the early twentieth century, while the other analysed labour conditions in the British West Indies. C. L. R. James in *The Life of Captain Cipriani* dealt primarily with the achievements of Cipriani in the context of political events in the colony.[6] James included brief references to Cipriani's links with England, particularly with the British Labour Party (BLP). W. Arthur Lewis' 1939 publication titled *Labour in the West Indies* described the intolerable conditions which served as a catalyst for protests that inspired the emergence of mass labour movements in the Caribbean.[7]

Studies based on personal involvement in the labour struggle include Albert Gomes' *Through a Maze of Colour*. His work is a particularly enlightening social and political analysis of Trinidad from the 1930s to the 1960s.[8] This autobiography from one of the colony's foremost politicians revealed the evolution and operation of the electoral system before the introduction of a formal party system. Gomes also addressed the conditions that led to the evolution of trade unions and the socio-economic problems facing the working class of the colony. Similarly, Bukka Rennie's *History of the Working Class in Twentieth Century Trinidad and Tobago* combined components of the early history of labour and chronicled the role of the working class and its influence on the development of labour organizations, reform groups, trade unions and political parties.[9]

The turbulent 1930s in Trinidad and Tobago, which was dominated by major working-class protests, have been fertile ground for social and political researchers of the 1970s and 1980s. W. Richard Jacobs in *Butler versus the King* analysed the trial of Butler.[10] Jacobs used primary sources, including court documents and colonial correspondence, to illustrate that Butler was a victim of a biased judiciary and an oppressive Crown Colony system. Ron Ramdin in *Chattel Slave to Wage Earner* provided a generalized account of the early origins of Trinidad's working-class movement with emphasis on the 1937 riots.[11] Nyahuma Obika's *An Introduction to the Life and Times of T.U.B. Butler* focused overwhelmingly on Butler's role in the 1937 protests.[12] This semi-autobiographical work lucidly illustrates Butler's contribution to labour development in the post-1937 era and the formation of his trade union. In 1987, Roy Thomas edited *The Trinidad*

Labour Riots of 1937, a compilation of papers written on the occasion of the fiftieth anniversary of the 1937 labour riots.[13] The study embraces a variety of themes including the ruling-class response, factors leading to the riots and the resultant investigations and commissions. Other historians who studied the 1930s included Susan Craig with *Smiles and Blood* in which she examined the socio-economic cleavages between labour and capital and the attitudes of the ruling class which created a volatile environment for the social eruption of 1937.[14]

In the 1990s and early twenty-first century, several historical works on working-class progress and challenges were published. Kelvin Singh's *Race and Class Struggles in a Colonial State* examined the complex relationships between classes and ethnic groups in the colony.[15] Singh analysed the rise of working-class protests within the context of local and imperial policy. O. Nigel Bolland in *On the March* gave a refreshing overview of the factors and consequences of protests in various Caribbean colonies.[16] In 1996, Ray Kiely in *The Politics of Labour and Development in Trinidad* employed Marxist methodology in his sociological analysis of political manifestations in Trinidad from 1937 to the early 1990s.[17] He argued that the consolidation of a united working class never materialized because of historically inherited social and economic divisions existing in the colony. In *The Politics of Labour in the British Caribbean*, O. Nigel Bolland provided an insight into the ferment and labour rebellions of the 1930s, the rise of trade unionism and the prominence of working-class organizations in the British West Indies.[18]

Sahadeo Basdeo in *Labour Organisation and Labour Reform in Trinidad* focuses on pre-Second World War labour reform as he highlights the uniqueness of Trinidad's labour organization among the British colonies.[19] This he attributed to a strong reform impulse in the TWA and later trade unions which convinced the colonial government, local employers and the British Parliament of the need for improvements in conditions of labour.

There were regional and international forces, including that of Garveyism, which guided and influenced the ideological and social outlook of the early labour leaders and working-class organizations. The secondary works which analysed Marcus Garvey's influence on the British

West Indies include W. F. Elkins' "Marcus Garvey, the *Negro World* and the British West Indies: 1919–1920."[20] He analysed the impact of Garvey's newspaper, *Negro World*, and the various attempts by West Indian governments to ban this publication. Tony Martin in *Race First* dissected the impact of the *Negro World* and the Universal Negro Improvement Association (UNIA) on the African diaspora in the circum-Caribbean region and North America.[21] This work examined the strong links at the leadership level between the UNIA and TWA. The edited work of Rupert Lewis and Maureen Warner-Lewis, *Garvey: Africa, Europe, The Americas*, placed much emphasis on the international appeal of Garveyism and his impact on the African diaspora in Europe.[22]

Selected articles in certain publications critically examined labour-related topics in the twentieth century. An illustration is Brinsley Samaroo in "The Trinidad Workingmen's Association and the Origins of Popular Protest in a Crown Colony" who considered the role of the TWA in improving workers' conditions and the influence of the association in the protest movements of the period 1897–1920.[23] Barry Simpson-Holley with "Members for Trinidad" added to the historiography on labour through his recognition of the contributions of two parliamentarians in the British House of Commons, Joseph Pointer and Thomas Summerbell, who raised and debated pertinent colonial labour issues, especially the concerns of the TWA in Trinidad and Tobago.[24] W. Richard Jacobs in "The Politics of Protest in Trinidad: The Strikes and Disturbances of 1937" emphasized that in 1937 there existed a strong interrelationship between the industrial sub-system and the larger socio-political structure in the colony.[25]

Sahadeo Basdeo in "Colonial Policy and Labour Organisation in the British Caribbean 1937–1939 – An Issue in Political Sovereignty" sought to examine the comprehensive and far-reaching effect of international events and policies in colonies such as Trinidad.[26] In another work, "The Role of the British Labour Movement in the Development of Labour Organisations in Trinidad 1929–1938," Basdeo considered the British assistance rendered to the TWA and the colony's early trade unions.[27] Likewise in "Foundations of British Working Class Cooperation: The Case of Trinidad and British Guiana, 1906–1914," Basdeo placed within the context of regional integration the efforts of the working-class relations between the two neighbouring colonies.[28]

Kelvin Singh's study titled "Adrian Cola Rienzi and the Labour Movement in Trinidad (1925–1944)" explored the extensive contributions of Adrian Cola Rienzi, one of the architects of the trade union movement in Trinidad. Singh examined both Rienzi's relationship with other leaders in the colony and his efforts in organizing the working class, particularly oil and sugar workers, during the formative years of trade unionism.[29] Brinsley Samaroo, another historian, provided a comprehensive account of Rienzi.[30]

Some Caribbean novels based on the 1920s and 1930s offer insight into various aspects of the labour movement in Trinidad and Tobago. Such authors as Arthur Calder-Marshall, George Lamming and Ralph de Boissiere made extensive references to working-class events in their works.[31] In 1939, Calder-Marshall in *Glory Dead* provided an investigative report that was partly impressionistic in highlighting the obstacles confronting the unions.[32] These included the negative stereotyping of unions by the colonial authorities which were anti-labour. One of Ralph de Boissiere's fictional characters served in Mesopotamia during the First World War but returned to Trinidad to work in the oilfield in Point Fortin. In the novel, the author talks about the problems facing the early labour movement and the incidence of strikes in the colony. Lamming's novel *In the Castle of My Skin* is set amidst a Barbadian village during the 1930s. His portrayal of colonial society is particularly useful for West Indian studies because of its references to the impact of racial factors such as Garveyism and the influence of the Italian-Ethiopian war on the working-class population.

Calypso is a unique mode of social commentary in Trinidad and Tobago, and, in the period under review, the art form was used as a medium both to expose perceived injustices and to express the grievances of the working class. During 1925–1946, such topics as the general elections, poverty, labour, class differences, administration of the colony, the Italian-Ethiopian War of 1935 and the 1937 riots provided material for calypsonians.[33]

A major methodological hurdle in this study is the frequent absence of objectivity in certain primary sources. Commissions appointed by the Colonial Office, secret despatches and reports from colonial officials portray labour in Trinidad and the British West Indies as subversive and incapable of operating as orderly British trade unions. On the contrary, pro-labour literature which was anti-government seemed to exaggerate membership numbers in organizations, crowd participation at meetings and influence of labour leaders. This illustrates how perilous and delicate the exercise can be to determine the veracity of extant material.

Primary sources include the despatches between the Governor of Trinidad and the Secretary of State for the Colonies and similar correspondence relating to the administration of the colony. The reports of various commissions sent to the West Indies reflect significant issues that affected the lives of workers in the British Caribbean. Documents in this category include the *Report by the Honourable E.F.L. Wood* (1922), *Report of the West Indian Sugar Commission* (1930), *West Indian Report of the Closer Union Commission* (1933), *Report of Major Orde-Browne* (1938) and F. Dalley's *Trade Union Organisation and Industrial Relations in Trinidad* (1947). Publications such as the *United Empire* and *The West India Committee Circular* were pro-British and emphasized the paternal role of Britain among her colonies.

The *Hansard* of the Legislative Council in Trinidad, Council Papers and Committee Reports provide insight into social, political and economic conditions in the colony. Local pamphlets also proved to be a vital storehouse of primary information on the evolution of the colony's working-class movement. Among these were David Headley's *Labour and Life* (1921), and two undated works: *Trinidad in Parliament* by Howard-Bishop and *Why and How the Workers Should Organize?* published by the Oilfield Workers' Trade Union (OWTU).

The daily newspapers included the *Port-of-Spain Gazette* which was generally pro-government and opposed to the TWA and the constitutional reformists; the *Trinidad Guardian* which supported the white ruling class in Trinidad; and *The Mirror* which sympathized with the political reform movements of the late nineteenth century. Both the *Port-of-Spain Gazette* and the *Trinidad Guardian* were often anti-labour and identified with the conservative status quo of the planters, merchants and the elite.

During the 1920s and 1930s, there were two labour-oriented weeklies – the *Labour Leader* (official organ of the TWA) and *The People* (representing African opinion) – which targeted working-class audiences and addressed labour issues ignored by the pro-capitalist daily newspapers. In addition, the *Argos*, *New Dawn*, *The Vanguard* and *The Clarion* provided a reflection of the struggles of the working class both in Trinidad and in other British colonies. Their selective coverage of the contributions of labour organizations was intended both to inform and to educate the working class. Some of the feature articles in these publications examine the difficulties experienced by Africans of the diaspora.

The Beacon, an anti-establishment publication, came off the press in Trinidad in March 1931. It was printed monthly, but it later became irregular, and publication eventually ceased in November 1933. Although constantly opposed to the daily newspapers, *The Beacon* briefly resurfaced in November 1939. It contained fiction, political and social commentary, reviews, poems and historical articles. Contributors included C. L. R. James and labour leaders such as A. A. Cipriani, Tito Achong, Ralph Mentor and Albert Gomes. In the past and present, persons were granted promotions and provided with jobs on the basis of race/ethnicity, class and political connections. Selection based on merit, qualifications and job experience were either overlooked or given secondary consideration.

Notes

1. Francis X. Mark, "The Rise and Development of Labour Movements in the British Caribbean with particular reference to British Guiana, Jamaica and Trinidad," PhD dissertation, University of Edinburgh, 1959.
2. Overand Padmore, "The Role of the Trade Union Movement in a Developing Economy: The Trinidad Experience," MA thesis, University of Toronto, 1962.
3. Basil Ince, "Politics before the People's National Movement: A Study of Parties and Elections in British Trinidad," PhD dissertation, New York University, 1966.
4. Brinsley Samaroo, "The Constitutional and Political Development in Trinidad 1898–1925," PhD dissertation, University of London, 1969.
5. Susan Campbell, "'En'less Pressure': The Struggles of a Caribbean Working Class in Their International Context Trinidad 1919–1956," PhD dissertation, Queen's University, 1995.
6. C. L. R. James, *The Life of Captain Cipriani – An Account of British Government in the West Indies* (Nelson, Lancaster: Coulton and Company, 1932).
7. W. A. Lewis, *Labour in the West Indies: The Birth of a Workers' Movement* (London: Victor Golancs, rep. Beacon Books, 1977).

8. Albert Gomes, *Through a Maze of Colour* (Port-of-Spain: Key Caribbean Publications, 1974).
9. Bukka Rennie, *History of the Working Class in Twentieth Century Trinidad and Tobago* (Trinidad: New Beginning Movement, 1973).
10. W. Richard Jacobs, ed., *Butler versus the King – Riots and Sedition in 1937* (Port-of-Spain: Key Caribbean Publications, 1976).
11. Ron Ramdin, *Chattel Slave to Wage Earner: A History of Trade Unionism in Trinidad and Tobago* (London: Martin Brian and O'Keeffe, 1982).
12. Nyahuma Obika, *An Introduction to the Life and Times of Tubal Uriah Butler* (St Joseph: College Press, 1983).
13. Roy Thomas, ed., *The Trinidad Labour Riots of 1937 – Perspectives 50 Years Later* (University of the West Indies, St Augustine: Extra Mural Studies, 1987).
14. Susan Craig, *Smiles and Blood – The Ruling Class Response to the Workers' Rebellion of 1937 in Trinidad and Tobago* (London: New Beacon, 1988).
15. Kelvin Singh, *Race and Class Struggles in a Colonial State: Trinidad 1917–1945* (Calgary: University of Calgary Press and Jamaica: The Press, University of the West Indies, 1994).
16. O. Nigel Bolland, *On the March – Labour Rebellions in the British Caribbean, 1934–1939* (Jamaica: Ian Randle Publishers, 1995).
17. Ray Kiely, *The Politics of Labour in Trinidad* (Jamaica: The Press, University of the West Indies, 1996).
18. O. Nigel Bolland, *The Politics of Labour in the British Caribbean* (Jamaica: Ian Randle Publishers, 2001).
19. Sahadeo Basdeo, *Labour Organisation and Labour Reform in Trinidad* (San Juan: Lexicon, 2003).
20. W. F. Elkins, "Marcus Garvey, the *Negro World* and the British West Indies: 1919–1920," *Science and Society* 36 (Spring 1972), 63–77.
21. Tony Martin, *Race First: The Ideological and Organizational Struggles of Marcus Garvey and the Universal Negro Improvement Association* (Westport: Greenwood, 1976).
22. Rupert Lewis and Maureen Warner-Lewis, *Garvey: Africa, Europe, The Americas* (Jamaica: ISER, rep. New Jersey: Africa World Press, 1994).
23. Brinsley Samaroo, "The Trinidad Workingmen's Association and the Origins of Popular Protest in a Crown Colony," *Social and Economic Studies* 21 (1972), 205–222.
24. Barry Simpson-Holley, "Members for Trinidad," *Journal of Caribbean History* 6 (May 1973), 81–93.
25. W. Richard Jacobs, "The Politics of Protest in Trinidad: The Strikes and Disturbances of 1937," *Caribbean Studies* 17 (April–July 1977), 5–54.
26. Sahadeo Basdeo, "Colonial Policy and Labour Organisation in the British Caribbean 1937–1939: An Issue in Political Sovereignty," *Boletin de estudio latinoamericanos y del Caribe* 32 (December 1981), 119–129.

27. Sahadeo Basdeo, "The Role of the British Labour Movement in the Development of Labour Organisations in Trinidad 1929–1938," *Social and Economic Studies* 31 (March 1982), 40–73.
28. Sahadeo Basdeo, "Foundations of British Working Class Cooperation: The Case of Trinidad and British Guiana, 1906–1944," *Journal of Caribbean Studies* 16 (Summer and Fall 2001), 45–60.
29. Kelvin Singh, "Adrian Cola Rienzi and the Labour Movement in Trinidad (1925–1944)," *Journal of Caribbean History* 16 (1982), 10–35.
30. Brinsley Samaroo, *Adrian Cola Rienzi: The Life and Times of an Indo-Caribbean Progressive* (Macoya: Royards Publishing Company, 2022).
31. Ralph de Boissiere, *Crown Jewel* (rep. London: Picador, 1981); George Lamming, *In the Castle of My Skin* (rep. London: Longman, 1973).
32. Arthur Calder-Marshall, *Glory Dead* (London: Michael Joseph, 1939).
33. The prominent bards of the era included Lord Protector (Patrick Jones), Lord Executor (Phillip Garcia), King Radio (Norman Span), Lord Beginner (Egbert Moore), Atilla the Hum (Raymond Quevedo), Growling Tiger (Neville Marcano) and Roaring Lion (Hubert Raphael Charles). See Gordon Rohlehr, *Calypso and Society in Pre-Independence Trinidad* (Trinidad: HEM Printers, 1990), 87–130.

CHAPTER 1

The Art of Exclusion and Failures

Some West Indian colonists were familiar with the representative system of government in Britain and felt comfortable with a government in Trinidad that included the Governor functioning as the King did in England; the Council operating as the House of Lords, and the General Assembly elected by the freeholders, substituting for the House of Commons. It is against this background of struggle and experiment at metropolitan control of the West Indian colonies that the constitutional and social evolution of Trinidad and Tobago is to be understood. Trinidad was added to the crown jewels through conquest and ratified against Napoleon Bonaparte's better wishes by the Peace of Amiens in 1802. Being the southernmost of the Caribbean islands, it remained undeveloped owing to Spanish neglect caused by the lack of precious metals such as gold and silver. Coming later, on the British colonial agenda, Trinidad never knew of the Proprietary System and the "old representative system."

The "old representative system" as a small-scale model of British parliamentary structure could not go beyond the eighteenth century. This system belonged to the pre-emancipation West Indian society when there were two social classes: an upper class comprising the planters, merchants and freeholders and the enslaved class, composed of people who were no more than material property and devoid of representation and franchise. The assemblies then, were representative of the only recognized social class, the plantocracy.[1] The emancipation of numerous enslaved Africans in 1838 created a new social order and therefore in subsequent decades of the nineteenth century, Crown Colony government was introduced as the preferred system of governance.

Political experiments

As early as 1801, the Governor of Trinidad appointed five upper-class whites to his Council of Advice to assist him in the administration of the colony.[2] The deficiency and apparent unrepresentative composition in such a limited selection of legislators is obvious when one considers the societal composition of Trinidad. In 1801, there were 2,153 whites in a total population of 27,000 in Trinidad.[3] By 1802, there were 1,166 Indigenous Indians, 19,709 enslaved Africans, 5,275 Free Coloureds and 2,201 whites.[4] While colonial policy unashamedly ignored the rights of Indigenous natives and the enslaved Africans, tensions were noticeable at the upper echelons of the social order between the Free Coloureds and whites in the struggle for power-sharing. Amongst the Free Coloureds, there were 1,751 Spaniards and 2,929 persons of French origin who were marginalized by the British due to concerns about their lack of support or loyalty. Hence, Governor Thomas Picton was distrustful of their intentions and branded them as one of the most radical groups in the colony.[5] The freedmen faced similar obstacles in other colonies; for instance, in Barbados, they were debarred from voting unless they owned land, while in Jamaica, freedmen were allowed to vote upon payment of taxes. However, in 1828, a British Order-in-Council removed these restrictions which disenfranchised the Free Coloureds.[6] Thus, with no elected representation from the wider citizenry in the ruling council and a parliamentary machinery responsible only to itself, it may not be unreasonable to agree with Morley Ayearst that Britain's control of her West Indian estate was that of "benevolent despotism" or with D. J. Murray who described the colonial policy as being a "benevolent autocracy."[7]

In an attempt to effect constitutional reform in 1831, a different form of government was introduced in Trinidad, Mauritius and St Lucia. Changes in Trinidad included the replacement of the Council of Advice by an Executive Council as well as the formation of the Legislative Council.[8] The Executive Council was nominated by the Crown and comprised six official and six unofficial members. The six official members included the Colonial Secretary, Attorney General and Chief Justice, whilst the six unofficial members, who were appointed by the Governor, represented vested economic interests. The Legislative Council, however, consisted of an equal number of official and unofficial members. The Governor's pre-eminence empowered him with a double vote in both the Executive and Legislative Councils, and he had the privilege of proposing subjects for debate in the council.[9] In accordance with colonial policy, the Governor's position remained unchallenged, and, as Ayearst concluded, "The Governor was, in effect, the Government."[10] This was to prevent the intentions of Britain from being derailed: "the unwillingness of the Colonial Office to permit more self-government in Trinidad at this time was the fear that a truly representative assembly with actual authority might block the humanitarian policies of the home government and especially its determination to end slavery."[11]

After the emancipation of enslaved persons, constitutional reform continued but did not benefit them and the Free Coloureds. Property continued to be one of the major criteria for eligibility of non-whites to membership in the Legislative Council. In the 1870s, the Governor's nomination of members to the Legislative Council was based on their financial status. Thus, the sugar planters comprised the majority membership and consequently represented a formidable economic caucus in the council.[12] During the 1880s, when cocoa was valued as much as sugar, the latter continued to be well-represented in the council. The plantation-dominated representation in the council was evident in 1897, in that the nine unofficial members comprised one lawyer, two traders (merchants) with ties to the planters and six sugar or cocoa planters.[13] Even those members outside the plantocracy had considerable connections with sugar and cocoa plantations.

Ensuring the Governor had the majority vote took precedence in matters of administration. But by 1850, Governor Lord Harris sought to have a few more members serving on the Legislative Council and suggested an extension of the vote.[14] This action was undertaken to increase the class interests represented in the Legislative Council. In 1877, mounting pressure from within the colony with 5,000 petitions from taxpayers seeking political representation failed to alter the composition of the council. The unofficial majority which existed from 1862 to 1892 was allowed to continue on the basis that the official vote would not be defeated.

The overwhelming presence of unofficial members and the preponderance of sugar interests in the council were seriously challenged by the reform movements of the 1880s and 1890s.[15] In the 1880s, sugar magnates continued to use the medium of the West India Committee to influence the Colonial Office. The plantocracy sought to diversify representation which would include professional and business interests; however, the planters were able to manipulate the middle-class reformers by favouring the wealthier middle-class merchants.[16]

Despite coverage in the press for reform during the 1880s, there was no legislation in the council for the implementation of constitutional reform. This reflected the myopic nature of the reform movements comprising conservative liberals. The condemnation emanating from the urban, Coloured, professional middle class was aimed at the narrow economic interest groups who had no desire to radically transform the political status quo. Those who were disillusioned with the attitude of arrogant officials and the existence of an inefficient administration complained of the inferior quality of certain governors appointed to Trinidad, while members of the Legislative Council were answerable to Britain rather than to those who governed the colony.[17] Despite clamouring for change, by the 1890s, the moderate reformers opposed universal suffrage[18] and thus excluded the African and East Indian working class from participation in the colony's political process. The social and political exclusion of this class was a major feature of the colonial attitude towards Trinidad and Tobago and became the source of much discontent.

The political, constitutional and social metamorphosis slowly unfolding in Trinidad and Tobago was not unique, as other colonies in the British West Indies were awakened to the necessity for reforms and began agitating for a more participatory system of governance. Dissatisfaction with the political administration and legislative structure became a common regional feature with parallel outbursts of discontent over the operation of the Crown Colony system. The Jamaican Assembly's "humble petition" of 1823 was a rejection of Britain's attempt to solely manage the affairs of the island. This resulted in the Jamaican Constitution Act of 1854, which created an Executive Committee comprising four members (one from the council and three from the assembly) and established a Legislative

Council that served as a second chamber without executive responsibilities. However, this form of the Legislative Council proved unsuccessful in its implementation in Tobago, Grenada and Antigua.[19]

In Jamaica, in the aftermath of the Morant Bay Rebellion in 1865, the island's assembly consisted of twenty-one estate owners from a total of forty-seven members. The political repercussions of that revolt resulted in the passage of a British Order-in-Council in 1866 which established the Crown Colony government in Jamaica. This marked the end of Jamaica's "old representative system" which had existed for approximately 200 years. Under a new form of government, the Governor was bestowed with the right to introduce legislation to the council and Jamaica's legislature comprised a minority of unofficial members and a majority of official members. This constitutional reform was welcomed by the ruling elite but caused considerable resentment among the disenfranchised. It was implemented in the British West Indies except for the Bahamas, Barbados and Bermuda.[20]

The link between political reform and social events was evident in the 1865 Morant Bay Rebellion in Jamaica. In 1871, a letter from Henry Taylor of the Colonial Office, who was supervising West Indian issues addressed to E. D. Fairfield, a clerk at the Colonial Office, made the following observation: "Then came the rebellion of 1865, and the Assembly in their panic made overtures to Governor Eyre (Governor of Jamaica 1864–1866) for a change in the policy."[21] However, their proposal was that the majority of members would still be elective and the Crown would have some votes.

In Jamaica in the 1880s, the widespread criticism against the Crown Colony system intensified. The evidence given to the West Indian Royal Commission in 1882 expressed the unwavering sentiments of the colonists: "Crown Colony Government is accused of discriminating against natives by excluding them from high office and by withholding the elective franchise from them."[22] One year later, in 1883, six Africans claiming to represent hundreds of Africans in Kingston submitted a letter to the West Indian Royal Commission indicating that they had never benefitted from popular representation. Furthermore, they claimed that "unofficial Members are wholly ignorant of measures of legislation until they are presented by an Official Member for the first time at the Legislative Council Chamber."[23] During this period, a petition (with 4,677 signatures from a population of 580,000) to colonial officials proposed a change for the creation of a Legislative Chamber comprising twenty-two members, of which eight were to be nominated by the Queen and fourteen to be elected with one from each parish.[24] Not surprisingly, this was ignored as Britain was not prepared to allow the selection of representatives by the working class who were deemed illiterate. By 1884, constitutional reform occurred as the new council comprised four ex-officio members (i.e. three officers who are served as ex-officio members of Director of Public Works and present council), nine elected members and five nominated members chosen by Britain.[25]

Other British West Indian islands also faced constitutional challenges in this era. In Barbados, an attempt was made in 1875 to introduce the Crown Colony system inclusive of a federation with the Windwards. However, planters rejected the federal principle because of the poverty existing in the Windwards. The Africans misunderstood the ensuing struggle between the Governor and assembly and, believing they would be disadvantaged in this anti-federation, began to riot on 22 April 1876.[26] In the 1857 election in St Kitts, only forty-seven electors were allowed to vote for twenty-two members to sit in the Legislative Council. In Barbados, likewise, only 1 per cent of the population was granted voting privileges. In 1861, Jamaican voters were estimated to be fewer than one in two hundred, and protests over political representation led to the creation of a group seeking reform in 1879.[27]

In 1871, the Leeward Islands belonged to a federation which was divided into six "Presidencies." Each Presidency possessed a Commissioner or Administrator and a local representative of the Governor. By 1898, reform was apparent as the local legislatures in the Leewards were entirely nominated with the Legislative Council comprising eight unofficial and eight official members. These former comprised three from Antigua, three from St Kitts-Nevis and two from Dominica. The Governor had ultimate authority as the legislatures contained an official majority. Among the Windwards (St Vincent, St Lucia, Grenadines and Grenada), each island retained its own government, while in the Leewards, there was no joint legislature. The Crown Colony system was not adopted in Antigua and Grenada until 1898 and survived longer in British Guiana, which kept its semi-representative system until 1928.

Influence of India

From the late nineteenth and early twentieth centuries, it was evident that Britain placed increasingly diminishing reliance on the British West Indies to support her economy. By this time India and possessions in Asia and Africa contributed significantly to England's economic fortunes. There were political and social developments in the British Empire that influenced, shaped and directly impacted the political evolution of the British Caribbean.

The political fortitude of Mohandas K. Gandhi in India proved to be an inspiration and model for colonists throughout the British Empire, including in the Caribbean, desiring political and economic freedom. Gandhi's philosophy of non-violence (*ahimsa*) aided his struggle against the British. He employed such tactics as fasting, marches and strikes (*hartals*).[28] During the 1920s, Gandhi sent a warning from India to Britain. The year 1921 marked the start of his campaign for *swadeshi* (economic and political independence of India) which was subsequently followed in 1922 by civil disobedience in Bardoli.

In 1929, Gandhi introduced the "Resolution for Complete Independence" and, in 1930, a "Pledge of Independence" was adopted throughout India. Gandhi's civil disobedience which continued during the 1930–1934 period coincided with anti-British sentiment throughout the colonies.[29] In India, the non-payment of rents and taxes created panic in the administration, and the problem intensified due to the collapse of agricultural prices in 1930–1931.[30] The peaceful march of Gandhi in 1930 to the sea at Dandi in protest against British Salt Laws further contributed to imposing non-violent tactics unto the campaign for self-government (*swaraj*) that was previously marked by violence, communal tension and division.

Gandhi's concept of a *swaraj* government was a democratic form of administration ruled by persons believing in the respectability and status of labour.[31] During this period, India experienced a vibrant movement to get rid of the yoke of British imperialism. Satyamurti, an elected member of the Madras Legislative Council and the representative of the Swarajist

(Home Rule) Party argued, "This cry for self rule in India is based not only on legitimate national sentiment, but also because Great Britain has failed to secure the people of India the rudiments of civilised life, and Indians want a chance to do what Great Britain has failed to do."[32] Gandhi's desire to end the British economic exploitation of India and secure India's political independence were goals strikingly similar to those of the labour leaders in Trinidad and Tobago and the rest of the British West Indies who passionately sought self-government.

Both Clem Seecharan in *India in the Caribbean* and Brinsley Samaroo in "The Mahatma in the Caribbean" provide ample evidence that the plantation Indian diaspora in the Caribbean benefited from the work of Gandhi. Despite Gandhi not being able to visit the Caribbean, the presence of his two emissaries – C. F. Andrews and Dr Durai Pandia – provided hope for the region's Indians.[33] Furthermore, reports in newspapers such as the *East Indian Weekly* and the *Daily Chronicle*, both in Trinidad and Tobago and in British Guiana, informed the public of the struggles of Gandhi. In addition. there were individuals such as Trinidad-born Inderjit Bahadursingh (1912–1988), a lawyer, who were part of India's struggle for freedom from Britain.[34]

International developments

In Trinidad and Tobago, the *Labour Leader*, the publication of the TWA, often reported on developments occurring among the global working class. For instance, in June 1925, whilst Cipriani was seeking to have legislation passed for an eight-hour day, there was an article about a similar struggle in Australia among the representatives of the working class.[35] In England, by 1925, apart from the BLP's success in the elections, competent men from the ranks of labour were chosen for the post of Mayors in Britain.[36] In 1930, Ceylon also experienced reforms as recommendations were approved in its council by a narrow margin of nineteen to seventeen. One of the main changes in Ceylon's new Constitution was the replacement of the existing Legislative Council by a State Council.[37] Undoubtedly, all of these events that were reported in the *Labour Leader* were influential in shaping public opinion.

It was obvious that the impressive territorial portfolio of Britain determined the slow pace of political and social reforms in the British West Indies. Thus, with such power concerns of constitutional reform and the granting of political representation to the working class or the general population, enacting social reforms or investing in developmental programmes in the British West Indies would not be viewed by Westminster as urgent or essential. Indeed, larger territories such as India, South and West Africa took precedence over the Caribbean.

The historical forces that were shaping the Britain Empire had an influence on the political and social evolution of the British West Indies. Events in Britain and other colonial dependencies throughout the world demonstrated parallel trends to those occurring in islands such as Trinidad and Tobago. Undoubtedly, the common bond of oppression, exploitation and the unrepresentative nature of political systems united the British colonies in a common purpose.

The frequency, militancy and determination of labour in its meetings were in response to the political marginalization of the masses coupled with economic injustices and inhumane living conditions of the working class. The stranglehold of vested, economic interests in Trinidad and Tobago and the frustration of the working class would be expressed in sporadic outbursts of discontent as evidenced by the 1919–1920 and 1934 disturbances. The bloody riots, industrial strike actions and civil disorder in the late 1930s in Trinidad and Tobago and the rest of the British Caribbean were due to the fact there were no other avenues of redress – certainly neither from the power brokers in the Caribbean nor London. Emerging from this climate of protest were the trade unions in the British Caribbean which represented the interests of the working class that led the workers' struggle with such irrepressible zeal that the Colonial Office was forced to respond.

Notes

1. For more on the Crown Colony, see James Millette, "Trinidadian Prototype: The Rise and Fall of the Crown Colony System," in *Foundation Readings on the History of Trinidad and Tobago* (Government of the Republic of Trinidad and Tobago: Ministry of Education, 2017), 177–204.

2. Hewan Craig, *The Legislative Council of Trinidad and Tobago* (London: Faber and Faber, 1951), 21.
3. James Millette, *Society and Politics in Colonial Trinidad* (rep. Avon: Zed Books, 1985), 105.
4. Millette, *Society and Politics in Colonial Trinidad*, 105.
5. Included in this category of Free Coloureds were 599 of British origin. Millette, *Society and Politics in Colonial Trinidad*, 106–110.
6. As early as 1797, the Free Coloureds were denied an active role in political affairs of Trinidad. However, for the next decade they remained a recognized force in the colony's parliamentary debates.
7. Morley Ayearst, *The British West Indies* (London: George Allen and Unwin, 1960), 41. See also, D. J. Murray, *The West Indies and the Development of Colonial Government* (Oxford: Clarendon Press, 1965), x.
8. Hume Wrong, *Government of the West Indies* (Oxford: Clarendon Press, 1923), 37–138. Also, Howard Johnson, "Crown Colony Government in Trinidad 1870–1897," PhD dissertation, Oxford University, 1969, 182; Murray, *The West Indies and the Development of Colonial Government*, 166–186, 230–232.
9. Murray, *The West Indies and the Development of Colonial Government*, 163–164. In March 1831, the new Commission and Instructions to the Governor changed the size of the Legislative Council from ten to twelve members.
10. Ayearst, *The British West Indies*, 79.
11. Ibid.
12. Johnson, "Crown Colony Government in Trinidad," 198–200.
13. Johnson, "Crown Colony Government in Trinidad," 162.
14. Elisabeth Wallace, *The British Caribbean: From the Decline of Colonialism to the End of Federation* (Toronto: University of Toronto Press, 1977), 14.
15. Bridget Brereton, *Race Relations in Colonial Trinidad 1870–1900* (Cambridge: Cambridge University Press, 1979), 32. There were two reform movements: 1885–1888 and 1892–1895. Some of the upper-class families associated with the reform movement of the 1880s were Rostant, Borde, Lange and de Verteuil. H. A. Will, *Constitutional Change in the British West Indies, 1880–1903* (Oxford: Clarendon Press, 1970), 162.
16. Will, *Constitutional Change in the British West Indies*, 153–154, 289–290.
17. Samaroo, "Constitutional and Political Development of Trinidad 1898–1925," 45–48.
18. Bridget Brereton, *A History of Modern Trinidad 1783–1962* (Port-of-Spain: Heinemann, 1981), 143–144.
19. Wallace, *The British Caribbean*, 14. Also Ayearst, *The British West Indies*, 26–27.
20. Wallace, *The British Caribbean*, 15.
21. Letter reprinted in the *Trinidad Guardian* 7 March 1926 (hereafter cited as *TG*).
22. W. Morrison, Evidence Given to the West India Royal Commission of 1882, supplement to the *Jamaica Gazette* 28 February 1884.
23. Letter addressed to Colonel William Crossman and George S. Baden-Powell, 17 February 1883 in *Papers Relating to Constitutional Development in Jamaica and*

Trinidad 1884–1931 (located at the West Indiana, University of the West Indies, St Augustine).

24. "The humble Petition of certain of her Majesty's subjects, inhabitants of the Island of Jamaica," Governor Sir A. Musgrave to the Earl of Derby in *Constitutional Development in Jamaica and Trinidad.*
25. Letter from the Earl of Derby to Governor Sir H. W. Norman, 28 May 1884 in *Constitutional Development in Jamaica and Trinidad.* See also Ayearst, *The British West Indies*, 31.
26. Ayearst, *The British West Indies*, 31.
27. Wallace, *The British Caribbean*, 15–16; Ayearst, *The British West Indies*, 26.
28. For the moral foundations of Gandhi's philosophy, see Ramashray Roy, *Gandhi – Soundings in Political Philosophy* (New Delhi: Chanakya Publications, 1984), 68–73. Also V. T. Patil, *Studies on Gandhi* (Bangalore: Sterling Publishers, 1983), 5–27.
29. See Harpinder Kaur, *Gandhi's Concept of Civil Disobedience* (New Delhi: Intellectual Publishing House, 1986).
30. R. J. Moore, *The Crisis of Indian Unity 1917–1940* (London: Oxford University Press, 1974), 194.
31. S. H. Patil, *Gandhi and Swaraj* (New Delhi: Deep and Deep Publications, 1983), 40.
32. *Labour Leader* 11 August 1925.
33. See Brinsley Samaroo, "The Mahatma in the Caribbean," in Rueben Gowricharn, ed., *Caribbean Transnationalism: Migration, Pluralization and Social Cohesion* (Maryland: Lexington Books, 2006), 139–153; Clem Seecharan, *India and the Shaping of the Indo-Guyanese Imagination* (Leeds: Peepal Tree Press, 1993).
34. Samaroo, "Mahatma in the Caribbean," 140.
35. *Labour Leader* 6 June 1925.
36. *Labour Leader* 12 December 1925.
37. *Labour Leader* 18 January 1930.

Bibliography

Brereton, Bridget. *Race Relations in Colonial Trinidad 1870–1900* (Cambridge: Cambridge University Press, 1979).

Brereton, Bridget. *A History of Modern Trinidad 1783–1962* (Port-of-Spain: Heinemann, 1981).

Craig, Hewan. *The Legislative Council of Trinidad and Tobago* (London: Faber and Faber, 1951).

Gowricharn, Rueben. *Caribbean Transnationalism: Migration, Pluralization and Social Cohesion* (Maryland: Lexington Books, 2006).

Kaur, Harpinder. *Gandhi's Concept of Civil Disobedience* (New Delhi: Intellectual Publishing House, 1986).

Millette, James. *Society and Politics in Colonial Trinidad* (rep. Avon: Zed Books, 1985).

Millette, James. "Trinidadian Prototype: The Rise and Fall of the Crown Colony System," in *Foundation Readings on the History of Trinidad and Tobago* (Government of the Republic of Trinidad and Tobago: Ministry of Education, 2017).

Moore, R. J. *The Crisis of Indian Unity 1917–1940* (London: Oxford University Press, 1974).

Patil, V. T. *Studies on Gandhi* (Bangalore: Sterling Publishers, 1983).

Roy, Ramashray. *Gandhi – Soundings in Political Philosophy* (New Delhi: Chanakya Publications, 1984).

Samaroo, Brinsley. "Constitutional and Political Development of Trinidad 1898–1925," PhD dissertation, University of London, 1969.

Seecharan, Clem. *India and the Shaping of the Indo-Guyanese Imagination* (Leeds: Peepal Tree Press, 1993).

Wallace, Elisabeth. *The British Caribbean: From the Decline of Colonialism to the End of Federation* (Toronto: University of Toronto Press, 1977).

Will, H. A. *Constitutional Change in the British West Indies, 1880–1903* (Oxford: Clarendon Press, 1970).

CHAPTER 2

The Birth of Party Politics

> For the first time since 1797, for the first time in 128 years of British rule, the people of Trinidad and Tobago, in a limited number had the right to elect a small proportion of their own representatives ... Thus did Trinidad and Tobago come to its first elections on February 7, 1925.[1]

Labour, particularly the TWA, though not a fully organized political party, contributed significantly to the historic concessions granted to the colony in its first-ever national elections in 1925. Previous representations, persistent dialogue and daring challenges to colonial rule in Trinidad gave new confidence to the TWA when its emissary William Howard-Bishop visited England in 1921. Howard-Bishop, General Secretary of the TWA, held discussions with British officials on labour issues in Trinidad and Tobago.

At the House of Commons in London, he met with W. Gillies of the BLP, S. Lindsay (Secretary of the Parliamentary Labour Party) and Ben Spoor (a labour MP). Howard-Bishop requested that the BLP arrange an interview for him with the Colonial Secretary, and he formally suggested that the party raise certain socio-political matters which affected Trinidad and Tobago in the House of Commons.[2] On 18 August 1921, Howard-Bishop met with Ben Spoor in the Whips' Room of the House of Commons where both men discussed such issues as trade union laws, the Seditious Publications Bill and representative government for Trinidad.[3]

It was primarily due to such efforts as those of Howard-Bishop that pertinent questions relating to working conditions and constitutional reform were later raised by labour MPs in the British Parliament. They appealed to the Parliament for the appointment of a commission to visit the West Indies, and in 1921, Britain appointed a Royal Commission headed by Major E. F. L. Wood. He visited the West Indies during the period December 1921–February 1922, "the visit of Major Wood to Trinidad, and, incidentally to the other islands of the West Indies and to British Guiana was primarily due to the representations made to the Parliamentary Committee of the Labour Party in the House of Commons and to the Under Secretary of State himself at the Colonial Office in Downing Street by the delegate of the Association in the summer of last year."[4]

During his visit, Wood conducted a number of interviews with organizations in Trinidad, particularly with regard to the urgent demand for representative government. Among those groups supportive of constitutional changes were the Legislative Reform Committee (LRC), the East Indian National Congress (EINC) and the TWA. Wood observed, "The East Indian National Congress advocated communal representation of the East Indian community as one group, on the ground that otherwise there was danger of their being outvoted."[5]

Even though the EINC was identified as being supportive of self-government, Rev. C. D. Lalla, a member of the organization, was accused by F. E. M. Hosein[6] of misrepresenting the views of all Indians in the colony. On 6 January 1922, Hosein quoted Lalla as being fearful of the impact of self-government on Indians, "The time has not yet come for East Indians to have elective representation. There is danger of their political identity being absorbed." Lalla's stance regarding Indians was later criticized by the *East Indian Weekly* as being "short-sighted."[7]

The LRC of 1921, with its majority membership being Black or Coloured men, acted as a pressure group in the colony as it sought to highlight and raise the need for electoral reform. Wood appreciated the influential stance of the TWA, and he recognized their proposals for the colony: "The Trinidad Working Men's Association, who were represented on the Legislative Reform Committee, also supported the demand for change. They advocated that the qualification for the vote should be an income of $20 a month, or payment of an annual rent of $96, and that the qualification for membership should be the possession of an income of $100 a month, or of £500."[8] Apparently, Wood wrongly identified the TWA as having representation on the LRC. On 2 September 1922, W. Howard-Bishop, in clarifying this misconception of the TWA being represented on the LRC, wrote an article in the *Labour Leader* protesting against what he thought was the exclusion of the TWA from the LRC.

There were also voices opposed to political reform such as those of the Agricultural Society and the Chamber of Commerce. Both organizations preferred the status quo since they already had representation in the Legislative Council. Opposition to representative government also included the East Indian National Association (EINA), which comprised a deputation of wealthy Indians from South Trinidad.[9] Being wealthy, educated and a minority group, they preferred the retention of the colonial administration rather than risk having representative government, which could potentially lead to the sharing of political power with Africans who formed the major ethnic group in the society.

Major Wood suggested that there should be an introduction of the elective principle in the colonial legislative system. He recommended that the officials should remain in the majority, the number of nominated officials be reduced and a limited number of members be elected to the Legislative Council (see Appendix 1). Wood's recommendations were eventually accepted by the Secretary of State for the Colonies and used as the basis for Trinidad and Tobago's new Constitution which came into effect on 21 August 1924.

In 1925, the new Legislative Council in the colony comprised twenty-six members. The number of unofficial members (nominated) was increased from eleven to thirteen (seven to be elected by voting and six being nominated). The number of official members, including the Attorney General, Treasurer and Colonial Secretary, was increased from ten to twelve, with the Governor having the casting vote to ensure an official majority (see Appendix 2).

Even though provisions were made for increased representation, the repository of power for the governance in the colony remained unchanged, since ultimate authority rested with the Governor and the Secretary of State for the Colonies. Furthermore, the Governor, with the support of the official and nominated unofficial members, would be able to veto easily any decision of the elected members. The concessions granted to the colony in preparation for the first elections were severely limited. The franchise restricted official political participation by the working masses. Therefore, in the 1925 elections, there were 15,632 registered voters in a total population of 364,828. However, on polling day, only 6,822 persons cast their ballots.[10]

Use of the media

The candidates contesting the municipal elections and the 1925, 1928, 1933 and 1938 national elections used the media as a powerful agent to publicize their campaigns, advertise their manifestoes and introduce themselves to the public. The newspapers functioned as an effective instrument in providing electoral information to the working class in Trinidad and Tobago. Advertisements for candidates were usually accompanied by a picture and/or summary of the candidate's intentions if elected to the Legislative Council. The term "manifesto" was occasionally used in advertisements to highlight the objectives of candidates seeking parliamentary office.

The use of the *Labour Leader*, especially during the 1925 elections, was paramount in the campaign of labour candidates since other newspapers had their own preferences in the coverage of non-labour candidates:

> The daily newspapers were patently partial in their reporting of the electoral campaign. They gave support to the candidates of their choice and since the owners of the newspapers belonged to the white conservative element of Trinidad society, their reporting tended to favour people with their economic interests. Thus their preference for Rust over Cipriani, Robinson over Teelucksingh, and Cory-Davies over Stollmeyer in the first election is not surprising.[11]

In the months prior to the 1925 election, there were advertisements in the *Labour Leader* sponsored by the labour candidates. Among these was C. H. Pierre, who, in July 1924, published an ad (with a picture) carrying the caption "The People's Candidate for Legislative honors to represent the parishes of St. David, Nariva, Mayaro and St. Andrews." This was further supported by a series of advertisements which sought to inform the electors of his candidacy:

> Electors of St. David, Nariva, Mayaro and St. Andrews
>
> Be Prepared
> TO VOTE FOR
> C. HENRY PIERRE

AT THE
Coming Elections.

With the Compliments of the Candidate.[12]

Two other candidates representing the working class, Cipriani and A. B. Gobin, used a similar format in their electoral campaigns in 1924 with advertisements in the *Labour Leader*. Such advertisements were regularly repeated in the working-class publication.[13]

These advertisements were strategically placed inside the TWA's newspaper among the editorials and important news items. The size of the advertisement also made it attractive and noticeable: for instance, Cipriani's ads were approximately 11 cm by 8.5 cm and included a passport-size (3.5 cm by 4 cm) picture of the candidate.[14] This strategy was important in ensuring that the working class was familiar with the candidate and his objectives.

In October 1924, during the municipal elections, Cipriani published a manifesto in the *Labour Leader*. It was addressed to the "Burgesses of the Southern Ward." Cipriani was nominated for all the wards, but he decided to serve the Southern Ward where he resided. He promised the people of his ward proper representation, "After three years of service on the Council, it is unnecessary for me to tell you anything appertaining to my policy, but it may be sufficient to state that if you return me as representative for the Southern Ward, your interests will be well looked after."[15]

The persuasive promotion of Cipriani was also apparent in the wording of the advertisements for the national elections, "The man of the people and the people's man who will run any man at the polls."[16] Other slogans incorporated in Cipriani's electoral advertisements were "Keep your eyes on The Man in the Corner" and "Capt. CIPRIANI The Workingman's Candidate and the poor man's friend."[17] In addition, notices of Cipriani's electioneering meetings were sometimes advertised on the front page of the TWA's paper.[18] In one instance, the first page of the *Labour Leader* had a notice of an election meeting at Queen's Park Savannah on 1 February whilst the back contained a full-page notice of a mass meeting at Princes Building scheduled for 6 February 1925.[19] The TWA adopted these measures to stimulate public interest and to ensure an overwhelming response at its meetings.

Entire pages of the *Labour Leader* were utilized to inform supporters of the importance of Cipriani winning the Port-of-Spain seat. For instance, on 22 January 1925, there was a full-page ad with the following appeal: "Electors of Port-of-Spain Vote for Cipriani All The Time."[20] This media blitz also repeated the following slogan in bold lettering at the top of the pages of the TWA's organ: "VOTE FOR CIPRIANI THE MAN OF THE PEOPLE."[21] Such an intensive campaign of Cipriani would have increased attendance at his meetings and contributed to his subsequent success at the polls.

The public and TWA's supporters were regularly invited and notified of the venue and time of meetings for labour candidates, primarily through information published in the *Labour Leader*. In August 1924, there were notices of Pierre's meetings in Toco as well as Gobin's meetings at Perseverance Village, Chaguanas,[22] and in late January 1925, a detailed fixture of Cipriani's electioneering campaign was published in the interest of his supporters.[23] The TWA had undertaken the task of promoting and associating with the four candidates who were contesting the elections. On 13 September 1924, there was an advertisement featuring Cipriani, Pierre, Albert Victor Stollmeyer and Gobin with the tagline "The String Who Will Stand For Labour."[24]

Although the majority of candidates contesting on a labour platform depended upon the TWA's paper for their election notices, other labour candidates such as Stollmeyer had advertisements placed in both the *Trinidad Guardian* and *Labour Leader*. In the latter, Stollmeyer's advertisements had the caption "The Progressive Labour candidate and the little man that worried the Chamber of Commerce in the fight for the Agricultural Bank."[25] In the *Trinidad Guardian*, Stollmeyer's advertisement carried the line "Vote for Stollmeyer" in bold print, and it included the venue and time of his public meetings.[26] The use of both newspapers would have allowed a wider group of persons to be aware of the meetings.

In addition, the *Labour Leader* urged citizens to participate in the municipal elections of 1924, "It is your municipality. Its troubles are your troubles, and its defects belong to you."[27] Almost a decade later, a similar appeal to the public was made by Levi Darlington in a pamphlet endorsing Mayor Alfred Richards:

> It is the duty of every burgess to vote for some candidate or other. To say he is not interested in politics, or he does not care who goes on the Council, and make these excuses the basis of his indifference, is both foolish and dangerous … The Mayor and Councillors, as aforementioned, are the governors of the City. They fix your water and house rates; they build your roads; they light your streets – in a word, they manage your city.[28]

Darlington also reminded the public of the power of their vote and that the dishonesty or honesty of the Mayor and Councillors would be reflected in their administration and the municipality:

> The Mayor and Councillors cannot occupy those positions unless you, the burgess, put them there; and you are permitted to make these appointments, only by means of your votes. Herein lies the gem of Representative Government, which is really Government by the people – one and all. A burgess, then who refuses to vote, and take an active part in the affairs of the Municipality, however small that part may be, is guilty of the worst type of truancy.[29]

Handbills were also printed to advertise the venues of meetings and sometimes stated the manifestoes of candidates.[30] The use of handbills was affordable for the candidates, and these could be circulated easily among villagers who could not afford or did not have regular access to the *Labour Leader* or the daily newspapers.

In 1932, during the tense electoral battle between Sarran Teelucksingh and Ernest A. Robinson, posters were used to increase support, "A poster war started yesterday. Chaguanas is ablaze with pink and white posters on almost every shop and hoarding. They proclaim in large type the merits of the respective candidates." The two posters in Chaguanas were "Vote for Robinson – the greatest good for the greatest number" and "Don't be misled: Vote for Teelucksingh, the Independent Labourite; the man who has never failed you."[31]

Labour's election rivals placed advertisements in the *Trinidad Guardian* in their appeal to the electorate for their support. In his electoral advertisement, Randolph T. Rust, a candidate for Port-of-Spain, dismissed rumours that his campaign expenses were funded by the Trinidad Lake Asphalt Company and the Barber Asphalt Company, "This report is a DELIBERATE LIE, I have had no interest in these Companies, and

I am merely the Shipping Agent for Asphalt shipped to Europe."[32] One of the rivals, Robinson, appealed to voters with his slogan published in the *Trinidad Guardian*: "The Greatest Good for the Greatest Number."[33] There was a noteworthy difference between the advertisements of labour and their rivals. The TWA, via the *Labour Leader*, allotted more space for ads of their candidates, as evident in their full-page advertisements of Cipriani. However, advertisements of Rust and Robinson were repeated in the *Trinidad Guardian* minus the propaganda style of promotion adopted by the TWA in which candidates were portrayed as being sympathetic to the working class. In contrast to frequent electoral information of labour's candidates in the *Labour Leader*, there was a noticeable absence of the announcements of candidates' meetings in the *Trinidad Guardian*. In one of the rare notices, A. Cory-Davies, the rival of Stollmeyer (the labour candidate), had a simple, unimpressive ad in which electors of the County of St George were invited to attend a meeting to be held on 15 January 1925 at the Government School, Tunapuna.[34] Labour's intense advertising of its candidates certainly provided an advantage over its rivals.

Certain fears were expressed by labour concerning campaigns for the 1925 elections. At one of the meetings for Cipriani, at Princes Building, on 7 August 1924, Howard-Bishop warned the listeners to beware of persons offering them money ($5.00 or $10.00), a drink or trip in a motor car to vote for a candidate other than Cipriani.[35] An editorial in the *Labour Leader* entitled "Bribery at the Elections" warned the electorate that it is illegal if candidates pay to transport voters to the polls. Furthermore, as in England, anyone guilty of bribery was permanently stripped of all electoral privileges. The view of the TWA was that the penalties for bribery in the colony were not a deterrent. "The penalties locally attaching to this nefarious practice might, at first sight, to the casual observer appear rather heavy; but when on reflection a correct estimate is put upon what might be the result of the law dealing lightly with this aspect of popular government then the law on the point of Trinidad is far from being what it should be."[36]

During the 1920s, electoral candidates used the local press as the medium to inform the public of their manifestoes. In the municipal election campaign of 1924, candidates such as Cecil W. E. T. Worrel, Murchison Rigsby and C. Geo. Archibald published their manifestoes in the *Labour*

Leader.[37] Timothy Roodal published advertisements in two newspapers, the *Trinidad Guardian* and *Port-of-Spain Gazette*, to increase the circulation of his election manifesto for the national elections.[38] Furthermore, Roodal also utilized the *Port-of-Spain Gazette* to inform the public of his meetings in St Patrick.[39]

Before his entry into the political arena, Teelucksingh was already well-known in Caroni and surrounding areas. In 1917, he built the Couva Electric Theatre and held the distinction of being the first person to build a cinema in the rural areas of Trinidad, "Sarran Teelucksingh was a pioneer in the film industry in Trinidad and Tobago. He was the first person to build a cinema in the rural areas that is outside Port-of-Spain and San Fernando. He had a "tent cinema" which was elongated and mobile which was carried to rural areas as far as San Juan. Later, he built permanent cinemas in Siparia, Palo Seco and Couva."[40] Teelucksingh's Electric Theatre in Couva was the venue for some of his election meetings. In addition, Teelucksingh owned a shop in Couva which was frequented by villagers. Both enterprises served to promote Teelucksingh's popularity during elections in Central Trinidad.

In 1928, Teelucksingh (the TWA candidate) also utilized the press in his campaign and in the *Labour Leader* gave seven reasons why he deserved the support from the electorate of Caroni (see Appendix 4). The publication also contained Teelucksingh's campaign itinerary indicating the time and date for meetings scheduled during February–March 1928 to be held in such venues as the Couva Theatre, Carapichaima E. C. School, Cunupia R. C. School, California Government School and the Court House in Chaguanas.[41]

E. Radcliffe-Clarke, one of Roodal's opponents in the contest for St Patrick, published, in January 1928, his "valediction" in the *Trinidad Guardian* and the *Port-of-Spain Gazette* which outlined his promises and a pledge to serve the electors of St Patrick, "I will earnestly but modestly represent to the Government the needs of my constituents brought to my notice, as also all genuine grievances whether by individuals or by numbers, and will endeavor to get justice done in all cases."[42] However, on 11 January, Radcliffe-Clarke, sensing defeat, announced his withdrawal from the election. Such a decision signalled a certain victory for Roodal and boosted the confidence of other labour candidates in the election.

During 1928 general elections, electioneering was less elaborate when compared to the publicity campaigns conducted by the labour candidates for the 1925 elections. Indeed, a major reason for the reduced publicity was that only three electoral campaigns were conducted since four of the candidates were reinstated unopposed to the Legislative Council (see Appendix 6). Those unopposed were Cipriani, F. E. M. Hosein, T. M. Kelshall and C. H. Pierre.[43] Interestingly, in November 1927, a frequent contributor to the *Labour Leader* "Poll Axe" predicted that certain candidates would be unopposed and gave an insight, "my opinion is that the seat for Port-of-Spain will be uncontested and that Captain Cipriani will be returned unopposed." Likewise, for Caroni, the writer believed that Teelucksingh had the whole-hearted support of thousands.[44] Furthermore, canvassers were employed to inform the electorate of matters pertaining to labour candidates. For instance, Roodal, who was considerably wealthy, ensured his campaign staff included canvassers. It was reported in the press that in St Patrick "the suffrage of the county had been industriously canvassed for over a month both privately and publicly."[45]

In the months prior to the 1933 elections, labour was disadvantaged in its publicity of candidates since the publication of the *Labour Leader* was discontinued.[46] The newly established working-class paper *The People* did not seem concerned with extensive coverage of the general elections, whereas labour's rivals continued to use the *Trinidad Guardian* to ensure that the public was informed of their political agenda. Robinson, in contesting the Caroni seat for the third consecutive time, published his manifesto in the *Trinidad Guardian* in which he sought to project himself to the electorate as being better than his challenger, Teelucksingh, "As an employer of labour, my duty necessarily brings me into more intimate and constant contact with the worker, and, consequently, I am better positioned to interpret his true feelings and aspirations than one whose knowledge of labour conditions is merely theoretical and therefore impractical."[47] Interestingly, in the final stage of the municipal election campaign of 1933, the editorial of *The People* advised the electorate to be wary of persons who portrayed themselves as sympathetic to labour, "One fact which has been referred to before, and which is now openly asserted, namely that persons of no possible labour convictions, assert themselves to be of the party, thereby making a tool of the labour organisation and a stepping stone to their attainment of political or municipal honours."[48] The editorial mentioned two candidates, A. P. T. Ambard and Edward Lai Fook, as persons who allowed themselves to be viewed as members of the TWA and sought assistance from the party. The TWA denied these claims of the candidates.

Another of the TWA's rivals was Harold Piper who, though not chosen by the TWA as its candidate, contested in Victoria as an "Independent Labour Candidate" and as a "Progressive Democrat." Piper's advertisement sought to explain the undemocratic and seemingly unjust decision by the TWA to reject his candidature, "The rejection of my candidature by the General Council of the T. W. A. in favour of one little known, and with no great claims to your suffrages, is a direct flouting of your wishes, a gross disregard of your rights, an insult to your intelligence, and a gratuitous and undeserved wounding of your feelings."[49]

A. C. B. Singh, the independent socialist contesting St George, had a series of ads in 1933 which described himself as follows: "The poor man's friend, The People's Candidate" and "The Man Who Shelters the Shelterless."[50] It was apparent from Singh's caption that he sought to portray himself as being similar to TWA candidates in sharing their concern for improved conditions of the working class.[51] Notice of meetings of labour's rivals received some publicity in the *East Indian Weekly*. An illustration is in 1932 when the newspaper published a notice of a meeting of Kelshall scheduled for 20 December at New Town Hall, San Fernando. Likewise, the readership was informed of the electioneering meeting for Teelucksingh, who had broken ranks with the TWA, on 22 December at Cunupia.[52] In 1933, there was a report of a "leaflet war" brewing among the candidates in Victoria.[53] The distribution of leaflets was not only to intensify the electoral contest but also to inform persons who did not purchase newspapers.

In the 1938 elections, Rienzi, the President General of the OWTU and All Trinidad Sugar Estates and Factories Workers' Trade Union (ATSE+FWTU), ventured into the political sphere. He was leader of the Unionist Party. In addition to support from the membership of both unions, he was endorsed by L. F. Walcott, editor of *The People*. One of the election ads for Rienzi had the captions "The Idol of the South" and "He Has The Support of 'The People.' "[54] Upon winning the Victoria seat, Rienzi was described by the newspaper as "The People's Candidate."[55]

Qualifications of candidates

Income and property qualifications of the candidates seeking election to the Legislative Council were compulsory requirements in Trinidad and Tobago. However, questions pertaining to the personal character and intelligence of the candidates were often raised by speakers and members of the public who attended electoral meetings. It became increasingly evident at gatherings that the electorate expressed the view that material wealth should not be a priority for membership in Parliament.

One of the weaknesses of the proposed elective principle was the limited franchise. This was due to high property and income qualifications for voters and candidates seeking election to the Legislative Council.[56] For all voters, the property qualifications included occupation of property rented at £12 10s per annum in a Borough or £10 elsewhere. Furthermore, the law stipulated that male voters must be over twenty-one years of age, whilst women were required to be thirty years and over. Some Indian women were able to vote as they owned small pieces of land in the rural areas of the colony.[57] And, for persons seeking to be elected to the Legislative Council, only men were eligible as candidates; also, they had to be literate in the English language and registered as voters. Furthermore, the electoral candidate had to possess income qualifications, earning at least £400 per annum, and also own property valued at least £2,500 or from which the annual income was at least £200.[58]

Among the candidates who contested the elections, there were variations in their social and professional status, and similarly, there were obvious differences in property ownership and wealth. There were large landowners like Ernest A. Robinson, candidate for Caroni, who owned considerable acreage in Chaguanas, including large citrus, rubber and cocoa estates. Robinson was also a barrister-at-law and the Managing Director of Woodford Lodge Sugar Estate. In contrast, Teelucksingh, Robinson's rival, was an entrepreneur owning business, which included the blending of rum for distribution to shops. In addition, Teelucksingh owned a dry goods store in Couva and operated the first rural tarpaulin cinema, which he took to several villages; later, he went on to build a permanent cinema house. During the 1920s and 1930s, Teelucksingh was also a landowner with one acre of land in Exchange Village, Couva.[59]

Other candidates who were either merchants or proprietors included Randolph Rust (merchant), Albert Cory-Davies (merchant and planter), Albert Victor Stollmeyer (merchant and proprietor), Ernest Radcliffe-Clarke (proprietor), Albert A. Sobrian (proprietor) and Isaac Hope (merchant). Also included in this category was Cipriani whose occupation was listed as "Planter, General Commission Agent, Trainer of Racehorses and Licensed Auctioneer." A considerable number of professionals also contested the election. Among them were three lawyers – Charles H. Pierre, Jules Mahabir and Gaston Johnson. Two other professionals were Thomas M. Kelshall (solicitor) and James A. Biggart (druggist).[60]

During the 1925 electoral campaign, it seemed that some members of the public felt morality should be one of the qualifications for membership in the Parliament. In November 1924, the *Labour Leader* published a letter (dated 24 October 1924) signed by Teelucksingh and his supporters, addressed to Rev. W. I. Green, Superintendent of the Canadian Presbyterian Mission Field in Couva.[61] The signatories complained that on the 3 October 1924, at one of Teelucksingh's electioneering meetings, H. D. Imamshah, a prominent Presbyterian layman made irresponsible public accusations against Teelucksingh: "Mr. H. D. Imamshah in opposing the candidacy of Mr. Teelucksingh thought it a fitting occasion, among other things, to refer to this gentleman's moral character by mentioning that a man with an immoral character was not fit to represent the people on the Legislative Council."[62] Furthermore, the letter to Green also criticized Imamshah for his behaviour at a public meeting in which he responded to a speech by F. E. M. Hosein: "He [Imamshah] incited the meeting by telling them that they [the people of Chaguanas] were grossly insulted, and they must not stand for such insults."[63] There is no further evidence to suggest that Imamshah disrupted or made further accusations against the candidate at subsequent election meetings. Imamshah was a probationer, preparing for the ministry of the Presbyterian Church, and it is possible that complaints to his supervisor would have deterred further slander on Teelucksingh's character. Imamshah's opposition to Teelucksingh hinged on the question of morality. The incident is an indication that morality, though not an official requirement, was another criterion in addition to property qualifications which the citizenry considered important for members of the Legislative Council.

During the 1928 electoral campaign, the matter of the character of candidates also became an issue on electioneering platforms. On 21 January 1928, a letter to the editor of the *Port-of-Spain Gazette*, signed "Middle Class voter," expressed disappointment with Pierre's performance in the Legislative Council and appealed to Gaston Johnston to perform an honourable public duty and contest the election. The writer saw it necessary to highlight Johnston's qualities, "His integrity, honour and abilities are preferable to Mr. Pierre's mediocrity."[64]

During the 1933 campaign, the unofficial qualification of education was desirable for election to the Legislative Council. In Trinidad Central, the education and experience of Robinson was seen by his supporters as an asset for election to the council. The editorial of the *Trinidad Guardian* championed Robinson's cause believing that members with a sound knowledge of agriculture was needed in the council.[65] In addition, at an election rally in Carapichaima, Captain W. F. Watson of Waterloo Estates Limited argued that Robinson's legal training would be an advantage in the Legislative Council. The ability to properly manage finances was highlighted by Robinson at a meeting in Mamoral. He told the crowd, "The difference between my opponent and myself is that I have made capital and he has lost it. I utilise my capital to bring relief by providing employment to hundreds of the poor of this country. Isn't that better than taking it and frittering it away."[66] At Tabaquite, Robinson told 600 supporters that if he was elected, they would not be disappointed.[67] This claim by Robinson was an attempt to prove to the electorate that he was sincere and trustworthy.

Membership and involvement in public life

In seeking the support of candidates at electoral meetings, there were allusions to their participation in public life, particularly any praiseworthy involvement in organizations, committees and association in the colony. For instance, on 18 January, at Tunapuna Government School, Michael Hamel-Smith, who chaired Stollmeyer's meeting, mentioned that the candidate was Chairman of the St Ann's and Diego Martin Local Road Board for many years and also served on the Committee of the Agricultural Society.[68] The TWA's spearheading of the establishment of an Agricultural Bank complemented Stollmeyer's involvement in the Agricultural Society.

Another labour candidate Harold Piper, in Princes Town, was praised by John Gordon (President of the Princes Town branch of the TWA) who emphasized that Piper was one of the zealous members of the Princes Town branch of the TWA. Another speaker supportive of the candidate, Mentor, claimed that the General Council of the TWA favoured Harold Mahabir because he was a former member of the League of Coloured Peoples in England.[69] Mahabir's membership in the league and his experience in working among the socially marginalized would have influenced the TWA's decision to approve his candidacy.

The rivals of labour candidates also placed considerable emphasis on their social contributions to communities. On 2 January 1925, in an election meeting for Robinson held at the Couva Court House, Watson, one of the speakers, encouraged the crowd to support Robinson because of his role in the Royal Commission of the Red House in investigating the Water Riots of 1903.[70] In a similar vein, in a gathering organized for Cory-Davies at San Juan, one of the speakers, Prince Robinson, drew attention to the candidate's social standing in society. The speaker revealed that Cory-Davies was Vice President of a premier club, the Queen's Park Cricket Club, whilst his rival Stollmeyer was President of the less prestigious San Juan Sporting Club.[71]

At Santa Cruz, on 22 January, at a meeting for Cory-Davies, C. Cudjoe moved a resolution supporting the candidate and identified Cory-Davies as a member of both the Chamber of Commerce and a large business concern in Port-of-Spain. The seconder of the resolution, F. D. Blackman, drew reference to the fact that the working class-candidate – Stollmeyer – was Chairman of the Local Road Board at Santa Cruz and, likewise, Cory-Davies was a member of the Tacarigua Local Road Board.[72] Such speakers were intent on demonstrating that their candidate was capable, as the TWA's choices, in serving the community and participating in the colony's affairs.

Other rivals of labour were also keen on emphasizing their service to the colony. For instance, at Victoria Hall, San Fernando, Kelshall drew references to the candidate's service on the Board of Education.[73] And, at an electioneering meeting for Sobrian at Fyzabad, the candidate's membership on the Board of Agriculture was highlighted. One of the speakers at this gathering referred to Sobrian's association with the Naparima District Agricultural Society.[74] At another meeting, C. B. Mathura publicly noted that Sobrian was a member of the Committee of the Truck Bill.[75] These pronouncements from non-labour were an attempt to portray their candidates as being industrious. However, the success of the labour candidates at the polls proved otherwise (see Appendix 3).

In the municipal election campaign of 1927, Tito Achong, in a letter to the editor of the *Labour Leader*, made a stirring appeal to the electorate to support Cipriani who honourably served in the British Army and was a good citizen. Achong also highlighted the Cipriani's service: "Capt. Cipriani is a man of parts. His activities are manifold; his knowledge of the wants and aspiration of the people intimate; his sympathy for the underdog beyond measure, and his cry for social justice not seldom thrill the land ... A vote for Cipriani is a vote for progress. A vote against Cipriani is a vote for class privilege. Vote Cipriani."[76]

In the course of the 1928 national elections, emphasis on the service of candidates also came through the medium of letters in the local press. On 12 January 1928, a letter to the *Port-of-Spain Gazette* praised Robinson's contacts with colonial officials at social and political affairs. The writer further stated that Robinson made annual visits to England and met with MPs and others who were interested in developments occurring in the colony.[77] Support for Sobrian's association with groups, as in the case of Robinson, came from editorial letters. For example, one letter to the editor of the *Port-of-Spain Gazette*, signed "Quality," sought to justify support of Sobrian by referring to the candidate's membership in the Legislative Council, Board of Agriculture and Agricultural Society.[78]

In 1938, Harold Piper contested the Victoria seat and was endorsed at a meeting held at the All Age Society Hall. The resolution of support was moved by Daniel Hackshaw, President of the All Age Friendly Society.[79] Such an endorsement was vital as this indicated that a group in society believed a candidate to be worthy of winning the election. In a similar fashion, speakers on Rienzi's platform endorsed the candidate's contribution to society. For instance, John Rojas, Second Vice President of the OWTU, highlighted the fact that Rienzi placed an important role in creating peace during the tumultuous 1937 disturbances.[80]

The constant references to membership in organizations and service to the colony were primarily aimed at promoting the candidate as being best suited as a representative in the Legislative Council. It also complemented the plan, manifesto and vision of a candidate. However, in some instances, recounting the achievements of electoral candidates concerned with improving the welfare of the working class and being involved in the colony's affairs neither increased one's chances nor guaranteed a candidate's success at the polls. An illustration is E. A. Robinson who, on three occasions, unsuccessfully contested the seat of Caroni. This, in spite of the fact that throughout the three electioneering campaigns, Robinson and platform speakers constantly touted the candidate as having made significant contributions to the economic and political development of Caroni and the rest of the colony.

Tobago

Tobago's participation in the national elections was not a new and unfamiliar exercise for the island. The political history of Tobago reflects its early association with representative institutions. In the early nineteenth century, Tobago was a self-governing colony possessing a bicameral legislature, unlike Trinidad with its Crown Colony status.[81] However, by 1874 the bicameral political system in Tobago was abolished and a single-chamber legislature was implemented.[82] Subsequently, on 20 October 1898, its political system would again be modified, with an Order-in-Council for both islands with Tobago as a ward of Trinidad. Susan Craig-James is accurate in describing the representation of Tobago in the Legislative Council from 1898 to February 1925 as "weak."[83] She contends that, during this time, poor representation of Tobago was due to factors such as inadequate sea communications between the two islands and that the Tobago planters did not possess the time and adequate finances.[84]

In preparation for the 1925 elections, the Ward of Tobago was allocated only one candidate among the seven to be elected for the twin-island legislature. However, the allocation of one representative did not diminish the enthusiasm among the island's residents: "Tobago is hot with the question of the coming election. This is the subject that is being freely discussed. It is not known to a certainty how many candidates will contest the seat for Tobago at the Legislative Council, but Mr. James A. Biggart is electrifying his countrymen to be up and doing in his favor, and many have caught his inspiration."[85] The electioneering campaign for candidates in Tobago contained features similar to that conducted in Trinidad. Candidates were publicly presented and endorsed by audiences at public meetings; manifestoes were outlined by rival candidates; and social and political issues were analysed by platform speakers.

On 10 September 1924, a public electoral meeting was held in the Anglican school in Scarborough to secure public approval for the nomination of James A. Biggart (1877–1932) as an electoral candidate. He was a licensed druggist and chemist. Chairman J. Prince and several other speakers unanimously supported the nomination. Also, the audience was fully supportive of Biggart. "They were asked to vote by show of hands, and they did it readily, notwithstanding the one or two discordant souls heard in the pit."[86] Biggart (the rival of labour) outlined his manifesto in which he promised to serve Tobago and offered plans for the island:

> There are some pressing needs of Tobago at the present time, which I regard as vital to her progress, and to the accomplishment of which I shall use my liveliest interest. Among them are: 1. Daily Communication with Trinidad; 2. Internal communication – opening up of new roads and proper maintenance of those now existing; 3. A Secondary School for Tobago; 4. Extension of the Jetty, Scarborough; erection of a jetty at Roxborough; 5. Borough Council for Town of Scarborough.[87]

A large audience attended another of Biggart's meetings at the Moravian school, in Moriah, in which his nomination was again approved. The issue of political representation was raised at the meeting with "captivating speeches in favour of Representative Government and Mr. Biggart's election to a seat in the Council were delivered by all the speakers."[88] The support and encouraging attendance for Biggart was also evident on 5 October 1924 at the Anglican school in Plymouth. Biggart's nomination was unanimously accepted by those in attendance, and the quality of presentations was high. "Captivating speeches in favour of Mr. Biggart were delivered by all the speakers who seemed to be thoroughly acquainted with their subject, by which they succeeded in completely arresting the attention of the entire audience."[89] Biggart's meetings later moved to the Roxborough E. C. and St Patrick's E. C. Schools.[90]

At this time, there were no newspapers printed in Tobago, but the island-ward received publications from Port-of-Spain. These media included columns dedicated to Tobago affairs. The *Trinidad Guardian* had regular reports on Tobago, the *Labour Leader* introduced a column entitled "Tobago News" and the *Port-of-Spain Gazette* had "Tobago Tidings."

Working-class representatives made only a few visits to Tobago, since the TWA's powerful support group based in Trinidad was busy with its extensive campaign throughout the island and would have certainly encountered difficulties in maintaining a physical presence in Tobago. Instead, the Tobago labour campaign was supported by the Trinidad-based TWA primarily through the *Labour Leader*, its official organ, and the association's branches in the sister island. Interestingly, the *Labour Leader* published Biggart's manifesto and reported on his meetings but did not support his candidature. The newspaper's opinion of Biggart's campaign was not favourable, and he was accused of being a liberal. The paper denounced, "His several electioneering speeches, too, do not ring true to a tune that bespeak sincerity of thought and action in the best interests of a people who are practically in the throes of industrial serfdom."[91] The coverage allotted to Biggart was to enlighten the labour supporters in Tobago on the inadequacies of the candidate as the island's representative.

The TWA endorsed the candidature of Isaac Hope (1865–1956), the rival of Biggart, in the contest for the Tobago seat. Hope was a building contractor and merchant. On 16 September 1924, a correspondent of the *Labour Leader* commended Isaac Hope to the electorate, "In this gentleman, the community must realise that they will have a representative who does not seek the seat because of personal aggrandisement, but because he feels he has a sacred duty to perform to his native island, his fellow country-men and to himself."[92] Following the views of this commendation, the *Labour Leader* led from its pages a major campaign in support of Hope, "We have no alternative than to endorse the views expressed above ... Mr. Hope touches at the very root of what is really needed to bring about better conditions not only in Tobago, but even in Trinidad."[93] This was true since Hope had businesses in Tobago and North Trinidad.[94] In addition, on 6 October, the *Labour Leader* published a picture of Hope with the title "Another addition to the Labour String."[95]

On 14 October 1924, Cipriani and Howard-Bishop, Executive members of the TWA, journeyed to Tobago and conducted two public meetings in Scarborough and Moriah – both were to garner public support for Hope. At Scarborough, George McEachnie (solicitor and conveyancer) presided the meeting, and Captain W. Havell, Cipriani, Howard-Bishop, and A. Peters (Headmaster of Mason Hall R. C. School) were among those on the platform. During Cipriani's address, he made reference to the labour government in England and a heckler replied, "But they are out of it now!" Cipriani responded, "Yes, but they are coming again with greater power to liberate you and others of your ilk from industrial serfdom and to lift the ban of cheap officialdom from your heads."[96] The heckler was reported to have remained "practically speechless and mute" for the rest of the meeting. Howard-Bishop denounced Biggart's manifesto as "cribbed, cabined and confined." This result was that someone from the crowd shouted a sarcastic reply – "Pretty," to which Howard-Bishop responded in a manner which made the heckler "crestfallen with drooping head."[97]

Biggart eventually won in Tobago and from reports, he seemed to be more organized and received more enthusiastic responses than Hope. A major factor responsible for Biggart's victory was his ability to connect with the Tobagonians. Biggart had been a co-founder of a cricket club and served on a committee to oversee the Tobago Public Library. In 1923, he helped create the Leeward District Agricultural Society in Scarborough. In addition, Biggart was President of the Scarborough Literary and Debating Club and assisted events held by St Andrew's Anglican Church in Scarborough.[98]

During the 1928 electoral campaign, there was reduced interest in the coverage of elections in the *Labour Leader* and *Trinidad Guardian*. Once more, the incumbent Biggart was the preferred candidate. A meeting was held on 22 January 1928 in Delaford to support his candidature, and the attendance included villagers from neighbouring communities such as King's Bay and Louis d'Or.[99] At this meeting, a supporter pledged allegiance to Biggart in an address: "In conclusion, we are glad to assure you sir, that in King's Bay, Delaford, and Louis d'Or you have the whole-hearted support of every man, woman and child from the big European planters to the ordinary street labourer."[100] Biggart, in his speech, sought to dismiss rumours that were being spread by his rival, Samuel Bonnett (the labour candidate), and supporters of the TWA: "They were telling the people that he (the speaker) had done absolutely nothing for them during the three years he had represented them on the Legislative Council and that he had caused the labourers to do longer hours of labour and other rubbish (voices, they are trying to fool the people)."[101] A meeting for Biggart was held on 5 February at Roxborough, where, in previous meetings, a proposal supporting his nomination was signed by residents of Roxborough. The statement expressed gratitude for Biggart's achievements, which included a grant to a secondary school, erection of a retaining wall at Military Road, allowance of stamping of scales and weights at Roxborough and the inclusion of Tobago as a port of call for Canadian steamers.[102]

Bonnett agreed to contest the seat on a "labour-socialist" platform and pledged, "it will always be my highest endeavour to aim at getting the greatest good for the greatest number of the people and a square deal for the underdog." Bonnett presented a plan for improvements in Tobago which included reduction of the present water tax, establishment of a Money Order Department in the Post Office at Moriah, construction of a Roxborough market, provision of better means of transport for travellers between Roxborough and Speyside, revision of the Teacher's Pension Scheme and competitive entry into the Civil Services. These proposals were included in the only major article in the *Labour Leader* on Bonnett's election campaign in Tobago.[103]

In Tobago, only a quarter of the total electorate voted. In a total electorate comprising 1,661 persons, Biggart polled 361 votes whilst the defeated

Bonnett could only muster 55 votes.[104] Biggart's victory was based on a 25 per cent voter turnout, but it nevertheless indicated that between these two candidates, both of whom were inclined to support working-class issues, the electorate was not attracted to the TWA's candidate. Also, the fact that *Labour Leader* lent scant support to Bonnett during his campaign would have contributed to his dismal defeat at the polls.

In 1933, the Tobago electoral campaign was conducted without Biggart who had died. Therefore, the candidates contesting the 1933 elections in Tobago were Isaac Hope (the defeated labour candidate of 1925), John I. King (proprietor and shopkeeper) of Moriah and G. F. Samuel (druggist) of Scarborough.[105] In May 1932, the General Council of the TWA recommended G. F. Samuel as the labour-socialist candidate for the elections in Tobago.[106] It was noteworthy that the incumbent Hope, despite being associated with the TWA in 1925, was not labour's choice in the 1933 elections. Political newcomer Samuel did not receive publicity in either the daily press or *The People*. In the 1933 elections, the ideological description that was displayed after each candidate's name was omitted for George F. Samuel. In the press, both Isaac Hope and John I. King were designated "independent" whilst George F. Samuel was identified as "unknown."[107] Since Samuel was endorsed by the TWA, he should have been identified as "socialist" as were other labour candidates in Trinidad. Even though the *Trinidad Guardian* reported of the "independents" and an "unknown" among the Tobago candidates, in one of its election reports, King is identified as socialist and not independent, "In Tobago, Mr. Isaac King, the Socialist candidate met with a stormy reception at his first meeting and was heckled and harangued by a small crowd."[108]

On 1 January 1933, Hope published his New Year greetings to the electors of Tobago in which he asked for their support, "I have no doubt that you will be afforded the opportunity of casting your vote definitely for the man you depend on to represent your country's and your interest at the Council."[109] He subsequently held a meeting on 13 January in which C. M. Tull, headteacher of Mason Hall Wesleyan School, presided, and after the Chairman's opening address, the candidate spoke on his plans, if re-elected for Tobago. Several members of the audience, upon being invited by the Chairman, spoke at the meeting in support of Hope. Other election gatherings for Hope were held in Montgomery and Scarborough.[110] The *Trinidad Guardian* reported a modest turnout at the 1933 polls in Tobago, with a 463 voter turnout from an electorate of 1,657 registered Tobagonians (see Table 1).

An election protest occurred in Tobago at the onset of the 1938 elections. The protest took the form of complaints to the government regarding the rejection of nomination papers of Samuel Bonnett, owner of Adventure Estate, by the Returning Officer, H. Maingot. According to the complaint, Maingot believed that the candidate arrived late and thus could not be accepted. However, Bonnett argued that he arrived one minute after the statutory time.[111] As a result of Bonnett's disqualification, two candidates, George de Nobriga and George F. Samuel, contested the lone Tobago seat. On 7 January, Samuel withdrew from the electoral race, and as a result, de Nobriga returned unopposed as the island's representative.[112] Even if there were opposing candidates, de Nobriga would have comfortably won. He was a planter, Director of a few companies including Trinidad Consolidated Telephone Company, Electric Ice Company and Tobago Plantations Limited. De Nobriga also had an appealing manifesto which included adequate sea communication, improvements in tourism, better roads and assistance to peasants.[113]

From the TWA's inception, it was no easy task to maintain a commanding presence in Tobago although there were branches established on

Table 1 Voting results for 1933 elections in Tobago

District	Candidates	
	I. Hope	J. King
Scarborough	226	64
Moriah	46	39
Roxborough	74	14
	346	117
Total votes accepted		463
Total votes rejected		30

Source: *Trinidad Guardian.*

this island. Furthermore, the Executive failed to maintain any enduring cohesion and control over the Tobago branches. During election campaigns, the *Labour Leader* was the principal source of electoral information to members and supporters of the TWA in Tobago. Certainly, the election thrust would have been enhanced with the regular presence of Cipriani and Executive TWA members on the platform of Tobagonian candidates. But, this was not to be as the Tobagonian candidates were virtually on their own.

Certain factors affected the performance of the TWA's candidates in the early elections. The difficulty in communication among branches in Trinidad and Tobago contributed to personal contacts being infrequent. Indeed, without the benefits of air travel, telephone and electronic media, the TWA's communication between the two islands rested largely upon the visits of cargo ships. The indirect exclusion of Tobago from the powerful TWA's electoral campaign in Trinidad would have contributed to the failure of the association's candidates in the colony's elections. Tobagonians would have felt, for the most part due to the relatively late interest of the TWA towards the Tobago elections during 1929–1930, that the TWA, a Trinidad-based organization, was primarily concerned about victory only in Trinidad.

Another plausible factor that mitigated against the TWA's chances at the polls was the voter eligibility of its supporters. Therefore, if Tobagonian supporters of the TWA did not possess the necessary income and property qualifications, labour candidates would be at a disadvantage. Reports of large crowds at TWA's public meetings in Tobago were no guarantee of electoral support since voting power may not have been in the hands of labour supporters.

However, the failure of the powerful TWA to influence the electorate in Tobago may have its roots in the political history of the island. Eric Williams noted, "This is how Tobago lived up to the 18th century – between Britain and France, or between France and Holland, or between Holland and Britain, now invaded by buccaneers, now attacked by Spain, now settled by Courlanders."[114] Then, finally by the Act of Union, Tobago became a ward of Trinidad and was united under a single government. But, prior to this, Tobago had its own representative government and electoral traditions. It enjoyed self-governing status with its own Governor. Therefore, the traditions of independence embedded in the psyche of Tobagonians must have been the operative principle in the 1925 elections and thereafter.

By 1930, there were TWA branches at Bethel, Canaan, Lambeaux Village, Plymouth, Scarborough, Roxborough and Glamorgan. The total membership was an impressive 1,000 persons. This identification with the Trinidad-based TWA ought not to be construed as a guarantee that the electorate in Tobago would align itself to a political culture, that of Trinidad, which was in its embryonic stages. The defeat of labour in the elections in Tobago may have sent signals that, the island, though a ward of Trinidad, was not prepared as yet to be politically controlled by Trinidad.

Undoubtedly, the 1925–1938 electoral exercises in Trinidad and Tobago signalled a new era in politics in the colony. This first stage in the planning and contest for seats in the Legislative Council undoubtedly produced intense campaigns and sustained interest from the candidates as well as from the electorate and the disenfranchised. The encounter between candidates and their rivals resulted in quality debates on the political stage indicative of the high level of political maturity already attained in the colony.

The struggle among fledgling "parties," like the TWA with their phalanx of speakers and core supporters, and the involvement of small but influential pressure groups such as the EINA clearly indicated the desirability and advantage of the "party" approach to elections. The TWA (and later as the TLP) in its mass appeal through its closely bonded network of branches in the colony was the precursor of the well-oiled political machinery of the People's National Movement (PNM) and Democratic Labour Party (DLP) which were to later develop in the colony.

Notes

1. Eric Williams, *History of the People of Trinidad and Tobago* (London: Andre Deutsch, 1964), 220–221.
2. A letter (dated 12 August 1921) from W. Gillies of the BLP to Howard-Bishop indicated the questions and dates on which they were to be asked in the House of Commons. *Labour Leader* 2 September 1922.

3. *Labour Leader* 2 September 1922. For more on Howard-Bishop's trip, see Singh, *Race and Class*, 48.
4. *Labour Leader* 26 August 1922.
5. *Report of the Honourable E.F.L. Wood (Parliamentary Under Secretary of State for the Colonies) on His Visit to the West Indies and British Guiana December 1921–February 1922* (London: HMSO, 1922), 24 (hereafter cited as *Wood Report*).
6. Hosein was a lawyer and advocate of civil rights and better treatment of Indians in the colony.
7. *East Indian Weekly* 12 January 1929.
8. *Wood Report*, 24.
9. *Wood Report*, 23, 25.
10. Williams, *History of the People of Trinidad and Tobago*, 220.
11. Ince, "Politics before the People's National Movement, 67.
12. See *Labour Leader* 6, 9, 11, 18 August, 20 September 1924.
13. Cipriani's ad stated: PORT-OF-SPAIN

    Be Prepared
    TO VOTE FOR
    Captain A Cipriani
    THE MAN OF THE PEOPLE AND
    FOR THE PEOPLE.
    AT THE
    COMING ELECTIONS

14. Pierre's ads were approximately 10.5 cm by 8.5 cm and also included the candidate's picture (3 cm by 4 cm).
15. *Labour Leader* 25 October 1924.
16. See *Labour Leader* 6, 8, 20 August 1924.
17. *Labour Leader* 15 November 1924.
18. *Labour Leader* 24, 28, 31 January 1925.
19. *Labour Leader* 31 January 1925.
20. *Labour Leader* 22 January 1925.
21. *Labour Leader* 16, 18, 20, 23 August 1925.
22. *Labour Leader* 9, 20, 23 August 1924.
23. The fixture included a mass meeting at the Olympic Theatre at 4.00 pm on Friday, 23 January, as well as meetings at Gaiety Theatre, St Joseph Road, at 3.30 pm, on the same day, and on Sunday, 25 January; and a street parade beginning at Woodford Square at 1.30 pm on 24 January. *Labour Leader* 22 January 1925.
24. *Labour Leader* 13 September 1924. See also 23, 30 August, 9 September 1924.
25. *Labour Leader* 2 August 1924.
26. *TG* 4, 15, 16, 17, 20, 23 January 1925.
27. *Labour Leader* 25 October 1924.

28. Levi Darlington, *Things the People Should Know: The Forthcoming Municipal Elections* (n.p.: n.d.).
29. Darlington, *Things the People Should Know*.
30. E. R. Blades, personal interview, 7 February 2001. Blades resides in Cumuto, and he celebrated his 107th birthday in 2009.
31. *TG* 8 December 1932.
32. *TG* 1, 6, 11, 18, January 1925.
33. *TG* 1, 3, 6, 7, 8, 10, January 1925.
34. *TG* 15 January 1925.
35. *Labour Leader* 9 August 1924.
36. *Labour Leader* 9 August 1924.
37. *Labour Leader* 25 October 1924.
38. *Port-of-Spain Gazette* 5, 6, 13, 15 January 1928 (hereafter cited as *POSG*).
39. *POSG* 26 January 1928. The meetings were to be held at Siparia (27 January), Erin (30 January), Cedros (4 March), La Brea (6 March) and Oropouche (8 March).
40. Godfrey Teelucksingh, personal interview, 27 April 2001. Godfrey lived in Calcutta (central Trinidad) and was the son of Sarran Teelucksingh.
41. *Labour Leader* 18 February 1928.
42. *POSG* 5, 7, 8, January 1928. Also *TG* 4, 5, 6, 7, 8, 10, January 1928 (size of the ads were approximately 11.5 cm by 21 cm).
43. See Ince, "Politics before the People's National Movement," 64.
44. *Labour Leader* 12 November 1927.
45. *TG* 12 February 1928.
46. The candidates returning unopposed were Cipriani and Pierre. Ince, , "Politics before the People's National Movement," 99.
47. *TG* 11, 18, 23 January 1933.
48. *The People* 28 October 1933.
49. *TG* 24, 26, 27, January 1933. There is mention of Piper's advertisement in Ince, "Politics before the People's National Movement," 101.
50. *TG* 5, 8, 15, 19, 22, 24, January 1933.
51. Ince suggests that the electorate would vote for those displaying sympathy with labour rather than candidates linked to big businesses. Ince, "Politics before the People's National Movement," 71.
52. *East Indian Weekly* 17 December 1932.
53. *TG* 22 January 1933.
54. *The People* 8 January 1938.
55. *The People* 29 January 1938.
56. Ayearst, *The British West Indies*, 33–34.
57. See Singh, *Race and Class*, 67.
58. *Labour Leader* 27 January 1923.
59. Teelucksingh, personal interview, 27 April 2001.

60. *TG* 18 January 1925.
61. Signatories included L. Ramjitsingh, Babu Lalsingh, James Headlie, C. W. Samlalsingh, H. Thesiger, Jas Alex. Amorgan. *Labour Leader* 22 November 1924. The article was entitled "Gutter Tactics to Obtain Political Victory."
62. *Labour Leader* 22 November 1924.
63. *Labour Leader* 22 November 1924.
64. *POSG* 21 January 1928.
65. *TG* 7 January 1933. Ten days later, another editorial of the newspaper praised Robinson for committing his views to paper. *TG* 17 January 1933.
66. *TG* 14 January 1933.
67. *TG* 18 January 1933.
68. *TG* 20 January 1925.
69. *POSG* 4 January 1933.
70. *TG* 3 January 1925.
71. *TG* 21 January 1925.
72. *TG* 23 January 1925.
73. *TG* 23 January 1925.
74. *POSG* 29 January 1928.
75. *POSG* 31 January 1928.
76. *Labour Leader* 2 January 1927.
77. *POSG* 12 January 1928.
78. *POSG* 29 January 1928.
79. *The People* 4 January 1938.
80. *The People* 6 January 1938.
81. For more on the early politics of Tobago, see K. O. Laurence, "Council, Assembly and Taxation in Tobago, 1793–1815," unpublished paper presented at the Association of Caribbean Historians Conference, St Augustine, 1990.
82. The new Legislative Council in Tobago comprised fourteen members (six nominated by the Governor and eight elected by Tobagonians). Williams, *History of the People of Trinidad and Tobago*, 133.
83. Susan Craig-James, *The Changing Society of Tobago, 1838–1938: A Fracture Whole, Volume II: 1900–1938* (Arima: Cornerstone Press, 2008), 95.
84. Craig-James, The Changing Society of Tobago, 95.
85. *Labour Leader* 6 September 1924.
86. *Labour Leader* 16 September 1924.
87. *Labour Leader* 13 September 1924.
88. *Labour Leader* 4 October 1924.
89. *Labour Leader* 18 October 1924.
90. *Labour Leader* 25 October, 10 November 1924. At Roxborough, the building was reportedly filled to capacity.

91. *Labour Leader* 1 November 1924.
92. *Labour Leader* 16 September 1924.
93. *Labour Leader* 16 September 1924.
94. Craig-James, *The Changing Society of Tobago*, 97.
95. *Labour Leader* 6 October 1924. His picture was reprinted on 11 October, *Labour Leader* 1 November 1924.
96. *Labour Leader* 1 November 1924.
97. *Labour Leader* 1 November 1924
98. Craig-James, *The Changing Society of Tobago*, 96.
99. Among those on the platform were Edward Macdougal, Clarence Ligoure, T. J. Baldwin, Hugo Massy and D. M. Stewart. *TG* 28 January 1928.
100. *TG* 28 January 1928.
101. *TG* 28 January 1928.
102. *TG* 12 February 1928.
103. *Labour Leader* 12 September 1927.
104. *TG* 12 February 1928.
105. *POSG* 6 January 1933.
106. *POSG* 1 January 1933.
107. See *TG* 5 January 1933.
108. *TG* 14 January 1933.
109. *POSG* 1 January 1933.
110. *POSG* 21 January 1933.
111. *TG* 4 January 1938.
112. *TG* 8 January 1938.
113. Craig-James, *Changing Society of Tobago*, 99.
114. Williams, *History of the People of Trinidad and Tobago*, 51.

Bibliography

Craig-James, Susan. *The Changing Society of Tobago, 1838–1938: A Fracture Whole, Volume II: 1900–1938* (Arima: Cornerstone Press, 2008).

Ince, Basil. "Politics before the People's National Movement: A Study of Parties and Elections in British Trinidad," PhD dissertation, New York University, 1966.

Report of the Honourable E.F.L. Wood (Parliamentary Under Secretary of State for the Colonies) on His Visit to the West Indies and British Guiana December 1921–February 1922 (London: HMSO, 1922).

Singh, Kelvin. *Race and Class Struggles in a Colonial State – Trinidad 1917–1945* (Jamaica: University of the West Indies, 1994).
Williams, Eric. *History of the People of Trinidad and Tobago* (London: Andre Deutsch, 1964).

CHAPTER 3

Conduct and Composition of Electoral Meetings

During the general elections of 1925, 1928, 1933 and 1938, candidates and their supporters used public electoral meetings as a significant instrument in their campaign. It was at these meetings that candidates were formally introduced to the electorate and their nomination given some measure of public approval since there were no constitutionally structured parties. Therefore, the TWA and their rivals adopted the procedure of proposing candidates and seeking confirmation at public meetings.

In anticipation of the 1925 elections, the campaign of Cyril Henry Pierre (of Indian and African descent) was initiated at the Oriental Hall, Port-of-Spain, in July 1924. This hall was owned by Indians and used for recreational purposes. Pierre, a barrister-at-law, was seeking to represent the counties of St David, Nariva, Mayaro and St Andrews. W. Howard-Bishop, of the TWA, formally declared the meeting open and asked James Reid, a proprietor, to act as Chairman, while others on the platform included A. A. Cipriani, H. A. Quash, Hugh Innis, A. L. Cezair, Emmanuel de Ravenu, Rev. Connell and Karim Bocas. A resolution was proposed in which the citizens of the counties of St David, Nariva, Mayaro and St Andrew accepted Pierre as their electoral candidate to the Legislative Council. Cipriani seconded the resolution and then addressed the crowd.[1]

During the second half of 1924, there were similar endorsements of candidates by other groups in the colony. For instance, on 10 August, the Chaguanas branch of the TWA held a public meeting at the Theatre Hall in Chaguanas. The gathering, comprising proprietors and farmers, approved and nominated A. Bharat Gobin to represent Caroni.[2] A similar format was adopted at a meeting convened at the office of the St Ann's and Diego Martin Local Road Board Office in Port-of-Spain to approve and confirm the nomination of Stollmeyer to contest a seat on the Legislative Council.[3]

Large-scale public meetings were held in strategic areas within constituencies. On 24 August 1924, the first in a series of electioneering meetings for Gobin was held at the Theatre Hall in Chaguanas. J. Fredericks (President of the Chaguanas branch of the TWA) presided over the gathering where Cipriani moved a resolution for the acceptance of Gobin's candidature. Howard-Bishop seconded the resolution and enumerated the good qualities of Gobin, and Cipriani then formally requested the confidence of the gathering and their pledge of support to Gobin. In reply, Gobin expressed pleasure and honour to be selected as a candidate, and the meeting ended with the vote of thanks by Cipriani and the singing of the national anthem.[4] It became a common feature to endorse candidates when they were initially presented at public electoral meetings.

Cipriani's election campaign received considerable support as evidenced by the responses at public gatherings. On 11 September 1924, at the second public meeting, which was held at Woodford Square, Port-of-Spain, the crowd was estimated to be 5,000 people.[5] On 9 January 1925, another meeting that was held for him at the London Electric Theatre in Woodbrook drew a massive crowd; the *Labour Leader* commented on the impressive attendance at this "monster meeting."[6] During the gathering, Howard-Bishop gave a brief address, then spoke of the sterling qualities of Dr Tito P. Achong whom he invited as Chairman of that meeting. Achong then made a speech and requested Howard-Bishop to move a resolution in support of Cipriani's candidature, which was subsequently accepted by a show of hands and unanimously passed.[7] A major advantage which Cipriani possessed over his electoral opponents was the support of the TWA, "In the Trinidad Workingmen's Association, Cipriani, the main opponent of Rust for the Port-of-Spain seat, had behind him what was virtually an organised political party, with an independent political organ, *The Labour Leader*."[8] This was an asset to Cipriani and other labour candidates associated with the TWA, particularly in this period of political individualism when the colony was yet to have the benefit of full-fledged operating political parties. Individuals assured of the support of organizations and influential groups certainly enjoyed an advantage in their campaigns.

In the municipal election campaigns, the meetings of candidates occasionally received extensive coverage. For instance, in November 1924, the

Labour Leader reported on Cipriani's meeting at Liberty Hall where he was endorsed as a candidate to contest a seat in the Port-of-Spain Borough Council. The newspaper reported that a "large and enthusiastic crowd" was present. People on the platform included A. V. Stollmeyer, A. P. Plimmer, Fred Adams, Leo Pujadas, M. Rigsby, Kitchener Thorpe and C. T. Worrell. Vivian Henry opened the meeting, and the proceedings were chaired by Deputy Mayor C. H. Pierre. Cipriani's rival for the seat in the city council was Alfred Richards, a former President of the TWA. This demonstrated one of the early splits in labour. Pierre paid tribute to Cipriani and sought to discourage electors from voting for Richards. In Cipriani's address, he dismissed Richards' manifesto as "merely an extract from the various reports of the City Council" and dubbed Richards an "unsuitable candidate."[9]

In the 1925 national elections, the candidates opposing labour employed campaign strategies similar to those of representatives of labour in the electoral contest. On 2 January 1925, E. A. Robinson (Managing Director of Woodford Lodge Sugar Estate) held his election meeting at Couva District House, Couva. The meeting was chaired by A. B. Carr and among those present were Sarran Teelucksingh (Robinson's rival), James Clarke (President of the Cane Farming Association), John Pierre and C. L. Peterson of the Central Electioneering Committee.[10] A. L. Challenger (Secretary of the Cane Farming Association) gave reasons for voting for Robinson, and these included the candidate's experience in the parliamentary procedure of the colony, his lack of arrogance and the fact that, as a barrister-at-law, he would be able to assist the government in making laws. Watson then moved a resolution, seconded by Peterson, that the electors of Caroni support Robinson. Then the candidate was formally invited to the podium to address the gathering.

In the national election campaign of 1928, there was no significant difference in the method of selection between a labour candidate and his rival. In 1928, Goberdhan,[11] head teacher of Fyzabad C. M. School approached Roodal and asked him to contest the election. Roodal initially declined and instead suggested Sobrian. However, Goberdhan refused to consider Sobrian, and Roodal was again requested, by influential persons from Cedros, to consider contesting the election.[12] Roodal eventually agreed to contest the election. Sometimes, in choosing a labour candidate, the

Executive of the TWA would select and ask an individual who professed to be sympathetic to the working class about his willingness to contest the seat. In one instance, there was more than one person vying to be a TWA candidate. In 1933, both Harold Piper and Harold Mahabir were screened by the Executive of the TWA, and the latter was chosen as the TWA's candidate for the Victoria seat. A non-labour candidate would usually be approached by a group of concerned members or prominent individuals of the particular county who would invite him to contest the election. For instance, on 26 January 1928, a deputation visited Robinson, the Managing Director of Woodford Lodge Sugar Estate, and asked him to seek election to the Legislative Council.[13]

The coverage of the electioneering meetings by the *Trinidad Guardian* usually involved a listing of prominent persons, in the district or colony, who were in attendance. For instance, at Robinson's meeting held at the Chaguanas Court House, the dignitaries included J. Ryan (solicitor) and K. Thorp (barrister-at-law).[14] At meetings of Cory-Davies, the candidate contesting in the district of St George, people from the upper echelons of society were in attendance. At his public meeting in Tunapuna, on 15 January, Sir Francis Watts was the Chairman and notable supporters on the platform were Professor H. A. Ballou of the Imperial College of Agriculture and Dr C. B. Reid.[15] One day later, on 16 January at Arima, the Mayor of Arima C. H. J. de Gannes presided over one such meeting of Cory-Davies and in attendance was G. Birdwood (Secretary of the Taxpayers Association).[16] Likewise, on 25 January, another of Cory-Davies' meetings was chaired by Lionel Clarke, President of the Tunapuna Literary and Debating Association.[17] This trend continued in the 1938 elections. Among those supporting Harold Piper was Mellizan, a large contractor of Brechin Castle and Usine Ste Madeleine Sugar Estate. The labour candidates also had prominent persons in society at their gatherings. Stollmeyer, who was the rival of Cory-Davies in St George, had a meeting at the San Juan Theatre on 26 January 1925. Among those on the platform were Tito P. Achong (TWA), A. Waterman, W. O. Prizzgar, C. Smith, George Wattley and Robert Webster.[18]

The results of the 1925 elections signalled a milestone for labour in the politics of Trinidad and Tobago as three of the five candidates whom labour supported – Cipriani, Pierre and Stollmeyer – won at the polls. In February 1925, the composition of the Legislative Council included the colony's first seven elected members: C. H. Pierre, T. M. Kelshall, J. A. A. Biggart, A. A. Cipriani, E. Radcliffe-Clarke, A. V. Stollmeyer and S. Teelucksingh. The term of the council commenced in February 1925 and ended on 10 December 1927.

Almost two years after the 1925 elections, another election was held. In June 1927, the public was informed that the government had embarked on the registration of electors in preparation for the next general elections in 1928.[19] There were two minor changes in the 1928 elections. First, the term of elected representatives was increased from three to five years. Second, the electoral list in 1925 had 21,794 voters, whilst in 1928, with only 33 voters added, this figure had increased to 21,827 voters.[20] Only three seats were contested – St Patrick (Sobrian and Roodal), Tobago (Biggart and Bonnett) and Caroni (Teelucksingh and Robinson).[21]

One of the methods employed by the TWA to assist in its campaigns was the recruitment of canvassers. This was evident on 31 January 1925 with the appeal from the TWA for 100 volunteers to assist in winning a "GLORIOUS VICTORY FOR DEMOCRACY."[22] These assistants served in house-to-house meetings, mobilized supporters and ensured the electorate was informed of the labour candidate in their county.

During these election campaigns, the present-day concept of "campaign managers," "party groups" and elaborate internal structures did not exist. The third Legislative Council ended on 17 December 1937 and Nomination Day for elected representatives was 4 January 1938. After Piper and Rienzi filed their nomination papers, the *Trinidad Guardian* reported that both candidates "spoke with their party chiefs, discussing campaign tactics."[23] A few weeks later, *The People* mentioned that a member of the San Fernando branch of the TLP was Piper's campaign manager.[24] Certain regular supporters who frequented electioneering meetings constituted a vital support group for candidates. This relatively small band of five to twelve loyal patrons would be either in the audience or on the platform offering verbal support to speakers. An illustration is Rienzi's campaign in the 1938 elections. He had dedicated and unflinching support from "lieutenants" of which some were in the Executive of his union: McDonald

Moses (Vice President of the OWTU) and E. R. Blades (Secretary of the OWTU).[25]

Electoral candidates included the appointment of special groups of supporters such as the "Teelucksingh Electioneering Campaign Committee" in their campaign organization. [26] Unfortunately, there is no evidence of these campaign managers being paid a salary. Certain questions remain unanswered: did the campaign manager and/or the candidate select the campaign committee? Did the candidate, wealthy supporters or the campaign committee pay for ads and flyers? Did the campaign manager choose and advertise the venues and speakers for election meetings? Who invited the press to these public meetings? Basil Ince preferred to describe such efforts and also the involvement of the TWA as "pseudo parties" as these were not full-fledged political parties.[27] Indeed, it would be more appropriate to use the terms "embryonic parties" or "nascent parties" to describe these evolving political entities.

Evidence of support groups is discernible from reports of Sobrian's meetings at which prominent citizens were in regular attendance. His public meetings in Penal, Fyzabad and Siparia were supported by C. B. Mathura, Major Randolph Rust, Kitchener Thorp, J. C. Anthony, N. K. Ablack, Goberdhan Maharaj, B. D. Edwards, L. Harban, H. C. B. Hickling and H. Atwell.[28] Furthermore, Colonel H. C. B. Hickling (General Manager of Apex Oilfields Company) chaired two of Sobrian's meetings.[29] Likewise, Sobrian's meeting in Siparia R. C. School on 28 January was chaired by R. G. Thompson (Manager of the Caura Estate). Usually, persons on the platform at political gatherings gave a public declaration of their agreement and support of the candidate's philosophy.[30]

In labour's electioneering campaign for the 1928 elections, prominent citizens continued to profess their support at public meetings. For example, in January 1928, at Isidore Hall, Penal, Cipriani presided over a meeting for Roodal, and among those on the platform were locally respected persons in the community: T. R. Mahabirsingh, A. Baldeo, G. H. Mahon, N. W. Ramcharan, J. A. Sargeant, L. William and Bhagwandin Maharaj.[31] Similarly, Cipriani, a member of the Legislative Council and Deputy Mayor, benefitted from the presence of distinguished citizens at his meetings. On 8 February 1928, at a congregation of Cipriani's supporters at Liberty

Hall, the meeting was chaired by Gaston Johnston, Mayor of Port-of-Spain, with Councillors Tito P. Achong and Leo Pujadas in attendance.[32] Likewise, at gatherings of Teelucksingh (endorsed by the TWA in 1928), two important members of the TWA were regularly present: Cipriani and Howard-Bishop. From 22 February to 1 March, election campaigns for Teelucksingh were held in Central Trinidad at the Couva Theatre, Cunupia R. C. School, Flanagin Town, Tabaquite, California Government School and Preysal Village.[33]

The conduct of the 1928 elections was marred by the rejection of the nomination papers of Sarran Teelucksingh (candidate for County Caroni) by the Returning Officer, John Menzies, Warden of the District who indicated there was an irregularity. The *Labour Leader* reported that, on 21 January 1928, Menzies was questioned three times by Teelucksingh as to the reason for claiming that his papers were not in order.[34] Subsequently, Teelucksingh, accompanied by Cipriani, called upon the Governor to protest the action of the Returning Officer. Also, a telegram of the candidate's protest was despatched to the Colonial Secretary, W. E. Jackson. Two days later, on 23 January, Teelucksingh sought legal advice from L. A. P. O'Reilly. On that day, Teelucksingh wrote to the Colonial Secretary indicating the refusal of the Warden to accept his Statutory Declaration.[35]

The Colonial Secretary replied to Teelucksingh's correspondence stating that the Governor advised that the Caroni seat be declared vacant, and furthermore, the issue of a new writ be given for the election of a representative for County Caroni.[36] The action of the Governor regarding the nomination issue was according to the legal framework of the country. One of the colony's earlier publications, the *Gazette Extraordinary* of 25 June 1924, stated that a writ for holding by-elections could be issued by the Governor.[37] In March 1928, in the aftermath of Teelucksingh's victory in the by-election, the refusal of the Returning Officer to accept Teelucksingh's papers was due to his omission on the electoral form to state he was of the male sex.[38] Such problems contributed to Rienzi's concerns at the onset of the 1938 elections. He contacted the Colonial Secretary and requested they assign neutral Presiding Officers. Rienzi lodged a protest against the appointment of three Presiding Officers at important polling stations.[39]

The new parliamentary term commenced in February 1928 in which the Governor appointed six nominated unofficial and official members. The results of the 1928 general elections, as it was in 1925, were favourable for labour with four candidates representing the working class: Cipriani, Roodal, Hosein and Teelucksingh. The *Labour Leader* was critical of the electoral tactics of non-labour candidates, "The opposition failed ignominiously because they made the same blunder at Caroni as was made by them at the St. Patrick's election. They left the substance and attacked the shadow. It was not Captain Cipriani who was standing for election, and yet they levelled all their attacks at him and not at Teelucksingh."[40] Since Cipriani (Port-of-Spain) and C. H. Pierre were returned unopposed, elections were conducted in the other four districts in 1933. In an interesting turn of events, Roodal's rival withdrew before the election. This withdrawal likely stemmed from the belief that Roodal would emerge victorious. In the 1933 elections, 4,790 persons voted from the total electorate of 11,000.

During the weeks prior to the 1933 elections, concerns were raised as to the conduct of the campaign in Victoria. On 20 January 1933, the *Trinidad Guardian* published in bold headlines: "100 DEAD PEOPLE ON A VOTERS' LIST."[41] The article claimed that election agents in Victoria indicated that there were names of at least 100 dead persons on the final voting list. An example was Buen Intente Road, in Savana Grande Ward, in which four of the thirty-three voters were dead.[42] Almost a week later, that newspaper's editorial entitled, "Dead and Nearly Dead Voters," mentioned the "intense surprise" among the public on hearing about the deceased voters on the electoral list. Furthermore, election agents indicated that 500 persons, qualified to vote in Victoria, were not registered and that the mandatory house-to-house inquiry, in preparation for the 1933 elections, was not conducted by the Registration Officers.[43] This troubling aspect of political history would repeat itself. During the 1970s, there were incidents of dead persons voting in the elections of Trinidad and Tobago.[44] Later, in the elections of 2000, there was evidence that dead people had voted in the elections.[45] It seemed that electoral fraud was a feature of the party politics of this small island state.

In Caroni, after the victory of Teelucksingh, there were protests from Robinson (the defeated candidate) and his supporters. On 30 June 1933,

Robinson and a deputation of Indians from Chaguanas met with the Governor and Colonial Secretary and outlined their grievances, which included the alleged use of hired vehicles to bring electors to the polls, impersonations of voters and the obstruction of persons from using the secret ballot. The decision of Robinson to allow a few Indians to accompany him was to give the impression that he was supported by Indians in Caroni. Furthermore, there were incidents in which individuals voted more than once while others whose names were not registered were allowed to vote.[46]

The discrepancies in Victoria and Caroni would not have significantly influenced labour's loss at the polls. The reason for the loss was that in Caroni, there were no labour candidates and in Victoria, Kelshall won by a considerable majority of votes. Interestingly, labour did not protest the conduct of the elections or query the results. In the 1933 elections, the non-labour candidates who won included T. M. Kelshall, S. Teelucksingh and I. Hope (see Appendix 8). Likewise, in 1938, Rienzi expressed disappointment that C. C. Abidh, a labour candidate, did not win the Caroni seat.[47]

Role of hecklers and supporters

The attendance at public political meetings included not merely the privileged electorate with voting rights but also disenfranchised citizens. The latter proved to be aware of political and social issues in the colony, and they made their presence felt when electoral candidates or supporting speakers addressed these public assemblies. Bridget Brereton in *A History of Modern Trinidad 1783–1962* acknowledged the role of hecklers and supporters who participated in the electoral process, thereby declaring, in at least an unofficial way, that they were ready for inclusion in the colony's voting list, "The unenfranchised majority influenced elections by disrupting meetings, heckling opponents and cheering popular candidates, especially in Port-of-Spain, and through the leadership and organization provided by TWA, the people gained experience in political organization and electioneering. This is the real significance of the 1925 constitutional reform, limited though it was. It accustomed the people to political organization and the electoral system."[48] The presence and participation of vocal labour supporters at public meetings contributed to disturbances during speeches and were intended to frustrate rival candidates. E. R. Blades who attended some of these meetings said that hecklers were a regular feature.[49]

Crowd participation at public meetings remained an important feature in preparation for elections. At a political meeting held in the San Juan Theatre in support of Cory-Davies, whilst the Chairman was introducing the candidate, a voice shouted "change the bowler," and this resulted in the embarrassed Chairman abruptly ending his opening remarks.[50] At an earlier meeting, Alfred Richards, who was initially contesting the 1925 national elections but eventually pulled out, was confronted with such choice comments as "Not a soul for you, boy! A good dose of Sedlitz please! Time up man. Away with Barrabas!"[51]

At Santa Cruz, Cory-Davies held a meeting where F. D. Blackman, a supporting speaker, referred to "Cory-Daviesites and the Stollmeyerites" in his speech. Blackman's reference to these two groups prompted a query from a labour supporter: "What about the Ciprianiites?" Such comments indicated the presence and unorthodox participation of labour supporters at meetings of rival candidates. Cory-Davies in his address to the crowd said that Stollmeyer did not address them, and this prompted a reply from the gathering "Not yet. He is following you." The candidate was interrupted by a heckler, Charles Smith, who was chastised by Cory-Davies. The *Trinidad Guardian* reported the unsavoury incident:

MR. DAVIES:	Mr. Smith, please don't interrupt you can think as much as you like, for I don't think your head will burst because it is too hard ... Mr. Charles Smith the interrupter again interposed a remark to which the candidate retorted, "You can show your sincerity more by walking home."
A VOICE:	Public meeting.
ANOTHER VOICE:	Private
MR. DAVIES:	Mr. Smith are you an elector for this district?
MR. SMITH:	No; You are not either.[52]

Certain responses and verbal exchanges through shouting insults and general heckling were meant to embarrass candidates. It was also apparent that hecklers were determined to discourage voters from supporting any rival candidates. An illustration is Gaston Johnston's meeting at Picadilly School in which he was unable to finish his speech due to frequent shouts of "Cipriani" from hecklers in the crowd.[53] The frequent reporting in the press of these critical comments suggests that the input from the crowd was considered relatively important in the proceedings of the meetings. Undoubtedly, the heckling by partisan elements at public meetings reflected their determination to give approval to labour candidates. Conversely, anti-labour hecklers participated in public meetings organized for labour candidates, but negative comments were noticeably absent from the *Labour Leader*.

Speakers usually ignored the distracting comments of hecklers. For example, on 24 January 1928, at an electioneering meeting for Sobrian at Penal, Rust claimed that Roodal had agreed that Sobrian was the better candidate. This statement was apparently inaccurate as opposition voices loudly responded saying, "He never said so" and "No such thing." Towards the end of the meeting, C. B. Mathura moved a resolution that the electorate of Penal support Sobrian. However, Mathura was greeted with defiant shouts, likely from labour supporters, of "No, no."[54] In another instance, Sobrian held an electioneering meeting at Fyzabad on 27 January in which the *Port-of-Spain Gazette* reported considerable opposition from the crowd, "A good deal of heckling was indulged in during the speeches of the various supporters but most of this seemed to have emanated from the less responsible element."[55] At the meeting, Mitra Sinanan, a platform speaker, in an attempt to bolster support for Sobrian, was jeered twice by supporters of the rival candidate. Sinanan proceeded to urge the crowd to vote for "the better man" and was interrupted by someone who exclaimed – "Which is Roodal." Later, another person shouted "No, no, Mr. Roodal" which prompted another speaker, G. T. MacDougal, to comment that the youngsters who were heckling did not possess voting rights and branded them as empty vessels making the most noise.[56] It was obvious that MacDougal sought to alleviate fears among supporters that Sobrian's future victory at the polls was in jeopardy.

Labour candidates were not immune to heckling. In the general elections of 1933, labour conducted a difficult campaign in Victoria as the two opposing candidates t were TWA members. It was a unique situation with Harold Mahabir, endorsed by the TWA, being challenged by Harold Piper, also a member of the TWA but not selected as a candidate by its Executive.

A meeting to approve Harold Mahabir's candidature was held on 10 January at Princes Town. In attendance were supporters of the rival candidate, Harold Piper. Every speaker, including Cipriani, was heckled. The meeting became so hostile that police from San Fernando arrived to restore calm. One of the supporters for Piper shouted, "Cipriani you have fooled us so long, you can't fool us any more."[57] This response indicated the dissatisfaction with Cipriani's endorsement of Mahabir. It was one of the rare instances in which Cipriani was confronted with hostile elements who questioned his motives at an election meeting. The charisma of Cipriani failed to persuade supporters of Piper who were vocal about the TWA's choice of an electoral candidate. The seriousness of labour's split in the county was clearly illustrated though the crowd's response at meetings of Mahabir. On 15 January, at another public meeting in support of Mahabir at Brothers Settlement, Cipriani was heckled, and one day later, another of Mahabir's meetings was abruptly dissolved due to interruptions caused by some individuals in attendance. Although such incidents of heckling were never serious enough to cause bodily harm to the candidates, there were meetings in which the disruptions led to supporters getting hurt.

Rust sought to circumvent the problem of heckling by issuing tickets to persons wishing to attend his electioneering campaigns. On 7 January 1925, at Brookland Hall, Woodbrook, Rust told his audience that his use of tickets was enforced "to prevent the great unwashed who had no votes from kicking up disturbances and breaking up a respectable meeting."[58] Rust, in retaliation to those who disturbed his meetings, contemptuously referred to them as, "people scraped up from the wharf, and who could not understand any more than pigs."[59] At another public gathering, Rust branded Cipriani's supporters as "a band of hooligans" and the "great unwashed."[60] This display of arrogance by Rust certainly contributed to his defeat at the polls.

Labour's election meetings included a noticeably supportive audience who encouraged and applauded the speakers. And, in contrast to their rivals, these meetings were usually not disrupted by interjections from hecklers. Cipriani had his faithful band of supporters who accompanied him in his campaign and who ensured that they spared no efforts to undermine any opposing candidates. Labour's presence in the electoral contest was dynamic and aggressive, "Cipriani had a great deal of vocal support from the rougher elements among the lower class, who, though without the franchise themselves, often interrupted the meetings of his opponents and intimidated the latter's respectable supporters."[61]

At public meetings, bands of TWA supporters made their presence felt as they cheered labour candidates and harassed rivals. There is no evidence that the TWA and their candidates instructed or advised hecklers to continue or desist from their activities at meetings. For instance, on 24 August 1924, at a national election meeting for A. B. Gobin held in Chaguanas, Cipriani was warmly applauded when he appealed to the crowd to support only Gobin and ignore the other rivals. A similar enthusiastic response was received by Gobin, who thanked the audience for their support.[62]

Vociferous pro-labour crowd responses were common at Cipriani's election meetings. At one of his meetings on 11 September 1924, at Woodford Square, his comment on Rust's nationality earned him loud applause and cheers. In addition, at a meeting for Cipriani held at Liberty Hall, Prince Street, on 15 January, Chairman of the meeting Vivian Henry appealed to the crowd to vote for Cipriani, whereupon supporters responded thus: "We must! We don't want Rust." Deafening cheers followed the Chairman's comment that Cipriani was the most popular man and worthy of being their parliamentary representative. Henry stated that two candidates were opposing Cipriani, Rust and Johnston, to which the supporters of labour cried, "We don't want them."[63]

Likewise, at a labour meeting in support of Stollmeyer, the crowd openly expressed their displeasure with Cory-Davies, the rival candidate. At that meeting in Tunapuna, during the address by one of the speakers, Jorsling, a voice sarcastically shouted, "Mr. Cory-Davies had to type write his address." Another speaker, Jugmohansingh, revealed that Cory-Davies was not registered as a voter in the district and subsequently enquired of the crowd what the rival candidate had accomplished for the district. In reply to Jugmohansingh's question, a supporter of labour sarcastically replied, "Give poor people notice to leave this land." During Stollmeyer's address, after Cory-Davies' name was mentioned, the crowd responded, "We want you, we want the better man, Stollmeyer for ever." There was a similar reaction from the audience with the passage of a resolution supporting Stollmeyer, when a voice shouted, "Don't call Mr. Cory-Davies' name here at all."[64]

In addition to heckling and vocal support for speakers, another aspect of crowd participation in which supporters of labour played a considerable role was the informal interaction and public dialogue between the platform speakers and the audience. Attendees were permitted to ask questions and seek the views of the candidate on issues, whereupon speakers paused to respond to specific queries.

At the San Juan Theatre, in January 1925, during Cory-Davies' speech, an audience member asked the candidate for his opinion on the Sedition Ordinance. Cory-Davies replied that only when elected would he be able to abolish it. In addition, the candidate agreed with a member of the crowd who asked whether he would advocate for applicants to the Civil Services to be employed on merit rather than on favouritism. At that meeting, someone asked Cory-Davies to allow him to use that forum to speak on behalf of the rival candidate, but the request was denied: "Another member of the audience rose to speak on behalf of Mr. Stollmeyer and Mr. Cory Davies pointed out to him that he had hired the hall for his meeting, he had allowed Mr. Stollmeyer's supporters to speak but it was getting late and he would allow no more."[65]

The report of a meeting held in Penal in 1928 to support Timothy Roodal illustrated the significant level of participation and political interest of labour supporters. Cipriani, after the presentation of the candidate, asked the crowd whether they would make "the fatal mistake of returning a man who guarded his selfish interests." This prompted cries of protest from the audience. Subsequently, Cipriani reminded the crowd that three years ago they elected Radcliffe-Clarke, and this prompted shouts of "We do not want him." N. W. Ramcharan, who seconded the resolution supporting Roodal, asked the gathering about the work which their representative for St Patrick had accomplished. In reply to this query, a voice shouted "Nothing!" The speaker proceeded to ask his listeners whether they would sell their birth right for a mess of pottage to which the crowd unanimously responded in the negative. When Roodal touched upon the lower price of gasoline in Barbados, there were shouts of "Shame!" and "Advantage!"[66] It was apparent that responses from the crowd were encouraged especially if speakers were favoured and rivals ridiculed.

At a meeting of Sobrian at the Siparia R. C. School on 28 January, mention was made of Roodal's character. Thorp cynically stated that Siparia was blind if persons thought that Roodal was better than Sobrian. In addition, when Thorp referred to Roodal as "an inferior being," this prompted someone to sarcastically reply, "Your position does not entitle you to speak of Roodal's integrity." Sobrian, in an effort to silence the few labour supporters, challenged them, "Heckle intelligently and don't indulge in silliness." This did not stem the tide of comments, and when the next speaker, C. B. Mathura was being questioned as to the fitness of Sobrian as a candidate, a crowd member responded, "Good, yes, but Roodal is better."[67] Rust, another speaker, referred to Roodal as a tool of Cipriani, and this prompted a member of the crowd to sarcastically shout, "A perfect tool but he needs a lot of sharpening." This was an attack on Roodal's ability as it suggests that he was incapable of functioning independently of Cipriani. Furthermore, at a previous political meeting Rust made an allegation that there was mismanagement of funds in the TWA, but this was summarily dismissed by labour supporters in the audience. Rust's questions were directed to TWA members when he queried who had all the money they subscribed to in the TWA, and this prompted the anonymous reply "Bishop." The speaker subsequently questioned the whereabouts of the organization's money to which voices from the gathering replied in unison, "It is in the bank."[68] The working-class members of the TWA, convinced of the accountability of their organization and its Secretary in financial matters, were willing to publicly defend the TWA at meetings. There is no evidence indicating the veracity of accusations hurled at Sobrian's competence, and such outbursts from the crowd suggest these were supporters of labour who were accustomed to "infiltrating" public meetings of rival candidates to erode the credibility of speakers and hope for a loss of electoral support.

There were occasional instances of disruptions which required police presence or their intervention at political meetings. In 1928, the tense political situation in St Patrick made it necessary for the police to be stationed at the polling stations in this county. This prompted Howard-Bishop to send a letter of protest to Governor Sir H. A. Byatt informing him of the repercussions of having the police present during voting: "the posting of armed squads of police constables at the various polling stations which they regard to have been not only unnecessary and fraught with an element of excitement of the people, but also as possible of having the effect of preventing persons at election time from going to exercise the right to vote."[69]

Teelucksingh, the winner of two previous elections, had serious disagreements with Cipriani and thus contested the 1933 elections without the support of the TWA. He faced hostility from supporters of Robinson and other disgruntled persons. On 15 December 1932, Teelucksingh held a public electoral meeting in Chaguanas at the Court house. During the meeting, in which C. C. Abidh, an Indian headmaster of the Charlie Village (later known as Charlieville) C. M. School, was the Chairman, the police evicted hecklers who were prominent Indian citizens in the community. Among those removed from the meeting were Shorab Khan (member of Caroni Local Road Board), Dinanath Ramcaran (teacher), Moohassar Maharaj and Nagassor Bhajan.[70]

Violent eruptions were usually short-lived and quickly contained by the police. Not surprisingly, the meetings of labour's rivals were prone to these disruptions since supporters of labour did not hesitate to demonstrate their opposition to other contestants for political power. In January 1933, at Robinson's meeting in Couva, crowd behaviour degenerated as his opponents taunted him. This story, as with most news related to the election activities in Central Trinidad, was reported by Seepersad Naipaul, father of world-renowned author and Nobel Prize winner V. S. Naipaul. The report noted Robinson's "sheer force of argument" and lucid expressions calmed disgruntled persons who were shouting "Sit down man! Sit down."[71] The feeling of calm was only temporary as continued disturbances by hecklers led to the arrival of six constables who tried to restore order. Eventually, fifty hecklers were removed from the meeting by the police. Upon resumption of the meeting, a water-filled bottle crashed through one of the windows. Even though there were no injuries, such crowd responses demonstrated the intensity of public involvement at meetings. The persons creating the disturbances were supporters of Teelucksingh (and also of the TWA) as evidenced by the fact that Henry Teelucksingh (a relative of the rival candidate Sarran Teelucksingh) was called upon by those in attendance to quell the disturbance.

There was an occasion in which a clash of supporters of rival candidates resulted in injuries to one of the persons attending a political meeting. In January 1933, Usuf Ali was hurt during a fight in one of Teelucksingh's meetings at Warrenville. Ali was injured in a struggle that ensued in the crowd when someone shouted, "Vote for Robinson" while a few of Teelucksingh's supporters responded, "Vote for Teelucksingh." In the following days, Robinson (candidate for Caroni), a retired lawyer, defended Ali at the Chaguanas Magistrate Court.[72] On 19 January, the *Trinidad Guardian* reported this on its front page, the sequel to the court case. The legal matter involving the assault on Ali was postponed to 1 February 1933.[73] The hearing of the case was set after the elections to prevent the outcome from affecting the results of the elections.

Often it was more than a few discontented persons at meetings. For example, on 7 January 1938, at one of Piper's election meetings at Allahar Hall, the entire audience exited the meeting before it ended. This was due to Piper's opposition to the introduction of unemployment insurance and the fact that he saw nothing wrong with the price of petrol. He further insulted the working class by claiming that if people wanted jobs, they should "get a fork and till the soil."[74] At an election meeting in New Grant, Piper was greeted with heckling and jeers. This was a surprise for Piper because the district was one of his strongholds in the last elections. He informed his listeners that if he was re-elected to the Legislative Council, he could deal with the flaws in the Cane Farming Control Ordinance within four months. Voices from the crowd immediately responded that in four months the crop season would end.[75] This hostile treatment was also meted out to the candidate in Gasparillo as the crowd derisively shouted, "Go back Piper, we don't want you" and "We want Rienzi."[76] Piper was humiliated when someone exclaimed, "Piper is against the working man. He is a tool."[77] At one of Piper's meetings, in Williamsville in 1938, a member of the audience shouted "We don't want you. We don't want any stool pigeon of big business." [78] Such responses provided an indicator to the electorate and public who would be the likely victor.

Instances of election violence coupled with the frequent crowd disruptions at meetings would have influenced the government's decision to provide additional police presence in certain areas on election day. For the general elections, on 8 February, seven police officers were sent to Chaguanas to assist the constabulary in preserving order; an equal number of officers were also despatched to Couva.[79]

The reports of heckling served as an indicator of the level of support t for a candidate and his chances of success at the polls. Writing letters to the editors of the newspapers complaining about candidates would have been more diplomatic and influenced more persons. However, the relatively high rate of illiteracy and the fact that letters might be rejected would have discouraged letter-writers. Heckling proved to be more direct and had the desired impact. Attendance at the election meetings would have been part of the recreational activity for the working class. Nonetheless, it also reflected a keen interest among a segment of the disenfranchised population in the colony's political developments.

Mudslinging

The attempts to sully the reputation of rival candidates constituted the political mudslinging. This was a regular feature on the election platforms. Slander of candidates' characters originated from labour candidates and their rivals.

The determination, and to a lesser extent the desperation, of candidates such as Rust to influence the voting public was discernible in his attacks on Cipriani and supporters of labour. On 14 January 1925, at a public meeting for Rust at the Belmont E. C. School, one of the platform speakers, E. McKenzie, accused Cipriani of being "a political maniac." This was an attempt to suggest that Cipriani was incapable of rational and logical decisions and thus an inferior candidate when compared to Rust. Rust dubbed Cipriani's policy as "queer" because the President of the TWA stated that he (Rust) had plans to abolish the Legislative Council. Also, Rust dismissed Cipriani's claims that the former held a grand dinner party on New Year's

Day for the colony's aristocrats. Rust responded to the allegations claiming they were false and that his wife had invited a few close friends.

At a political meeting at Woodbrook on 12 January, William Howard-Bishop, (an Executive member of the TWA), said that Rust had derogatorily referred to Cipriani as a "stable-boy." In response to Rust's comment, Cipriani said he was not ashamed to be a one-time "stable-boy."[80] There was another attempt by labour on 15 January at Liberty Hall (on Prince Street) to refute allegations made by Rust. Chairman Henry Bishop condemned Rust's previous statement that Cipriani never hosted a dinner. Supportive of Bishop's stance was Tito Achong who questioned Rust's goodwill, "The charity he is now doling out to a few individuals was a sort of advertisement (loud cheers) and was the very cheap sort of advertisement. If he distributed a few dollars to this community it would not help the 400,000 who were now underfed and unshod."[81]

At Rust's meeting at Margaret's Hall, Belmont, he accused Cipriani of being a wrong choice as a candidate and that the Secretary of the TWA was an "unworthy man." Rust was berated by a labour supporter in attendance to account for the rumour about his dealing with a cheque.[82] By not responding to this allegation, Rust would have fuelled speculation and created doubts in the minds of some people in attendance.

Whenever appropriate, Cipriani responded to charges and claims made by Rust, dismissing them as inaccuracies. The President of the TWA said that Rust's claim to be the pioneer of the oil industry is the "most insidious propaganda flouted upon the people."[83] Rust's claim had some validity, especially considering his involvement in the oil industry in Trinidad. Rust had joined John Lee Lum in oil exploration, and together they successfully discovered the mineral resource. Lum, originally from Kwan Tung in China, arrived in Trinidad in 1885 and became involved in cocoa and the provision business.[84]

Allegations, criticisms and charges were part of electoral mudslinging tactics in Trinidad and Tobago. At Robinson's election campaign in Couva on 2 January, Watson told the gathering that Teelucksingh indicated he would support Robinson's candidature if the latter was elected to the Legislative Council. Ironically, Teelucksingh was in the crowd and vehemently denied ever uttering such a statement.[85] A similar situation occurred at the San Juan Theatre at a meeting of Cory-Davies. The candidate refuted Stollmeyer's accusations of the speaker being "an undischarged bankrupt."[86]

Harold Piper, the "independent socialist" candidate contesting Victoria, held a meeting at Princes Town on 29 December 1932. One of labour's supporters from Sangre Grande, Ralph Mentor, attempted to explain the selection of Piper's rival, Harold Mahabir, by the TWA, "Mr. Mahabir was eventually selected by the General Council and it was done because Mr. Roodal said he was completely under his thumb. I heard those words myself by Mr. Roodal at the general meeting."[87] Mentor added that Julien Brathwaite (Vice President of the TWA) said that whatever Cipriani says or does must not be opposed. This prompted a voice to say "That is tomfoolery." The speaker was also critical of Kelshall, another electoral candidate, and identified him as being a coward who shirks his duty: "Mr. Kelshall is a man with a compact-mentalized mentality which makes him a psychological monstrosity."[88]

In 1938, Shorab Khan, a speaker at one of Teelucksingh's meetings in Flanagin Town, said that it would be a "political catastrophe" if Abidh won the elections. Khan, who had previously been critical of Teelucksingh, sought to portray the challenger as lacking ambition, "Mr. Abidh taught as a Third Class Schoolmaster for 43 years in the same school; he never progressed in his profession and if a man was stagnant in his own job he would surely be a dumb aspirant to legislative honours."[89] At another of Teelucksingh's meeting in Couva, L. R. Lalsingh contended that Abidh was Secretary of the Cane Farmers' Standing Committee but he did not do anything to benefit cane farmers.[90] This type of mudslinging was meant to reveal the ineptitude and laziness of candidates vying for electoral support.

Piper was also on the receiving end of criticisms from Rienzi's supporters. One week before the elections, *The People* referred to Piper as the "Rip Van Winkle candidate."[91] This portrayal of the candidate as someone who was not aware of the existing problems facing the populace was a serious blow which undermined the credibility of Piper. At a meeting in Barrackpore, Blades compared Rienzi and Piper to horses in a race. The speaker said that five years ago Piper had his legs "broken" in the last election race.[92]

The results of the elections painted a different picture of the feelings and decisions of the electorate. For instance, in 1925, although Teelucksingh's integrity was questioned by a prominent citizen of Central Trinidad, he emerged victorious during the 1925, 1928, 1933 and 1938 elections. Similarly, speakers in Sobrian's campaign in 1928 attacked Roodal's honesty and the TWA's management of funds, but this failed to convince the electorate that Sobrian was the better choice. In 1933, efforts to portray Robinson's honest and wise management of finances did not threaten the incumbent Teelucksingh. It is evident that the morality and integrity of candidates were not an influential factor in the outcome of the elections. Factors such as popularity among the citizens of the specific county, being the incumbent, the persuasiveness of advertisements and the issue of race would have determined the voters' decisions and the success of a candidate.

Participation of women

The majority of women in Trinidad and Tobago did not satisfy the necessary income and property qualifications for voting in the 1925, 1928, 1933 and 1938 elections. There were no female candidates contesting the early elections, but they attended meetings, sat on political platforms and addressed crowds. An estimated twenty to thirty women attended the larger election meetings.[93] In Tobago, a considerable female presence was reported in an election meeting, "Notwithstanding the constant showers of rain which fell for nearly the whole of the day a large number of both sexes found themselves there."[94] Women's participation in the electoral campaign was noticeable among both labour and their rivals.

At an election campaign for Cipriani on 9 January 1925, at the London Electric Theatre in Woodbrook, several women were in attendance. Among those on the platform were Miss Estelle Smith, Miss Hilda Charles, Mrs E. J. Louis, Miss Augusta Bishop, Mrs F. Adams, Mrs J. O. O'Brien, Miss A. Husband and Mrs W. Placide. One woman, Mrs A. H. Charles, who was unable to attend, sent her greetings to the gathering.

Mrs E. J. Louis addressed the gathering and gave a reason for voting for Cipriani, "My answer flows directly from his manifesto, which I am sure the majority of you, have either read or listened to a number of times. Captain Cipriani has a policy, he has a platform, supported by strong and sturdy planks, each of which indicates the great doctrine of Christ himself – The Fatherhood of God and the brotherhood of man."[95] Her speech was favourably received by the crowd. Likewise, Mrs W. Placide was greeted by "uproarious cheers" as she arose to address the audience. She described Gaston Johnston as "erudite and well-informed" but did not believe his "spontaneous public activities" were sufficient to earn the suffrage of the people.[96]

At a meeting in Woodbrook, on 9 January, Mrs Adams advised her listeners not to believe their vote will be missed in a poll of thousands, "Remember every vote counts, and every vote will stand out prominently when the tellers make their declarations."[97] After Cipriani's address, Miss Bishop gave a vote of thanks to the Chairman of the evening's proceedings. On 12 January 1925, a gathering described by the *Labour Leader* as a "monster meeting" was held in Market Street, Woodbrook. Mrs A. H. Charles, who had spoken at a previous meeting, was critical of the *Trinidad Guardian* which boycotted the meeting and also misrepresented labour in their reports, "By the *Trinidad Guardian* we have been styled, in effect, sedition-mongers, preachers of race-hatred and class-prejudice, and in exceedingly vulgar terms, those of my sex who have sallied forth to save our children and our homes, from being ruthlessly kept under the broad heel capitalised might, have been referred to as 'women.' "[98] It was evident that the women appearing on the labour platform were outspoken and, like other labour candidates, were fearlessly critical of the *Trinidad Guardian*.

On 15 January, labour organized a meeting at Liberty Hall, Prince Street, in Port-of-Spain and due to the tremendous response, hundreds of supporters were reportedly turned away from the venue. As in previous meetings, the news report included the noticeable presence of female supporters on the platform. Among these were Mrs W. Placide, Mrs A. H. Charles, Mrs Fred Adams, Miss Hilda Charles, Miss E. Charles and Mrs

R. Faveck. At this gathering, Mrs Charles was given the opportunity to address the supporters and friends of labour.[99]

The election meetings of labour's rival candidates, such as Cory-Davies, also saw active participation from women. For instance, on 15 January 1925, a public meeting was held for him at Tunapuna and supporters on the platform included Mrs J. H. Knights and Mrs Rene Rostant.[100] A similar assembly was organized for Cory-Davies at San Juan Theatre and among the women present were Mrs Cory-Davies, Mrs M. Rapsey, and Mrs O. Burke. In addition, Miss Millicent Humphrey spoke on behalf of the candidate and was critical of his rival, "Only one class of people Mr. Stollmeyer catered for and those were his servants in the cocoa field."[101] The surnames of these women, such as Rostant and Humprey, suggest they are from the upper class. In January, Cory-Davies' wife was present at his political meetings at Maracas Government School and St James E. C. School.[102] The support given by Mrs Cory-Davies to her husband was unique and was not reported in the other campaigns.

On 25 January 1925, a Cory-Davies meeting was convened at the Estate buildings at La Concordia, Caura, and among those on the platform were Mrs Vignale, Miss George Williams, Miss Cephas E. Vidale and Miss E. Guyton. Two meetings followed in close succession in support of the candidature of Cory-Davies, and both had a visible presence of women. On 27 January, Mrs C. Williams and Mrs Cory-Davies were present on the platform to support him at the schoolroom of Maraval Girls' R. C. School.[103] A comparison of the reports of political meetings of labour and their rivals suggests that more women featured on the labour platform. Furthermore, labour encouraged more women than their rival candidates, such as Cory-Davies, to address their audiences.

Reports of persons addressing crowds and of hecklers reflected a predominantly male-dominated election campaign in 1928. One of the exceptions was labour's meeting on 9 January 1928 at Penal in which women were briefly mentioned. There, Roodal told his supporters in South Trinidad that the oil industry provided prosperity for a minority whilst poverty continued to exist. During his speech, two women in the crowd exclaimed thus: "That is true Sir!" and "We trust so."[104]

Women had a prominent presence during the 1933 elections, and they actively participated in the campaign meetings. In December 1932, the Young Ladies Debating Association organized an assembly at Town Hall, San Fernando, to support the candidacy of T. Kelshall. One of the women, Mrs Beatrice Greig, praised the candidate, "Mr. Kelshall is a man of unquestionable integrity. And he is an accepted leader of thought in the West Indies."[105]

At the meeting held for Harold Piper at the Princes Town Drill Hall on 29 December 1932, women on the platform offering support to the candidate were Mrs Saunders (of the Indian Walk branch of the TWA), Miss Kathleen Piper and Mrs R. Cooper (of the Princes Town branch of the TWA). The *Port-of-Spain Gazette* reported the speech of one of the women speakers, "Miss Kathleen Piper, one of his supporters made an equal appeal to her hearers when she essayed a vigorous reply to an attack on her sex by the opposing Labour Candidate on another occasion a short while ago."[106] In addressing this gathering at Princes Town, Miss Piper said that a few weeks ago, a group of Lady Social Workers at a meeting at San Fernando publicly supported one of the candidates for Victoria. This action by the women had infuriated Harold Mahabir, a candidate contesting Victoria, who cynically referred to this group of women as "voteless flappers" and advised them to "stick to what they know about." Miss Piper strongly condemned Mahabir's gender-biased comments and her view was supported by someone in the audience who shouted – "Shame!"[107] The candidates received support from women even on voting day as seen in the 1938 election. Among those backing Piper in Victoria were his sister and Audrey Jeffers.[108] Jeffers would later become the first female member of the Port-of-Spain City Council in 1936 and the first woman on the Trinidad Legislature in 1946.

Press reports of the inclusion of some women on the platforms and reports of their presence proved they were actively involved, though often "invisible," in the election campaigns. Even though women were disenfranchised, they were a formidable presence during the electoral campaigns. In retrospect, the quality of platform speeches by women speakers demonstrated their capability for engaging in debates of a calibre similar to that of their male counterparts. These women were outspoken, politically aware and excellent orators.

Notes

1. *Labour Leader* 26 July 1924. For a brief overview of the early elections, see Kirk Meighoo, *Politics in a "Half-Made Society": Trinidad and Tobago, 1925–2001* (Kingston: Ian Randle Publishers, 2003), 10–13.
2. *Labour Leader* 11 August 1924. Cipriani and Howard-Bishop were also present at this meeting.
3. *Labour Leader* 16 September 1924.
4. *Labour Leader* 27 August 1924. Among those present was Habib (an Indian catechist and schoolmaster).
5. Among those attending were C. H. Pierre (Deputy Mayor) who presided, Drs H. S. Hartley and T. P. Achong, Fred Adams, S. Roberts, W. Howard-Bishop and A. Rigault. *Labour Leader* 13 September 1924.
6. *Labour Leader* 10 January 1925. The London Electric Theatre was opened on 2 February 1911 and was located at French Street, Woodbrook. Blades estimated Cipriani's meetings were attended by 500 to 600 persons. Blades, personal interview, 7 February 2001.
7. *Labour Leader* 10 January 1925.
8. Singh, *Race and Class*, 126.
9. *Labour Leader* 25 October 1924.
10. Others present were J. W. Arbuckle, J. J. McLeod, N. McLeod, F. Grant, J. C. Macaulay, David Colley, Edward Caine, W. Cumberbatch and Rev. W. I. Green (a Canadian missionary of the Presbyterian Church serving in the Couva-Balmain pastoral charge). *TG* 3 January 1925.
11. No first name was recorded for Goberdhan.
12. *POSG* 28 January 1928.
13. This deputation comprised C. C. Watson, H. Dolival, J. Pierre, D. Warren, C. L. Peterson, L. A. Challenger, D. Sealy, Siriram Maharaj (representing Hindus), Thomas Gibbs, J. E. Armugam and Nazar Hosein (representing Muslims). *POSG* 28 January 1928.
14. *TG* 15 January 1925.
15. *TG* 17 January 1925.
16. *TG* 17 January 1925.
17. *TG* 27 January 1925.
18. *TG* 27 January 1925.
19. *Labour Leader* 25 June 1927.
20. *POSG* 13 January 1928. Also TG 14 January 1928.
21. *TG* 22 January 1928. On 11 January 1928, E. Radcliffe-Clarke announced he would no longer stand for election in St Patrick. *TG* 12 January 1928.
22. *Labour Leader* 31 January 1925.

23. *TG* 6 January 1938.
24. *The People* 22 January 1938.
25. *The People* 15 January 1938.
26. *TG* 9 February 1928.
27. Ince, "Politics before the People's National Movement," 58.
28. *TG* 26, 29 January, 5, 7, February 1928. Also *POSG* 26, 29, 31 January, 2 February 1928.
29. *TG* 29 January, 5 February 1928.
30. Ince, "Politics before the People's National Movement," 49.
31. *POSG* 14 January 1928.
32. Others present included Jonathan Ryan, Vivian E. Henry, J. de Verteuil, A. M. Holte and S. Patrick. *POSG* 10 February 1928. *TG* 10 February 1928.
33. *Labour Leader* 18 February 1928.
34. *Labour Leader* 28 February 1928.
35. *TG* 27 January 1928.
36. *TG* 27 January 1928.
37. *POSG* 24 January 1928.
38. *Labour Leader* 10 March 1928.
39. *POSG* 20 January 1938.
40. *Labour Leader* 10 March 1928.
41. *TG* 20 January 1933.
42. *TG* 20 January 1933.
43. *TG* 26 January 1933.
44. Raffique Shah, "Mysterious Maths," *Independent* 3 January 2001.
45. "Dead Man Voting," http://www.trinicenter.com/TrinidadandTobagoNews/2001/Feb/
46. *TG* 31 January 1933.
47. *The People* 29 January 1938.
48. Brereton, *History of Modern Trinidad*, 167.
49. Blades, personal interview, 7 February 2001.
50. *TG* 21 January 1925.
51. Ince, "Politics before the People's National Movement," 49.
52. *TG* 23 January 1925.
53. Ince, "Politics before the People's National Movement," 49.
54. *TG* 26 January 1928.
55. *POSG* 29 January 1928.
56. *POSG* 29 January 1928.
57. *TG* 12 January 1933. This was a front-page story with the bold headline: "CAPT. CIPRIANI 'HOWLED DOWN' IN PRINCES TOWN."
58. *TG* 8 January 1925.
59. *TG* 15 January 1925.
60. *Labour Leader* 24 January 1925.

61. Singh, *Race and Class*, 126.
62. *Labour Leader* 27 August 1924.
63. *Labour Leader* 20 January 1925.
64. *TG* 20 January 1925.
65. *TG* 21 January 1925.
66. *POSG* 14 January 1928.
67. *POSG* 31 January 1928.
68. *POSG* 31 January 1928.
69. *Labour Leader* 3 March 1928.
70. *East Indian Weekly* 17 December 1932.
71. *TG* 22 January 1933.
72. *TG* 13 January 1933.
73. *TG* 19 January 1933.
74. *The People* 15 January 1938.
75. *The People* 22 January 1938.
76. *The People* 22 January 1938.
77. *The People* 22 January 1938.
78. *The People* 15 January 1938.
79. *TG* 15 January 1933.
80. After Cipriani's victory at the polls, a poem by "Fairplay" was published. The last verse had a reference to Cipriani being a stable-boy:

    When his rivals see their danger
    They say all things to annoy.
    But Christ was born in a manger
    So we'd have this stable-boy.

81. *TG* 20 January 1925.
82. The report of the meeting was recorded in the "Lizzie and Joe" column. *Labour Leader* 17 January 1925.
83. *TG* 22 January 1925.
84. The first oil well was drilled in Trinidad in 1867 by Walter Darwent of San Fernando. See Michael Anthony, *First in Trinidad* (Cascade: Paria Publishing, 2003), 85.
85. *TG* 3 January 1925.
86. *TG* 21 January 1925.
87. *POSG* 4 January 1933.
88. *POSG* 4 January 1933.
89. *POSG* 14 January 1938.
90. *TG* 12 January 1938.
91. *The People* 15 January 1938.
92. *The People* 15 January 1938.
93. Interview with McDonald Moses, San Juan, 1 January 2001.

94. *Labour Leader* 16 September 1924.
95. *Labour Leader* 10 January 1925.
96. *Labour Leader* 10 January 1925.
97. *Labour Leader* 14 January 1925.
98. *Labour Leader* 17 January 1925.
99. *Labour Leader* 20 January 1925.
100. *TG* 17 January 1925.
101. *TG* 21 January 1925.
102. *TG* 20, 29 January 1925.
103. *TG* 28 January 1925.
104. *POSG* 14 January 1928.
105. *East Indian Weekly* 10 December 1932.
106. *POSG* 4 January 1933.
107. *POSG* 4 January 1933.
108. *The People* 29 January 1938.

Bibliography

Anthony, Michael. *First in Trinidad* (Cascade: Paria Publishing, 2003).
Meighoo, Kirk. *Politics in a "Half-Made Society": Trinidad and Tobago, 1925–2001* (Kingston: Ian Randle Publishers, 2003).

CHAPTER 4

Local, National and International Issues

Political and racial/ethnic issues pertinent to the development of Trinidad and Tobago featured prominently on the agenda of public meetings in 1925, 1928, 1933 and 1938. Candidates and supporting speakers reiterated the urgency for a decision on constitutional reform for the colony. Other significant concerns included the improvement of social services, the amelioration of conditions of labour and the proper management of the islands' industries.

Self-government

Colonial authorities were undoubtedly aware of these issues as these were analysed by radical politicians on the electoral platform or featured in the media during elections in Trinidad and Tobago. Prior to the 1925 elections, the Secretary of State for the Colonies received Major Wood's *Report* which indicated concerns and dissatisfaction as well as grievances and demands of the West Indian colonies. The *Wood Report* gave an assessment of the state of the British West Indian sugar industry and also reminded the Home Office of the restless agitation for representative government. Wood added, "Other matters of intercolonial importance brought to my notice in Trinidad were, cable and wireless communications, the question of shipping rates, the Canadian preference, health and water supply, education and export tax on oil."[1] Furthermore, Wood acknowledged the leadership role of the TWA in the colony's affairs, "My attention was drawn to Labour questions by the Trinidad Working Men's Association. Most of the matters they brought up were within the province of local Government."[2]

British colonial policy was rigid and uncompromising in response to the proponents of representative government in Trinidad and Tobago. Wood's recommendation to the Home Office reflected the prevailing metropolitan sentiments on representative government for the colonies, "The comparative smallness and isolation of many of the islands make it questionable whether the experiment of responsible government would be practicable without greater change in their economic position than their physical conditions seem to follow."[3] His assessment was that Trinidad's population was "backward and undeveloped" and that self-government was impracticable because of the limited number of persons who were enfranchised.[4]

The colony's protagonists for self-government would not be deterred, and their convictions were given primacy even in the preparatory stages for the colony's first election. In anticipation of the 1925 elections, the TWA conducted a public meeting in July 1924 in support of Charles Henry Pierre. At that gathering, Cipriani condemned the opposing candidate, Robinson, for not identifying with the TWA in its efforts to secure representative government.[5] Cipriani recalled that Robinson and his supporters were glaringly absent from earlier campaigns for self-government. However, there is evidence to suggest that although Robinson did not identify with the TWA in its early public meetings on representative government, nevertheless, in his campaign, he appealed to the electorate for support and declared his preference for this type of governance for the colony. In the *Trinidad Guardian*, Robinson placed notices during his campaign with the caption "Representative Government"[6] and openly signalled his intention to work towards achieving that status of governance for the colony.

The TWA was emphatic in its pursuance of self-government for the colony, and the *Labour Leader* was used to give extensive coverage of the views of labour candidates to reinforce the urgent need for constitutional reform. For instance, in advertisements supportive of Pierre and Cipriani, the headline "Representative Government" frequently occurred in bold print.[7]

In January 1925, an assessment of the electoral candidates was undertaken by Tito P. Achong who wrote in the *Labour Leader* and focused on the virtue of electing legislators who were committed to the struggle for representative government. He thought that one of the prerequisites in selecting a suitable candidate was that he should be "a man whose sympathies are with the aspirations of the people in their legitimate struggle for economic independence."[8] Achong was critical of Randolph Rust and Gaston Johnston, who opposed Cipriani. He said that Rust did not arouse enthusiasm among the electors and was not a proper rallying personality for the colony's national spirit, whereas Johnston was deemed unsuitable partly due to the publication of an essay to the electors in Port-of-Spain which was described by Achong as "too sophomoric and unsophisticated."

Furthermore, Achong's choice of Cipriani as a worthy parliamentary representative was confirmed in the candidate's slogan – "Trinidad for the Trinidadians" – which embodied the best hope in giving direction and unity to Trinidad and Tobago.[9] However, this was not a novel initiative because the slogan "Trinidad for Trinidadians" was used during the 1890s by persons involved in the reform movement.[10] Another of Cipriani's slogans which appealed to labour's supporters was "Votes for sons of the soil."[11] Achong believed Cipriani possessed the necessary qualities to promote the movement for achieving self-government, economic justice, fair play and political democracy. Such statements portraying Cipriani as embodying the spirit of nationalism encouraged the TWA members and other electors to support him at meetings and at the polls.

Other rival candidates such as Cory-Davies and Kelshall also made noteworthy contributions to the debate on representative government. For instance, at a meeting held in Arima for Cory-Davies on 15 January, various speakers attacked Cipriani's concept of representative government. C. Birdwood (Secretary of the Taxpayer's Association, Tunapuna) described Cipriani's slogan, "Trinidad for Trinidadian," as being "stupid" and "narrow minded." Similarly, C. C. Jordan, another platform speaker, felt the people of Arima were not ignorant and, thus, would not associate with any group espousing Cipriani's slogan. This strategy used by the rivals in associating support for Cipriani with ignorance was merely an attempt to undermine labour's support in Arima. Another speaker, J. O'Laughlin, discredited Cipriani's slogan and urged the audience to vote solidly for Cory-Davies.[12] Denouncing electioneering issues propounded by labour candidates was part of the opposition's strategy to destabilize the TWA's support base.

During January–February 1925, articles supporting Cipriani's stance on representative government were published in the *Labour Leader*. The writer, using the nom de plume "The Gentleman in Black," urged voters to support Cipriani.[13] Two weeks later on 28 January, the *Labour Leader* published an article "The Final Word" by "The Gentleman in Black" who criticized Johnson's boast of being a good debt collector. The writer felt the colony needed sound legislation and not prompt debt collection.[14] And, on 7 February, the said writer again offered support to Cipriani portraying him as proactive and capable of securing self-rule for the colony.[15] Such viewpoints complemented Cipriani's pronouncements at public meetings supportive of the type of governance which preferred wider public participation in the colony's political affairs.

Among labour's rival candidates, the issue of representative government was also debated and utilized as a means to secure votes. Stollmeyer, a candidate endorsed by the TWA, also supported the concept of representative government. At a public gathering on 18 January, at Tunapuna, Stollmeyer claimed that the faster the colony was granted representative government, the better it was for the citizens.[16] Likewise, Robinson, contesting the Caroni seat, claimed to be for representative government but, in contrast to Cipriani, believed it could be achieved under the British administration. Indeed, Robinson concluded that British was "a government of honesty," "stood for freedom of all peoples" and capable of ruling the colony's racially diverse population, "They were a conglomery of many fragments of people – Portuguese, Chinese, Indians, Africans, and every sort of people and it was only because they lived under a Government which held the rein firmly and properly for all classes, all races, all colours that they could come there and achieve what had been achieved."[17]

The issue of representative government was addressed at one of Robinson's political meetings in Caroni on 14 January 1925. He defended himself against accusations that he opposed political change and claimed to have never made any statement critical of this particular type of governance, "It had been said of him that he was against self-government but he did not know when he had made any speech that was against self-government. What he would say was that they had to be very careful with the measure given them."[18] In effect, Robinson sought to adopt a moderate stance in order to avoid offending the ruling class and still be able to appeal to the working class.

At a political meeting for Cory-Davies held at Maracas Government School on 18 January 1925, the candidate sought to dismiss a rumour, circulated among labour supporters, that at a recent meeting of the Chamber of Commerce he opposed the idea of representative government, "Gentlemen without representation and political importance etc., this great cosmopolitan people in this island are getting along so happily together. My view is that introducing this representation in a tropical climate will cause uncontrolled dissension loss of love one man for another, and for this reason, I am not supporting it."[19] According to Cory-Davies' explanation, he was seeking to avoid divisions that arose among the citizens as a result of the introduction of a new political system – representative government.

The issue of governance of Trinidad and Tobago prominently featured in speeches at a meeting for T. M. Kelshall at Victoria Hall, San Fernando. Dr P. T. Vilain gave brief remarks on the benefits of representative government. Another speaker, Wharton, recalled having met Kelshall sixteen years ago at E. Lazare's Chambers in Port-of-Spain for one of a series of meetings to discuss representative government. A member of the clergy, Rev. D. L. Evans, in his address, hoped that in the future there would be a larger measure of representative government in the colony.[20]

On 24 January 1928, Rust, one of the speakers at Sobrian's meeting at St Isidore Lodge Room, Penal, highlighted matters related to representative government during his speech. Rust dubbed himself the "Godfather of the Constitution" and claimed that, for thirty-five years, he fought to get voting rights for the people and to send their representatives to the Legislative Council.[21] At Sobrian's meeting at Siparia R. C. School on 29 January, C. B. Mathura mentioned Rust's fight for representative government for the past forty-five years.[22] Rust and his supporters hoped to convince the electorate that the TWA, when compared to Rust's contribution, was a virtual newcomer despite their portrayal as stalwarts of representative government.

The issue of representative government continued to be prominent on the electoral platforms in 1933. Labour maintained its conviction that it was desirable for the colony. Others such as Harold Piper, candidate for

Victoria, voiced their reservations on representative government for the colony. Piper declared,

> A great deal of talking has been done within the last two years about federation and Self-Government … But I, for one, say now is not the time for that. Only when the people have acquired such a sense of responsibility as not to allow political agitators, professional politicians and others to misguide them and have them at their bidding, then and only then shall we be fully fit, and each one of us will be absolutely safe under such a Government.[23]

In the 1938 elections, Rienzi had a manifesto which included self-government and universal suffrage.[24] The editorial of the *Trinidad Guardian* sought to criticize his ranking of self-government on the list, "Mr. Rienzi has outlined an eleven-point programme to the electorate. At the bottom of the list he puts self-government and universal suffrage, feeling possibly that it is too impractical a proposal to be given a more prominent place."[25] The newspaper further argued that Piper advocated "the more common-sense immediate step of increased representation in the Legislature."[26]

Analyses of the state of politics in the early twentieth century reflected the political maturity of the colony's middle and working classes. Prior to the 1928 elections, "The Curate," a frequent contributor to the *Labour Leader*, was critical of the nature of the colony's political rule. The writer was critical of the non-elected members of the Legislative Council, particularly, the officials who seemed to be concerned with "seizing the pleasures of the coming day" and their role as mere "pawns" and "political mummies" whose "yea" or "nay" is dragged out of their mouths by the government. In addition, "The Curate" condemned the nominated officials as limited and as "pandering … to Government's point of view, only to retain that favour and the title of honourable, which they evidently feel assured that no intelligent electorate would bestow upon them."[27] This was one of the early appeals for constitutional reform which pointed out the inadequacies of the Westminster system copied from Britain.

Almost a decade later, in January 1938, four candidates were returned unopposed: A. A. Cipriani (Port-of-Spain), Aldwyn Maillard (St George East), Timothy Roodal (St Patrick) and E. V. Wharton (eastern counties).

The *Port-of-Spain Gazette* interpreted this as an indicator that the electorate was either absolutely satisfied or reflected a feeling of apathy not caring who was the representative.[28] Tito P. Achong, a member of the TLP, condemned the Legislative Council as being woefully inadequate, "Examined dispassionately, constitutionally, practically and morally, it is difficult to find anything in favour of the existence of such an instrument."[29] Two weeks later, Achong harshly condemned the electives of the council as being "destitute of all moral cohesion and strong patriotic feeling."[30] It was obvious that the working-class citizens were discontented with the system of governance and prepared to voice their opinions.

International trade

Since the late eighteenth century, a vibrant trade occurred between the British North American colonies and the West Indies.[31] The North American colonies provided provisions to the Caribbean whilst the latter supplied molasses and rum. Scholars such as J. A. Stagg and Peter Newman provided evidence that, despite international tension, this trade continued in the nineteenth and early twentieth centuries.[32] The subject of trade was featured during the 1925 elections. At Tunapuna on 18 January, Stollmeyer criticized Canadian reciprocity as being beneficial to Canada but injurious to Trinidad, "That was nothing but exploitation. Why should they give to Canada anything at all? Trinidad could afford to do without Canada and her people would be better off freed from monopolies."[33] The *Trinidad Guardian* reported that the crowd applauded after Stollmeyer expressed his opinion on the trade relations with Canada. Such a reaction from the audience suggests the existence of a growing sense of nationalism and their understanding of at least certain external trade agreements. Even though Cory-Davies was not a labour candidate, he endorsed Stollmeyer's viewpoint on the Canada-Trinidad trade relations. At the San Juan Theatre, Cory-Davies said that Canadian reciprocity was a measure which prevented people in the colony from using all the sugar they needed.[34]

There was also an increasing concern among organizations such as the Chamber of Commerce which were critical of trade relations between Trinidad and Tobago and Canada. The colony extended preferential treatment to the products of Newfoundland and received similar benefits in return. This prompted the chamber to address the issue at a local forum. On 21 January 1925, amidst election campaigns, a meeting was held at the Chamber of Commerce to receive and extend a welcome to Hance J. Logan (delegate to the government of Canada) to discuss closer trading links with Canada. Groups attending included the Sugar Manufacturers' Association (SMA) and the Agricultural Society. Stollmeyer was also present, and at this meeting, Cory-Davies, Vice President of the Chamber of Commerce, moved a resolution, which was supported by the members present, asking the government of Newfoundland to consider adopting reciprocal trade relations with Trinidad and Tobago. The editorial of the *Trinidad Guardian* believed this discussion was a sincere attempt by Canada to adjust its trade policy to ensure a mutual advantage between the two countries.[35] The discussion of trade relations on the platform partly suggests the political maturity of the candidates.

Citizenship of candidates

During the campaign of the general elections in Trinidad and Tobago in 2000, members of the PNM expressed concern that two elected MPs from the United National Congress (UNC), William Chaitan and Winston "Gypsy" Peters, should be disqualified from being elected to the House of Representatives. Both Chaitan and Peters were accused of possessing dual nationality and thereby ineligible to contest the elections. Earlier, in the campaign of the 1925 elections, the issue of the nationality of candidates was hotly debated. In September 1924, at an electoral meeting, Cipriani questioned whether Rust could truly represent the national spirit because he was not a Trinidadian, "I cannot see how the appointment of an Englishman, no matter how deserving would argue that we are getting any closer to *Self-Government* and even if Major Rust did actually give us all the representation that could be given when Major Rust is dead and gone 10 or 20 years hence the local enemies of Representative gov't, the Colonial Office, and our Masters in Downing Street, will make use of it against us."[36]

The year 1925 began with a public meeting in support of Rust at Woodbrook, where the question of citizenship, pertaining to the ability of an Englishman or foreigner to successfully serve the interests of the people, was raised. The Chairman, C. G. Archibald, emphasized the absurdity in attempting to establish the principle that any person born outside of Trinidad should be debarred from being elected to the Legislative Council. Archibald further added that the electorate should consider the fact that Major Rust had lived in the colony for forty-three years.[37] Rust was born in Somerset, England, and arrived in Trinidad in 1881, where he spent the rest of his life.

On 9 January 1925, the *Trinidad Guardian* carried a report of a political meeting in support of Stollmeyer in Port-of-Spain. Stollmeyer told the gathering that he hoped his opponent would not be an Englishman.[38] This statement alluded to Cory-Davies who hailed from Kent, England.[39] The issue of foreign nationality was highlighted repeatedly at subsequent meetings of both Stollmeyer and Cory-Davies. At one such meeting in Tunapuna on 18 January, Stollmeyer raised the topic of nationality and claimed that one of the differences between himself and Cory-Davies was that the latter was English-born.[40]

There was a strong response from Cory-Davies and his supporters to the issue of citizenship. Henry Clark, speaking on behalf of the people of St Joseph, at a meeting for Cory-Davies at Tunapuna on 15 January, defended the candidate:

> The only criticism that could be levelled at his head by the supporters of Mr. Stollmeyer was the fact that he is an Englishman but the fact remained that what they wanted was a representative, a proper representative whether he be a Chinaman or a Portuguese. That was not a racial or religious question, it was a communal question, one that affected this particular community, and he believed all things considered that Mr. Davies had the ability and influence to represent them properly.[41]

Cory-Davies sought to assure the electorate that his abilities would not be affected by English citizenship. To prove this, at some of his meetings,

Cory-Davies spoke in patois to identify with the locals.[42] On 16 January at Arima, a meeting for Cory-Davies was held in which J. O'Laughlin appealed to the electorate not to ignore candidates especially those from England by whom they are governed. In defending his status, Cory-Davies stated that he had been in the West Indies for thirty-one years and lived in Trinidad for twenty-eight years.[43] Similarly, at a meeting of Cory-Davies held on 18 January at Maracas Government School, the Chairman, F. D. Blackman, told the crowd that for twenty-seven years Cory-Davies lived in Trinidad. Another speaker, C. A. Cudjoe, who seconded the resolution supporting the candidate, declared that Cory-Davies was "a great Englishman." Cudjoe added that the candidate had married a Trinidadian and his children were born in Trinidad.[44]

Two days later, on 20 January in San Juan, at another of Cory-Davies' meetings, a supporting speaker, Prince Robinson, made a plea for electors to ignore the issue of nationality when selecting a candidate. Robinson added that Bonar Law, a Canadian by birth, became the Prime Minister of England.[45] On 22 January, at Santa Cruz, Cory-Davies held a meeting in which Cudjoe commented on the candidate's nationality, "Mr. Cory Davies had come all the way from England to Trinidad, had liked their country, had lived in it, as well, had married a daughter of Trinidad and had children born in Trinidad."[46]

In addition to being a citizen of England, it was evident that being a national of another Caribbean island was also an issue of debate. F. D. Blackman, another speaker at Cory-Davies' meeting, alluded to Stollmeyer's nationality revealing that he was not a Trinidadian, but a Barbadian.[47] In another instance, on 14 January, Robinson reassured supporters that being a Barbadian would not hamper his ability to effectively serve in the Legislative Council. The candidate claimed he was a resident of Trinidad for thirty years.[48]

It may be a matter of conjecture as to the effect of the question of the nationality of candidates on the elections in the period under review. Cory-Davies was English-born, and he lost at the polls; Rust was an Englishman resident in Trinidad, and he also suffered defeat. But Stollmeyer, Barbadian-born, won his seat in the Legislative Council on a TWA ticket. Most likely the endorsement by the TWA saved Stollmeyer from the fate of Rust and Cory-Davies at the polls.

Prior to 7 February 1925, British colonial policy precluded elections in Trinidad. Therefore, these first elections in the colony offered an opportunity for limited participation in political governance. Those who previously agitated for greater involvement in the administration of the colony used the electoral platform to further raise awareness among the electorate about the need to consider Trinidadians, rather than foreigners, as best suited for the Legislative Council.

It was convenient for opponents to attack such candidates as Stollmeyer who were West Indian-born but not Trinidadian. However, the greater objective was to undermine and replace the dominating presence of the English in the colony's administration. Therefore, this was an opportune time for reformers to launch another salvo at colonial rule, particularly in challenging the electors to reject any "great Englishman" at the polls.

Race and the Indian vote

The Royal Commission of 1888 revealed the extent of race consciousness in the colony. For instance, in evidence before the Royal Commission, Philip Hill, an African from an Indian village in Fifth Company, Savana Grande, was in favour of elected members who belonged to his race. Hill also stated that he would trust an elected member belonging to his class.[49]

The issue of representation for Indians in Trinidad was addressed in 1910 by the Sanderson Commission. Lord Sanderson headed the commission which was appointed by the Secretary of State for the Colonies, Earl of Crewe, on 3 March 1909 to study the question of the Indian presence in the British colonies. The commission observed the absence of political participation of Indians at the level of the Legislative Council and therefore made a recommendation that this be rectified, "The East Indian population of the island numbers about 30 per cent of the whole, and we think that the suggestion of the witness who gave evidence on their behalf that they are entitled to have a representative of their own community on the Legislative Council deserves sympathetic consideration."[50]

There was already an African presence in the Legislative Council with the appointment of C. P. David in 1904; David went on to serve the council until 1911.[51]

The Sanderson Commission was not the first to observe the social and political alienation of Indians in the colony. There were organizations such as the East Indian National Association (EINA), formed in 1897, and the East Indian National Congress (EINC), in 1909, which agitated for opportunities to permit greater Indian participation in the colony's administration. After the visit of Joseph Pointer (labour MP) in 1911, another Indian-based group called the Trinidad Democratic League was inaugurated in 1912. The main objective of the league was to encourage Indians to be proactive in the island's political affairs.[52] The existence and function of these groups were influential in the appointment of the first East Indian in the Legislative Council in 1912: "They secured the alleviation of a number of grievances suffered by their community and in 1912, obtained representation on the nominated Legislative Council when George Fitz-Patrick, a lawyer and President of the EINA, was called to the house. From this time to the introduction of a partly elective Council in 1925, an attempt was maintained by the colonial government to have at least one representative on the Council who was an East Indian."[53] Upon the death of George Fitz-Patrick in 1920, Rev. C. D. Lalla (an ordained minister of the Presbyterian Church) replaced him as a nominated member of the Legislative Council. The visit of Major Wood to Trinidad increased awareness of the need for greater Indian representation. Thus, with A. A. Sobrian's appointment, there were two East Indians in the Legislative Council.

On 23 February 1925, Krishna Deonarine (who later changed his name to Adrian Cola Rienzi) wrote a letter to the editor of the *Labour Leader* informing the readership of a mass meeting held on 7 February at the Oriental Hall. The purpose of the meeting was to pass a resolution of protest and to appoint delegates to convey their dissatisfaction to the Governor who failed to appoint Indians in the nominated unofficial section of the Legislative Council. Deonarine moved a historic resolution that representation be made to the government demanding the need for more political representation for the East Indian community. At this gathering, delegates were appointed to interview the Governor and expressed dissatisfaction with the fact that the appointment of East Indians among the unofficial members in the Legislative Council was overlooked.[54] This was one of the first bold attempts by an Indian to challenge the political status quo.

In these early elections held in the colony, the race factor was obviously decisive, particularly in the electoral districts of St Patrick and Caroni with their considerable Indian populations. Samaroo believed that in the 1925 elections, race and colour were important determinants in influencing the colony's voters.[55] The media, as indicated in its detailed reports, showed a definite interest in the role of Indians in the electoral process. From these extensive reports, it is obvious that Indians attended electoral rallies and participated in platform presentations. Indian candidates for elections included Jules Mahabir, A. A. Sobrian, S. Teelucksingh, F. E. M. Hosein and Timothy Roodal.[56]

The absence of Indians on the electoral platform of certain non-Indian candidates featured in media reports. In January 1925, at one of Robinson's meetings, the prominent persons listed were non-Indians; these included Rev. Green, A. B. Carr, J. J. McLeod, F. E. Grant, C. Macaulay, David Colley, James Clarke, W. Cumberbatch, K. A. Kipps and J. Ryan.[57] There is evidence proving that some Indians were affiliated and supported non-Indian candidates. At one of Kelshall's meetings at Victoria Hall, among those Indians reported in attendance were Charles Mootoo, A. W. Armoogam and Ralph Soodeen. At another of his meetings, three Indians shared his platform – D. Chadee, J. Lahouri and A. Dookie – while others listed were of different races.[58] A report in the *Trinidad Guardian* indicated a similar trend, showing that very few or no Indians could be identified at meetings for Johnston, Cory-Davies or Rust. At one of Rust's meetings in Woodbrook on 8 January 1925, no Indians were present despite a relatively large Indian community in the nearby county of St James.[59]

At election rallies in 1928 for Sobrian and Roodal, the *Trinidad Guardian* reported that Indians were on the platform and in attendance. During the 1928 campaign, some of the Indians appearing on Sobrian's platform included A. Rampersad, C. B. Mathura, Mooklassar Maharaj, Ramcheran Maraj, A. J. Mohomed, Goberdan Pundit and Harry Persad.[60] Likewise, Roodal attracted a visible Indian presence on his platform. At one of his meetings in Penal, some of the Indians present were

T. R. Mahabirsingh, A. Baldeo, Ramputi Rampaul, Juman Meah, N. C. Goberdhan, Bhagwandin Maharaj and N. W. Ramcharan.[61]

After his defeats in 1925 and 1928, Robinson believed that having more Indians visible on his platform as speakers would increase his chances at the polls. In December 1932, he held a meeting at Caroni in which a number of Indian speakers participated. The *East Indian Weekly*'s report listed the following Indians as being present at the meeting: A. Jamadar (barrister-at-law), S. Mohamed, M. G. Sinanan, Dinnath Ramcheran, Shorab Khan and A. C. B. Singh.[62] At another of Robinson's meetings, among the speakers were Charles Ramkhelawan, Shorab Khan and S. M. Hosein.[63] The use of Indians as speakers on Robinson's platform was a conscious attempt to win the votes of enfranchised Indians, especially from among those supporting Teelucksingh.

In addition to the political involvement of the EINC and EINA, there were other associations which played a role in party politics. Three groups representing Indians – the East Indian Mutual Help Friendly Society, the East Indian Recreation Club and the East Indian Debating Association – held a meeting on 24 August 1924 to pass a resolution to support the candidacy of C. H. Pierre.[64] The support given by these prominent Indian groups to Pierre, who was of mixed descent (Indian and African), provides evidence of one of the early instances in which race played an influential factor in the quest for the "Indian vote."

Gobin, one of labour's choices, also received considerable support from the Indian segment of the population. On 24 August 1924, at Gobin's meeting at Theatre Hall, Chaguanas, there was a large representative gathering of Indians from all classes. One of the speakers, Habib (an Indian catechist and schoolmaster), addressed the gathering in English and Hindi. The speaker urged Indians to vote for Gobin and explained the manner in which they should exercise their vote.[65] In Caroni, the race factor was decisive particularly with two Indian candidates in contention – Teelucksingh and Gobin. Samaroo believed that "the emergence of two prominent Indian creoles threatened to split the Trinidad Indian vote, thus making it possible for a third candidate of another race to capture the seat."[66] The dilemma was eventually resolved with the intervention of the EINC which met with both Indian candidates and their supporters. After discussions, it was finally agreed that Gobin would withdraw from the electoral contest.[67] The decision of Gobin, who was supported by the TWA, not to contest the election prevented the split in the "Indian vote" and ensured that Robinson, the white rival candidate, was not successful.

Certain electoral speeches at public meetings provide evidence of deliberate efforts to emphasize racial differences between candidates as being a criterion for voters' support. This occurred at an election meeting to support Robinson which was held on 14 January 1925 at the Chaguanas Court House. L. A. Pujadas, supporting Robinson, appealed to the East Indians in the crowd not to be prejudiced by the caste system and not to allow the EINC to influence their vote. In his address, Robinson dismissed allegations (by Teelucksingh) that he was not always available to listen to the complaints of cane farmers. In response to Robinson's statement, implying Teelucksingh was a liar, a voice from the crowd shouted, "It belongs to his race."[68] Robinson was adamant that the EINC deliberately wielded race in the Caroni campaign, and he appealed for the electorate to choose on merit rather than race:

> The election was not being fought on the merits of the candidates but it was being fought or attempted to be fought by the East Indian Congress on race. That was not the proper way to attempt to represent the divergent peoples of the Colony. The Colony did not contain only East Indians but white, black and every other colour and the proper thing to do if self-government was to be a success was to look at the merits of the candidates who came before them, irrespective of race, colour and everything else and say who was the man best fitted to represent their interests.[69]

Similarly, Randolph Rust experienced racial antagonism in his electoral campaign. In January 1925, the column "Lizzie and Joe" in the *Labour Leader* commented on Rust's campaign in Port-of-Spain. "Joe" queried the absence of Rust's white friends since the candidate's supporters on the platform were predominantly African.[70] In January 1925, Rust launched a vitriolic attack on Johnston claiming that his rival lacked knowledge of oil companies and was "as ignorant as a Hottentot."[71] Rust's comparison of his rival's paucity of intelligence to that of a Hottentot, a tribe in Africa, could also be interpreted as a racial reproach. Detractors of Cipriani sometimes placed him in the category of "white," but supporters of labour accepted him as a white sympathetic to labour. In one instance, a letter signed "A daughter of Iere" published in the *Labour Leader* defended Cipriani's credibility and character as being different from those of other whites, "Who does not know of the prejudice, the bitter racial scorn, that exists in the bosoms of the whites or so called whites in the Island? … Arthur Andrew Cipriani has taken the people's cause for his own, and has taught them the value of strong but quiet and law-abiding perseverance, blended with Unity, instead of the doctrines his accusers so wickedly and untruthfully accuse him of."[72]

It is apparent that in predominantly Indian communities, there was no guarantee of unanimous Indian support for any candidate. Furthermore, divisions of the Indian vote or any significantly low voter turnout could be detrimental for a candidate whose reliance was on the Indian vote. In Caroni, the composition of the electorate was working class, petite bourgeoisie and peasant.[73] The EINC provided Teelucksingh with an organizational base in Caroni akin to the one provided by the TWA for Cipriani in Port-of-Spain. Even though Teelucksingh, Vice President of the TWA, defeated Robinson in 1925, the association needed to downplay its Pan-African outlook if it desired to attract Indians to its membership. Kelvin Singh in *Race and Class Struggles in a Colonial State – Trinidad 1917–1945* contended that "neither Teelucksingh nor the EINC had the political stature or the *potential* for trans-ethnic appeal that the TWA had, once it relegated its Pan-African orientation in favour of a Socialist ideology, as it did after Cipriani had consolidated his leadership."[74]

The electoral situation in Caroni was not repeated in St Patrick. Sobrian, an Indian planter, was defeated by Radcliffe-Clarke, a white planter. The rejection of Sobrian reflected the political weakening of the EINA which had offered him support. Another factor to be considered is the low voter turnout in St Patrick. This meant a considerable segment of the qualified middle-class Indians did not exercise their franchise.[75] The issue of race was a determinant in the outcome of the results in St Patrick since Sobrian depended on the support and voting strength not only of the EINA but also of the Indians who did not vote.

Another interesting development occurred in St George, a constituency which produced a low voter turnout. Two white candidates contested here: Stollmeyer and Cory-Davies. Stollmeyer, the victor, is credited as possessing twin advantages of his popularity among the electorate and his association with Cipriani.[76] In such instances where candidates were of similar race/ethnicity, the decisive factors of publicity, association with the working class and issues debated became crucial criteria for success at the polls.

The results of the colony's elections in 1925 caused a degree of concern among officials, particularly regarding the absence of an elected Indian candidate in the Legislative Council. On 18 May 1925, the Secretary of State wrote to the Governor of Trinidad and Tobago, Sir H. A. Byatt, suggesting that the Indians in the colony should have a representative in the Legislative Council:

> I note that Mr. A. A. Sobrian, a member of the East Indian community, was not returned by the Electorate of St. Patrick, and that there is therefore only one East Indian, an elected member, represented in the Legislative Council. In view of the large numbers of East Indians resident in the Colony, I attach importance to one of their number being represented on the Council as a Nominated Unofficial Member and I should be glad to learn your reasons for being unable to nominate an East Indian other than Mr. Sobrian for one of the six nominated Unofficial seats.[77]

However, Governor Byatt was hesitant to nominate any individual who had lost the elections to the position of unofficial member. The Secretary of State acknowledged Byatt's decision and added that the Governor's choice of nominated members was "to redress any lack of balance in Legislative Council due to the hazards of an election."[78] The outcome of the election was also a matter of concern for the Secretary of State who queried the race and political outlook of the successful candidates: "I should be glad to learn to which race each of the seven Elected Members belongs and also their attitude on political questions generally as displayed at the election and whether they have in the past been prominent either as supporters or opponents of the Government."[79]

The TWA endorsed the candidacy of three Indians (Hosein, Teelucksingh and Roodal) who were contesting the 1928 election. Although fundamentally Afro-based, the association supported these candidates especially because no Africans were contesting the election in Trinidad. On the contrary, the two candidates in Tobago were Africans. Furthermore, Sobrian and Robinson, who were considered capitalists, opposed Teelucksingh and Roodal.[80] Indeed, the three Indians were not actively involved in the TWA, and, as Kelvin Singh argued, "even though these Indian candidates were not ideologically committed to the working-class movement, they were generally supportive of its causes."[81]

In the 1928 electoral campaign, race continued to be a significant factor in platform speeches at public meetings. On 9 January 1928, at a meeting held at St Isidore Hall, Penal, an attempt was made by Roodal to downplay the issue of race. Roodal not only acknowledged being an Indian but also assured his listeners that he would prioritize the interests of the constituents regardless of colour, class or creed.[82] The effort to dismiss race as a central issue in the campaign in St Patrick received a setback. A letter by "Trinidad" sent to the editor of the *Port-of-Spain Gazette* was critical of Roodal's policies and noted that the candidate did not have a "Prohibition plank." This was an indirect reference to the notorious alcohol addiction among Indians. The writer further queried the apathy among the colony's Indians in dealing with the poor in their comments:

> Might I ask the benevolent Mr. Roodal in which community the greatest amount of poverty exists, due in most cases to infirmity and old age? His answer would be "the East Indian community." Every community in the Colony other than the East Indian does something for its poor outside of government aid ... has any individual or deputation of East Indians at any time waited on the Government suggesting a measure by which with an annual contribution from them and with the aid of the government this visible distress might be relevant.[83]

At Sobrian's campaign meeting in Penal on 24 January 1928, the issue of race surfaced. During his address, Sobrian indicated that he had incurred the wrath of his Indian friends when he agreed to contest the elections for St Patrick only after being persuaded by Colonel Hickling, a white. This prompted cynical cries of "Sure! sure!" from the crowd, which seemed to comprise a considerable number of Roodal's supporters. Upon Sobrian's announcing that he was born in Trinidad and a Trinidadian first, someone in attendance loudly replied, "I am Indian first and Trinidadian after."[84] The candidate ignored the remarks and insisted he was not "a tool of the white man." Sobrian's rash comment brought a flurry of responses such as "You are a tool" and "We don't want you."[85] The defensive and apologetic nature of his speech as well as the crowd's deliberate rejection of the candidate's alliances with the white colonel were indicative of the strategic significance of the Indian vote at the polls in such districts as St Patrick.

At Sobrian's other meetings in 1928, he continued his efforts to capture and appeal to Indian voters. At Fyzabad, on 27 January, Sinanan, one of his supporting speakers, stressed the importance of the Indian vote as there were 1,933 electors in St Patrick of whom 833 were Indians. He further advised his predominantly Indian audience to act wisely as they (Indians) comprised a powerful segment of the population in Penal, Siparia and Fyzabad. The Chairman, Colonel Hickling, later indicated that the Secretary of the EINA would be a guest speaker at another meeting supporting Sobrian.[86] A similar scenario unfolded on 28 January at Sobrian's meeting in the Siparia R. C. School where Rust indicated that people were opposed to voting for Sobrian because of the support and endorsement he received from a white person – Hickling. Rust, a white, was supportive of Sobrian and appealed to the Indians in the crowd to refrain from repeating the mistakes of those who opposed that candidate. To any Indians who were inclined to reject the white presence in elections, Rust reminded them that Cipriani was white. This elicited an immediate response from the crowd when someone retorted, "No, no"; then another added, "He is a son of the soil."[87] Eventually, at the polls, Roodal was the victorious candidate. Apart from his support by the TWA, his campaign and success at the polls in a predominantly Indian district would have been strengthened by Indian voters who withdrew their support for Sobrian.

Teelucksingh, the labour candidate in Caroni, received public support from the EINC of which he was President.[88] He also received extensive support due to his involvement in another Indian organization. In 1932, the Sanatan Dharma Board of Control was established and Teelucksingh saw this as a political and social threat. He subsequently established and became President of a Hindu group called the Sanatan Dharma Association.[89]

At a monthly meeting of the EINC on 2 February at the Couva Theatre, a motion was moved and unanimously agreed upon by members to support the candidature of Teelucksingh. Furthermore, the members of the EINC formed themselves into a special committee to lend support to Teelucksingh's campaign.[90] This EINC Committee also collaborated with the "Teelucksingh Electioneering Campaign Committee" which had a considerable number of Indians including Abidh, Imamshah, Duarka Maraj, Bridgelal Maraj, Baboo Ramsingh, Gheesa Maraj, Teeluckram Maraj, Lachee D. Bissessar, Ramsubhag Maraj and Ramnewas Maraj.[91] Robinson's campaign also included an "election committee" and the Indians among his ten-member committee were J. E. Armoorgam, J. Ramoutar, Nazeer Hosein and Siriam Maraj.[92] It was obvious that, with this visible Indian element in his committee, Robinson was keen on attracting the support of the Indian electorate in Caroni.

By 1928, it was apparent that Indians were taking an active political role in the colony. Of the fifteen candidates who participated in the 1925 and 1928 elections, there were five East Indians – Teelucksingh, Roodal, Sobrian, Mahabir and Hosein. The results of the 1928 elections, especially with the victory of Indian labour candidates, had a positive impact on increasing the potential of the African-based TWA to develop into a "genuinely multi-racial organization."[93] The Indian labour candidates would have been part of the relatively small Indian middle class who undertook the role of the "modernizing elite"[94] within the colony's population.

In May 1928, a few months after labour's success in the general elections, there was an increase in middle-class Indian membership in the TWA, "At this stage it appeared to be mostly the literate, westernised Indians who were gravitating to the organization."[95] The editorial of the *East Indian Weekly* in March 1928 proudly attested to the selection of Indians and their active involvement in the political administration and social life of the colony, "East Indians today are occupying no less than three seats on the Legislative Council, one on the City Council, and two on the Borough Council of San Fernando, links being found in prominent positions in all the professions and in almost every rank and walk of life in our midst."[96]

During the conduct of the 1933 election campaign, the issue of race continued to be an obvious factor in the electoral districts of St Patrick and Caroni. As in the two previous elections (1925 and 1928), speakers and candidates utilized racial differences to attract voters' support. In the contest for Victoria, Piper (the rejected TWA candidate) held a meeting at Princes Town Hall where Roodal was criticized and his tribal politics exposed in his campaign for the St Patrick seat. L. R. Sinkia, a speaker, revealed that Roodal and his party conducted a racially biased campaign, "They made a house to house canvass of the Indian gentleman of that district and appealed to them in this way: It is a national question we have to put up, an Indian candidate and you have got to vote for him."[97] In addition, Sinkia publicly revealed that Roodal, in a derogatory manner, told residents of Tableland, "Mr. Piper is only a negro." Also at this meeting was Ralph Mentor of the Sangre Grande branch of the TWA, who made disclosures which illustrated that the TWA appreciated the race factor in the electoral process. He reported that he attended the general meeting of the TWA in which Mahabir was selected as an electoral candidate and that the General Council of the TWA chose Mahabir for two reasons: first, he was a member of the League of Coloured Peoples in England. Second, Mahabir, being an Indian, would be able to attract the Indian votes in Victoria.[98] This decision of the TWA to choose and support an Indian candidate indicated the organization's awareness of race consciousness among the Indians in the county. The selection of Mahabir and support by the TWA demonstrated a conscious attempt to win Victoria not only with a manifesto and impressive speakers but also by appealing to the race factor.

The TWA was also intent on retaining St Patrick and sought to use race in its bid to achieve electoral success. Two candidates of East Indian descent – Timothy Roodal (endorsed by the TWA) and Premchand Bunsee – were contesting the St Patrick seat. In an effort to prevent a split in Indian votes, a group of prominent Indians encouraged Bunsee to withdraw from the electoral contest. The delegation comprised Pundit Dinnanath Tewarri, Aiknath Ramcharan, Charles Ramkhalawan, Dr C. W. Chandisingh (former Vice President of the EINC), Gobardhan Pundit and Pundit Ramlochan. On 9 January, Bunsee cancelled his nomination at the Siparia Warden Office. Subsequently, Roodal was unopposed and declared elected by A. J. Bernard, the Returning Officer for St Patrick.[99]

At Robinson's election rally in Carapichaima on 5 January 1933, Mitra G. Sinanan, a twenty-three-year-old barrister from San Fernando, told his audience, "I see a good many full-blooded Africans here and I am going to speak good creole English to them." The speaker sought to discredit the opposition by emphasizing an apparent anomaly in Teelucksingh's advice to the electorate not to vote for Robinson because he was white. Sinanan stated that the EINC was receptive to the ideals of the Indian Congress in India and then asked the crowd "Who founded the Indian Congress?" to which someone replied, "A white man." Then, Sinanan asked, "Who was one of the most trusted leaders of Mahatma Gandhi?" to which a member of the crowd quickly responded, "Mirabai – a white woman otherwise known as Miss Slade, daughter of an Admiral."[100] The reply reflected the depth of knowledge of the crowd. Sinanan acknowledged the accuracy of the answers and questioned the motives of Teelucksingh, dubbed the local Mahatma Gandhi, in highlighting the issue of Robinson's racial background. At this meeting, Robinson sought to enlighten the crowd on his policy of equity among the races, "This country is a country of different races – Chinese, Hindus, Muslims, Spaniards. Is it decent for anyone to say that the people must vote for a particular race?"[101]

Allegations of racial bias haunted the Robinson/Teelucksingh campaign. At Las Lomas, Robinson categorically denied accusations made by Teelucksingh that the former paid $25.00 for the upkeep of a dog at a hotel but spent only $15.00 to pay an East Indian who cared for the animal. On 19 January 1933 at a meeting in the Anglican school in Couva, Robinson sought to counter Teelucksingh's racial attacks. Robinson mentioned that representatives of all races comprised his election committee and willingly supported his candidature. In retaliation, Robinson criticized the EINC which comprised officers who were either friends or relatives of Teelucksingh and resided in Couva or San Fernando. Robinson believed that "the whole truth is that Mr. Teelucksingh is the Congress and the Congress is Mr. Teelucksingh."[102] Robinson was aware that the EINC included three persons: S. Teelucksingh (President), Rev. C. D. Lalla (Auditor) who was a relative of Teelucksingh and P. Jhurisingh (Treasurer), a friend of the candidate.[103] Robinson inferred that the EINC lacked support from the majority of Indians and Teelucksingh manipulated and provided direction for the EINC.

The electoral contest in Chaguanas brought into focus a significant factor that was particularly dangerous for Indian solidarity at the level of elections as well as for communal harmony. On 23 December 1932 at the Charlie Village Mosque, Muslims assembled to discuss certain public comments made by Teelucksingh. Hadgi [*sic*] Rukmudin, spiritual leader of Trinidad Muslims, presided as the judge. Shorab Khan, Secretary of the Hindu-Muslim School, appeared in the capacity of the chief complainant, whilst M. S. Hosein, a Muslim from San Fernando, and Aiknath Ramcharan of Chaguanas supported Khan's accusations "that Mr. Teelucksingh told certain Chaguanas Indians connected with the Management of the Hindu-Muslim School, that unless they exclude Muslim children from the school he would not support them in the Legislature and would do nothing conducive to the Government placing their school in the list of Assisted Schools."[104]

Teelucksingh, elected member for Caroni and prospective candidate in the 1933 elections, was found guilty of uttering "derogatory statements" against Muslims in the colony. However, the Hadgi preferred conciliation and subsequently advised the Muslims to forgive Teelucksingh keeping in mind the service he had rendered to the Indian community in the past. The Muslims at the gathering were not eager to accept the advice of their leader. Teelucksingh had denied the allegations of "infidelity to Hindus and Muslims" which had been broadcast by his opponents in Chaguanas. At election meetings, he responded with the slogan "Vote for Teelucksingh and down with traitors." There is no evidence of hostilities between Hindus and Muslims in the Chaguanas-Charlieville community during that electoral year, and nor can it be substantiated that it seriously affected Indian voting patterns since Teelucksingh was easily returned to the Legislative Council.

In the aftermath of the 1933 elections, there was a minor outbreak of violence in Chaguanas. The *Trinidad Guardian* reported that "a civil war" almost erupted between supporters of Teelucksingh and Robinson, "Bands of Couva men riding on motor-cars and on motor lorries trooped down into Chaguanas to give battle to the defeated Robinsonites … Stalwart negroes in short sleeves turned up to give battle, but the Couva men beat a hasty retreat."[105] There were an estimated 800 people, armed with sticks and stones, walking through the streets of Chaguanas. Police arrived quickly on the scene and attempted to disarm and disperse the crowd. A report published by the *Trinidad Guardian* mentioned the racial composition of the groups in conflict in Chaguanas. Of note is the fact that "stalwart negroes" joined others in defence of Robinson while the Couva group, who belonged to the Teelucksingh camp, must have comprised Indians. This further indicated the intensity of race politics and the volatile race relations in Central Trinidad. It is obvious that, here, in a predominantly Indian district, there was a split in the political allegiance of the African and Indian groups. The "stalwart negroes" were supportive of Robinson whilst Teelucksingh relied on the Indian constituents.

Robinson did not contest the 1938 elections in Caroni, and thus race was not an influential factor as in previous years. C. C. Abidh, a former member of Teelucksingh's Campaign Committee in 1928, had broken ties with Teelucksingh and challenged him for the Caroni seat. Both Abidh and Teelucksingh were Indians, and this prompted the formation of an ad hoc Conciliation Committee, appointed by the EINC, which met on 7 January to avoid an election contest between both men. The *Trinidad Guardian* reported the intention of the meeting, "During the past few weeks there has been a growing feeling among the Indian community, particularly in the County of Caroni, that an election battle at this time between two well-known Indian leaders would serve no useful purpose … it would be wiser and far more expedient if a reasonable and friendly settlement were reached between both parties and their supporters."[106] The incumbent was able to garner sufficient support and claim a victory. Teelucksingh polled 574 votes whilst his contender gained a respectable 468 votes. The details in six electoral districts reflect strong support for Abidh in Cunupia, Chaguanas and Todd's Road (see Table 2).

In the 1938 elections, the EINC came under attack from A. C. B. Singh who described the organization as "a small body virtually defunct most of the time, which suddenly springs to life when certain Indian gentlemen desire to air certain views."[107] This criticism from Singh is not surprising because in the 1938 elections, he spoke on the platform of Robinson who lost to Teelucksingh. The EINC also endured criticism from *The People*, "They are forever reminding us that Indians form one-third of the island's population; and do not hesitate to demand special minority privileges, although Indians enjoy the same rights under the law as other sections of the community."[108]

Table 2 Table indicating results of 6 electoral districts in central Trinidad, 1938 election

Cunupia	Teelucksingh	31
	Abidh	98
Flanagin Town	Teelucksingh	59
	Abidh	40
Couva	Teelucksingh	217
	Abidh	74
Chaguanas	Teelucksingh	162
	Abidh	189
Todd's Road	Teelucksingh	11
	Abidh	35
Gran Couva	Teelucksingh	94
	Abidh	32

Source: *Sunday Guardian*, 23 January 1938.

The issue of race was a determining factor in the contest for Victoria. In mid-January 1938, *The People* reported that Piper was "trying to hoodwink the electorate with racial propaganda. But the intelligent electors smile complacently at such poor tactics."[109] The voting patterns in the electoral district strongly suggested voting according to race. For instance, in areas predominantly populated by Indians, such as South Naparima and San Fernando South, Rienzi claimed a wide margin of victory. However, in mixed areas such as Princes Town and Ortoire, Piper had relatively strong support. And, in Moruga, where the population was mostly African, Piper was able to narrowly defeat Rienzi (see Table 3).

In the aftermath of the election, a letter to the *Sunday Guardian* criticizing Rienzi was considered by *The People* as "rude and offensive." The working-class newspaper stated that the writer failed to appreciate the fact that Rienzi was the leader of the sugar union which had 70 per cent Indians and the OWTU which had 90 per cent Indians.[110]

The Couva-Chaguanas sugar belt with its predominantly Indian population ensured victories in four elections for Teelucksingh, a wealthy Couva

Table 3 Table indicating results of Victoria in 1938 elections

	Rienzi	Piper
North Naparima	126	9
San Fernando South	628	122
Moruga	24	30
South Naparima	400	32
Pointe-a-Pierre	131	75
San Fernando North	337	63
Princes Town	232	151
Ortoire	125	65
Total	2,003	547

Source: *The People*, 29 January 1938.

Indian. Furthermore, Teelucksingh received the support of prominent Presbyterians such as Abidh, and even Canadian missionary Rev. Green who sometimes attended Teelucksingh's meetings. Robinson, though a sugar estate magnate of European descent, relied on support from the Africans, a few Indians and whites. Consequently, he suffered defeat at the polls, and even though he had moral support from his employees, these workers did not possess the necessary income and property qualifications for voting.

In these fiercely contested elections in the colony, the platform debates and media analysis of topics deliberately exposed the disaster of colonial neglect of the island. Furthermore, the intentional and methodical analysis of the existing social and economic structure served as a powerful weapon to undermine public confidence against a harsh colonial administration.

The level of participation in the national elections conspicuously heralded the intention of local politicians to take up the cudgels in the struggle against colonial domination. They refused to be satisfied with the few seats offered to them in the legislature. Seven out of twenty-six seats reflected tokenism. The new 1924 Constitution bestowed national elections, but the Governor continued as the virtual autocrat of the colony. The benevolent constitutional "gift" permitted the local electorate to have their say, but colonial authority was selfishly preserved. The Governor's voice in the Legislative Council continued to be dominant:

> a Governor with near absolute powers, whose autocracy was reinforced by the inherited despotic character of the old Spanish governorship and the old French notion of paternal government; ... the governor, a despot locally, was simply, in the irreverent language of a daringly outspoken nominated member at a later period, a functionary regarded by the Council Office merely as the servant of the centurion.[111]

Although not distinctly manifested, the course of the early elections in Trinidad and Tobago was indicative of the rise of a vigorous national spirit which served as the beacon to inspire future efforts along the road to self-government.

Notes

1. *Wood Report*, 81.
2. *Wood Report*, 81.
3. *Wood Report*, 7.
4. *Wood Report*, 7.
5. *Labour Leader* 26 July 1924.
6. *TG* 3, 6, 7, 8, 10, 18, January 1925.
7. See *Labour Leader* 2, 6, August 1924.
8. *Labour Leader* 7 January 1925.
9. *Labour Leader* 3 February 1925.
10. Samaroo, "Constitutional and Political Development," 185.
11. Ramdin, *Chattel Slave to Wage*, 72.
12. *TG* 17 January 1925.
13. *Labour Leader* 14 January 1925.
14. *Labour Leader* 28 January 1925.
15. *Labour Leader* 7 February 1925. The article had the headline "Representative Government."
16. *TG* 20 January 1925.
17. *TG* 3 January 1925.
18. *TG* 15 January 1925.
19. *TG* 20 January 1925.

20. *TG* 23 January 1925.
21. *TG* 26 January 1928.
22. *POSG* 31 January 1928.
23. *TG* 20 January 1933.
24. *TG* 6 January 1938.
25. *TG* 8 January 1938.
26. *TG* 8 January 1938.
27. *Labour Leader* 18 June 1927.
28. *POSG* 8 January 1938.
29. *The People* 8 January 1938.
30. *The People* 22 January 1938.
31. See S. Basdeo and H. Robertson, "The Nova Scotia-British West Indies Commercial Experiment in the Aftermath of the American Revolution, 1783–1802," in Brian Douglas Tennyson, ed., *Canada and the Commonwealth Caribbean* (Maryland: University Press of America, 1988), 25–49.
32. J. C. A. Stagg, "James Madison and the Coercion of Great Britain: Canada, the West Indies, and the War of 1812," in Tennyson, ed., *Canada and the Commonwealth Caribbean*, 51–103. Peter K. Newman, "Canada's Role in West Indian Trade before 1912," in Tennyson, ed., *Canada and the Commonwealth Caribbean*, 105–135.
33. *TG* 20 January 1925.
34. *TG* 21 January 1925.
35. *TG* 22 January 1925.
36. *Labour Leader* 13 September 1924.
37. *TG* 8 January 1925.
38. There was a calypso in 1925 which dealt with the issue of nationality.
39. *TG* 9 January 1925.
40. *TG* 20 January 1925.
41. *TG* 17 January 1925.
42. Ince, "Politics before the People's National Movement," 51–52.
43. *TG* 17 January 1925.
44. *TG* 20 January 1925.
45. *TG* 21 January 1925.
46. *TG* 23 January 1925.
47. *TG* 23 January 1925.
48. *TG* 15 January 1925.
49. Evidence Given at the commission's eighth meeting on 9 April 1888: The Royal Commission to Consider and Report as to the Proposed Franchise and Division of the Colony into Electoral Districts 1888.
50. *Report of the Committee on Emigration from Indian to the Crown Colonies and Protectorates* (London: HMSO, 1910), 101.

51. Brinsley Samaroo, "Cyrus Prudhomme David – A Case Study in the Emergence of the Black Man in Trinidad Politics," *Journal of Caribbean History* 3 (November 1971), 76–86.
52. John La Guerre, Brinsley Samaroo and George Sammy, eds, *East Indians and the Present Crisis* (Aranguez: Print-Rite, 1973), 2.
53. La Guerre, Samaroo and Sammy, *East Indians*, 2.
54. The resolution was seconded by Joseph Rattan and supported by Henry Gobin. Among those attending this meeting were Rev. Rameshwar, James Mungal, J. T. Namsoo, Charles Mootoo, A. R. Sinanan, C. Soodeen, A. Ogeerally, Mohammed Haniff, Shaffie Mohammed and A. Harbance. *Labour Leader* 28 February 1925.
55. Samaroo, "Constitutional and Political Development," 185.
56. See Singh, *Race and Class*, 125–126. Non-Indian candidates included R. Rust (white), T. M. Kelshall (Coloured), A. Cory-Davies (white), A. Stollmeyer (white), Gaston Johnston (Coloured), E. A. Robinson (white), C. H. Pierre (Indian and African descent), I. A. Hope (African) and A. Cipriani (white).
57. *TG* 3 January, 15 January 1925,
58. At Victoria Hall, others present included A. A. Ritchie, H. Monsegue, T. G. Luke, H. Gordon, E. T. Billouin, W. F. Harewood, G. McSween, Laurence Brown and A. Montano. *TG* 20 January 1925. Others in attendance on the 21 January were G. T. Macdougall. Rev. D. I. Evans, Dr P. T. Vilain, J. B. Parker, A. H. Dascent, F. A. Durity, B. Reynolds and H. Hart. *TG* 23 January 1925. One report identified some Indians at Stollmeyer's meeting: G. P. Jugmohansingh and J. Mohamed. Other persons supporting Stollmeyer included J. M. Perez, J. Ryan, H. Legendre, W. T. Cunningham, O. Springer, C. R. Smith, Edgar Jorsling, Thomas James, J. R. Govia, C. M. Lastique, R. M. T. Prizgar, Michael Hamel-Smith, G. Lyndon Kerr, A. A. Waterman and R. Fitzgerald. *TG* 20 January 1925. Another labour candidate, Pierre, had a considerable number of Indians at his meeting held at the Rio Claro Canadian Mission School. Among those present were S. Ramotar, Baldeosingh, Noorally, J. Bajnan, Ofi Mahommed, Rahamally, Gobin and Koban. *TG* 11 January 1925.
59. From the reported list of persons on Rust's platform at Woodbrook, there seemed to be no Indians: C. G. Archibald, Dr G. H. Masson, Rev. Dr W. H. Mayhew, J. Milton Thorne, R. M. T. Prizgar, W. O. Prizgar, A. Joseph and W. E. Murray.
60. *TG* 26, 29 January, 5 February 1928.
61. *POSG* 14 January 1928.
62. *POSG* 14 January 1928.
63. *TG* 8 January 1933.
64. *Labour Leader* 20 August 1924. Pierre was a barrister in Port-of-Spain and owner of a cocoa estate. Samaroo, "Constitutional and Political Development," 187.
65. *Labour Leader* 27 August 1924.
66. Samaroo, "Constitutional and Political Development," 187.

67. *POSG* 30 December 1924. Also Samaroo, "Constitutional and Political Development," 187.
68. *TG* 15 January 1925.
69. *TG* 15 January 1925.
70. *Labour Leader* 10 January 1925.
71. *TG* 8 January 1925.
72. *Labour Leader* 7 February 1925.
73. Singh, *Race and Class*, 128.
74. Singh, *Race and Class*, 128.
75. Singh, *Race and Class*, 129.
76. Singh, *Race and Class*, 130.
77. Letter from L. S. Amery to Governor H. A. Byatt, 18 May 1925, Confidential Despatches from Secretary of State to Governor 1923–1925, National Archives, Trinidad (hereafter cited as Confidential Despatches).
78. Letter from L. S. Amery to Governor H. A. Byatt, 18 May 1925, Confidential Despatches.
79. This was the second letter which Amery wrote to Byatt, 18 May 1925, Confidential Despatches.
80. Singh, *Race and Class*, 134.
81. Singh, *Race and Class*, 135.
82. *POSG* 14 January 1928.
83. *POSG* 20 January 1928.
84. See Ince, "Politics before the People's National Movement," 60. *TG* 26 January 1928.
85. *TG* 26 January 1928.
86. *POSG* 29 January 1928.
87. *POSG* 31 January 1928. Both Hickling and Rust were also involved in the colony's oil industry.
88. See *TG* 2 February 1928.
89. See Kelvin Singh, "Conflict and Collaboration: Tradition and Modernizing Indo-Trinidadian Elites (1917–1956)," *New West Indian Guide* 70 (1996), 239.
90. *TG* 9 February 1928.
91. *TG* 9 February 1928.
92. Others on Robinson's election committee included C. C. Watson, J. Ford, H. Dolival, Mathew Sagan, W. Henry Edwards and Michael Llanos (Honorary Reporter to the committee). *POSG* 12 February 1928.
93. Singh, *Race and Class*, 136.
94. See Singh, "Conflict and Collaboration," 230.
95. Singh, *Race and Class*, 136.
96. *East Indian Weekly* 7 March 1928.
97. *POSG* 4 January 1933.
98. *POSG* 4 January 1933.

99. *TG* 10 January 1933. Bunsee assured his supporters that the planks of his platform would be supported by Roodal.
100. *TG* 8 January 1933.
101. *TG* 8 January 1933.
102. *TG* 22 January 1933.
103. *TG* 22 January 1933.
104. *Sunday Guardian* 25 December 1932.
105. *TG* 31 January 1933.
106. *TG* 8 January 1938.
107. *The People* 5 March 1938.
108. *The People* 5 March 1938.
109. *The People* 15 January 1938.
110. *The People* 5 March 1938.
111. Gordon Lewis, *Growth of the Modern West Indies* (New York: Monthly Review Press, 1968), 198–199.

Bibliography

La Guerre, John, Samaroo, Brinsley and Sammy, George, eds. *East Indians and the Present Crisis* (Aranguez: Print-Rite, 1973).

Lewis, Gordon. *Growth of the Modern West Indies* (New York: Monthly Review Press, 1968).

Ramdin, Ron. *Chattel Slave to Wage Earner: A History of Trade Unionism in Trinidad and Tobago* (London: Martin Brian and O'Keeffe, 1982).

Samaroo, Brinsley. "Cyrus Prudhomme David – A Case Study in the Emergence of the Black Man in Trinidad Politics," *Journal of Caribbean History* 3 (November 1971), 76–86.

Singh, Kelvin. "Conflict and Collaboration: Tradition and Modernizing Indo-Trinidadian Elites (1917–1956)," *New West Indian Guide* 70 (1996), 229–253.

Tennyson, Brian, ed. *Canada and the Commonwealth Caribbean* (Maryland: University Press of America, 1988).

CHAPTER 5

Beyond Race: Debatable and Divisive Topics

Agriculture

Various issues affecting agriculture in the colony, especially concerns of the working class, were frequently highlighted during the early electioneering campaigns. Support for the establishment of an Agricultural Loan Bank drew considerable attention among speakers in the 1925 elections. Candidates emphasized the urgent need for such a bank particularly to assist the working class with small agricultural holdings. In July 1924, Cipriani publicly accused Robinson of not attending meetings that supported the idea of an Agricultural Loan Bank.

In response to Cipriani's accusations of Robinson's apathy towards the Agricultural Loan Bank, on 2 January 1925, Robinson clarified two misrepresentations: his stance towards the Agricultural Loan Bank and his support for cane farmers. Robinson, at a public meeting, claimed that he championed the case for the bank but did not want a loan mortgaged bank to be a burdensome millstone for the taxpayers. And, he also claimed to be supportive of the cane farmers as he sought to encourage them to harvest their canes at the right time and deliver them in a clean condition to the factories.[1]

At another meeting of Robinson, held in Caroni on 14 January, the platform speakers stressed the candidate's commitment to supporting agriculture. For instance, K. Thorp assured his listeners that Robinson was genuinely interested in the cane farming industry, while L. A. Pujadas advised the crowd that Robinson was always eager to listen to their grievances. Robinson claimed to be responsible for assisting the cane farming industry and for doubling the acreage of cane cultivation.[2]

At a meeting held on 18 January in Maracas, Cory-Davies made references to the government's passage of legislation creating the Agricultural Relief Ordinance and the Mortgages Extension Ordinance declaring a moratorium on mortgages. Cory-Davies compared cocoa prices and also argued that a man could not afford to pay a high mortgage and maintain his property. He suggested that the deadline for proprietors be extended to 30 June 1926 to ensure they benefitted from the next crop.[3] Two days later, another meeting was held for Cory-Davies at the San Juan Theatre. Prince Robinson highlighted the candidate's offer to assist the Agricultural Loan Bank at St Joseph with a payment of $500.[4] At this meeting, Cory-Davies said he did not oppose the Agricultural Loan Bank but the manner in which it operated. Furthermore, he claimed to have supported such an institution which was useful to the people if the bank was properly controlled.[5]

In an island where agriculture was of critical importance to the working class, electoral candidates utilized any opportunity not only to indicate their stance on such a sensitive issue but also to vehemently accuse rivals of their non-support of the industry. Though sugar occupied a significant place in the island's economy, there were cocoa proprietors such as Stollmeyer who proudly declared their commitment to the overall development of the colony's agriculture.

On 18 January 1925 at a public meeting in Tunapuna, Harold Smith, the Chairman, reminded the audience that Stollmeyer was always interested in the colony's agriculture, particularly in the cocoa and fruit industry.[6] Furthermore, Stollmeyer was aware of the delicate relationship which existed between employers and cane farmers, as he advised the factories and proprietors on the need to pay attention to the conditions of workers, of whom he said, "Their interests had to be protected. It did not matter what the factories did, but so long as they (farmers) were treated squarely, he would ask them to treat them (factory owners) in return squarely (applause)."[7] Indeed, the inherent diplomacy in such a statement would have served to bolster electoral support from those enfranchised in both categories.

During the 1928 campaign, agriculture continued to be relevant in the public debates and generated interest among the detractors of labour. For instance, a letter to the editor of the *Port-of-Spain Gazette* by "Trinidad" was critical of Teelucksingh's term of office, particularly with respect to his agricultural policy: "Has he defined to factory owners a means by which they can pay you a higher rate per ton of canes? Has he ever debated at any Agricultural Board the pros and cons of any argument for the betterment of agricultural conditions? … No Sirs! Electors of Caroni, appeal to Mr. E. A. Robinson."[8]

In 1925 and 1928, Robinson highlighted his involvement in agriculture but failed to win the approval of the electorate. Despite losing twice, in the 1933 campaign, he once again sought to use agriculture to demonstrate his concern for the welfare of the working class. These previous defeats did not deter him, and at an electioneering meeting for him at Las Lomas R. C. School, in January 1933, the candidate discussed the reason for imposing a 7 per cent interest on loans to farmers. Although this was apparently burdensome to farmers, Robinson explained that it was necessary due to stipulations attached to a loan of £140,000 from the government to estate owners. Owing to his experience as the Managing Director of the Woodford Lodge Sugar Estate, Robinson was able to explain that the conditions required that the estate be mortgaged. In addition, if the price of cane did not fall below £10 10s, the farmer should not get less than 12s for a ton of cane. Furthermore, Robinson accused Teelucksingh of being against the division of districts on territorial arrangements which benefitted estate owners and farmers. At this meeting, Robinson refuted allegations that he was paying a small price to farmers for their canes, "I am being painted as a very unmerciful man, a despot. I am not a despot. But I don't buy trash and tops; I buy cane."[9]

Apart from his links with Woodford Lodge and cane farming, Robinson was knowledgeable about the economic state of the colony. At a meeting at Todd's Road on 17 January, Robinson identified the need for reduced taxation, "Prices in our staple industries have dropped to such a level that the more taxes Government impose, the less will be the revenue."[10] Robinson referred to his proposal to establish a thriving banana industry and also suggested the benefits of growing grapefruits on a large scale, "Trinidad grapefruits are so good that I feel they are able to oust the Californian grapefruit and secure an excellent demand in the Canadian market and elsewhere."[11] Despite having knowledge of the domestic and international agricultural markets as well as presenting a clear manifesto, these aspects did not appeal to the electorate, once again leading to Robinson's defeat in 1933.

Social services

The quality and efficiency of social services offered in the colony was a major issue addressed in the colony's early elections. This included the state of the roads, health services, water supply and level of taxation. At Cipriani's electioneering meeting in August 1924, at Princes Building, Port-of-Spain, his working-class concerns were outlined. Among the ten planks of Cipriani's platform were poor relief, protection and development of agriculture, unemployment and general public health.[12] On 9 January 1925, at his meeting in Woodbrook, Cipriani criticized Rust's proposal that the working class should encourage their children to pursue manual jobs that require skills rather than becoming frustrated in seeking government employment. This was an attempt by Rust to preserve Civil Service jobs for the privileged class. Cipriani argued that his opponent's statement was not in the interests of the poorer class and was designed to limit vacancies in the Civil Services to children of the "upper tens."[13] Cipriani and the labourites did not fail to analyse their opponent's views within the context of benefits and relevance for the working class. Therefore, electoral promises on economic and social development were to be measured according to overall working-class needs.

Stollmeyer, contesting the election as a labour candidate, sought to highlight concerns affecting the working class. At Tunapuna on 18 January 1925, Michael Hamel-Smith, the Chairman of the meeting, told his listeners that Stollmeyer was in favour of providing water supply for all citizens, "Mr. Stollmeyer supported Scheme 'A' which provided a water supply for the whole Colony. He had taken an interest in the roads of the Colony and had sat on the Central Road Board as well as he had been a member of the Development Committee."[14] Stollmeyer, as the TWA candidate, openly indicated his concerns for labour, "What Trinidad is suffering from is underpaid labour (applause). There is no doubt about that. How are we going to bring about a change? There is only one way to do it and that is to have men in the Council who are going to be able to advance progressive ideas, who are going to think out schemes that are going to develop this island."[15]

Cory-Davies also brought concerns on social amenities – similar to those identified by the labour candidates – to the electoral platform. On 15 January at Tunapuna Government School, Cory-Davies addressed the vexing issue of the insufficient water supply in Tunapuna and the incomplete state of the road to Blanchisseuse.[16] At Maracas Government School, Cory-Davies was able to link the importance of education to good health:

> Dealing with education Mr. Cory-Davies said there was nothing grander than the enlightenment of the people, but the only way in which the children could get education on a higher plane would be by seeing after their health. It was one of the taxpayers' duties to look after the multitude and get their bodies in good form so that they might absorb the education being extended to them. The primary education was that of sanitation.[17]

A few days later, he held a meeting at San Juan where a variety of issues affecting the population was addressed, including the Tramway operations between St Joseph and Tunapuna.[18] The candidate illustrated his concerns for the welfare of the citizens which he hoped would increase his chances at the polls.

On 7 January 1925, Rust (a rival of labour) held an election meeting at Brookland Hall, Woodbrook. The candidate referred to the relatively small wages of teachers and the unsightly barrack yards which spoilt the beautiful city of Port-of-Spain. As a representative of the area, he believed that improvements could be made and the issue of alleviating poverty be addressed. Rust claimed that Johnston did not accomplish tangible benefits for the poor. Subsequently, Rev. W. H. Mayhew, who moved a resolution supporting Rust, suggested to the crowd that they ask the three candidates – Rust, Johnston and Cipriani – to prepare a payroll showing the amount each had paid to poor persons during the past decade.[19] The request of the speaker was to highlight the financial contributions of Rust to the poorer class, which Mayhew assumed would have been more than the two other rivals contesting Port-of-Spain.

The portrayal of Rust as being sympathetic to the plight of the working class was evident at other meetings too. At Belmont E. C. School, Murchison Rigsby introduced the candidate as someone who made "the people's cause his own cause." Rust openly staked his claim as an advocate for the working class, "I want to see the working classes housed in decent dwellings and I want to see the children of this country properly educated. I also want to see the status of teachers improved."[20] In addressing these issues, Rust attempted to project himself as a friend of the working class and, in effect, patterned his campaign on the TWA's concerns for the common man in the colony. Rust's failure to defeat Cipriani at the polls was an indication that the enfranchised citizens of the city were not easily swayed by mere rhetoric. In contrast, Cipriani's involvement with the TWA complemented his platform speeches on social and economic issues affecting the working class. Gaston Johnston also aired social concerns at Princes Building, Port-of-Spain. Johnston, who was contesting Port-of-Spain, believed that any candidate aspiring to enter the Legislative Council should examine such issues as the asphalt concession, distribution of revenues of the oil industry, the state of education and taxation of the poor. And, Johnston, like Stollmeyer, was concerned about the adoption of "Scheme A" of the water supply.[21]

Issues affecting the working class were given prominence in the campaign for the 1928 general elections. Water supply for the depressed areas featured prominently as indicated in an article in the *Labour Leader* of March 1927. The writer was critical of Stollmeyer's actions in the Legislative Council: "It is quite true, that he is not the *persona gratia* with his constituents today which he was two years ago. Like most men in the Council he has made blunders; the most remarkable being his negative vote to obtain for the people of the Central division of the Island a healthy water supply."[22] Even though Stollmeyer did not contest the 1928 elections, such a view by the *Labour Leader* demonstrated the continued focus on the provision of proper social services for the colony was an essential criterion for candidates seeking to be endorsed by the TWA.

At Penal, on 9 January 1928, Timothy Roodal told his supporters that in Penal the drinking water was polluted and teeming with disease-causing germs.[23] Roodal, the candidate endorsed by the TWA and contesting St

Patrick, outlined his plans to improve the living and working conditions in the colony in his manifesto. Singh claimed that some Indian candidates such as Roodal were supportive of the TWA's causes but had not adopted an ideological commitment to the working-class movement in the colony.[24] In January at a meeting in Penal, Roodal claimed the residents of Penal found it impossible to travel on certain roads during the rainy season. The candidate emphasized how badly this affected sick persons who were unable to travel on poorly laid roads. In addition, peasant proprietors experienced severe hardships due to the lack of proper access roads from the fields.

Taxes and the eight-hour day

During the 1928 elections, the eleven planks of Roodal's platform included minimum wage for workers, better housing, repeal of the Seditious Publications Ordinance, control by the government of the price of gasoline, poor relief and retrenchment.[25] Roodal also revealed that the price of gasoline in Barbados (twenty-eight cents per gallon) was cheaper than the price in Trinidad (forty cents a gallon).[26] This was a cause for concern, especially because Trinidad had oil reserves and refineries.

In 1928, Roodal argued that taxes were too high, and thus, the working class was unable to buy "bread and butter" and provide an education for their children. Among the issues outlined in Roodal's manifesto were poor relief, better housing accommodation, reduction of taxes and the introduction of a statutory eight-hour day. At an election meeting, Cipriani revealed that thousands of dollars from the oil and asphalt industries went directly to the American and English capitalists.[27] Both Radcliffe-Clarke and Robinson had publicly opposed the abolition of child labour on the colony's plantations.[28] Also, Cipriani claimed that Radcliffe-Clarke opposed the bill for the abolition of child labour and the passage of legislation to implement the eight-hour day. In 1928, this was the usual procedure of election rallies, especially for labour, which comprehensively dealt with a host of social and economic issues affecting the colony.

Roodal's manifesto prompted a response in an editorial letter, signed by a writer using the nom de plume "Trinidad." On 6 January 1928, the writer, who was not sympathetic to TWA candidates, condemned the idea of an eight-hour work day and further stated, "It is true that Messrs. Roodal Bros. have undertaken several oil field compacts but did they apportion to their employees a fair proportion of their fair earnings?" In addition, the letter contained advice to the electorate based on the work of Roodal, "Oh Trinidad and your people! Beware of whom you are sending up to represent you on the Legislative Council. There are plenty of good men down South if you, electors of St. Patrick, do not desire your present representative, who in my opinion has done silent but good work, you have Colonel Hickling, Fred Grant and others."[29] Such comments would have served as an incentive for Roodal, in his election campaign, to emphasize his concern for the improvement of social services.

Letters to the editor of the *Port-of-Spain Gazette* criticized Roodal's suggestions for improvements in the colony, particularly his appeal for a tax on oil which was dismissed by "Trinidad" who believed labourers in the oilfield would be affected. The writer also appealed for electors to support Robinson as someone who provides employment, circulates more money and gives more medical aid than any person in the colony.[30] In another letter, the writer expressed how it was impossible for Roodal to implement a law to pay an employee doubled earnings for his work.[31] The political leanings of "Trinidad" were apparent as he or she saw it fit not to attack the proposed plans of Sobrian and Robinson but was critical of Roodal's policies.[32]

Sobrian, contesting against Roodal for St Patrick, also made a conscious effort to address social and economic issues affecting Trinidad and Tobago. At Fyzabad, on 27 January, he attacked Roodal's policies, warning that such persons vying for political honours would make empty promises for better housing and reduction of taxes; however, only after they are elected will they realize their political limitations. This was an attempt to discredit Roodal's comprehensive manifesto as Sobrian described Roodal's policy on poor relief and minimum wage as "certainly childish in the extreme."

He also criticized his opponent's arguments as "ridiculous" and noted, "It showed they did not think about what they were saying."[33]

At another of Sobrian's meetings, Rust (one of the speakers) sought to highlight the divergent views between Cipriani and Roodal. Rust criticized Cipriani for his portrayal of the oil company as a curse to the colony and found this peculiar, "Roodal was oil, oil, oil and yet this great champion was decrying oil."[34] Why not give him a seat? Also, at the meeting, Sobrian attacked Roodal's manifesto regarding the reduction of taxes. The opponents of labour made an effort to unmask apparent contradictions, flaws and shortcomings in the promises and plans of the labour candidates. However, the arguments and criticisms of the opponents of labour and letters to the press did not seem to have a significant impact on the decision of voters as Roodal comfortably won his seat.

During the 1933 elections, the issues debated held the same importance as in the two previous elections. At Carapichaima, on 5 January, Robinson sought to dismiss allegations that he opposed compulsory education, "Gentlemen, if my influence was so strong that I influenced the Education Committee to make education compulsory up to 12 years of age then for that reason alone, you should send me in the Legislative Council."[35] Robinson also sought to address the misconception that Teelucksingh obtained water for the colony's citizens, "But I advocated for water when Mr. Teelucksingh was yet a boy. If you read the newspapers of 50 years ago, it will bear out what I said. I spoke to Sir John Chancellor about the scheme and today it is intended to supply water throughout Central Trinidad."[36] This response from Robinson was intended to demonstrate that his initiative was taken by Teelucksingh and paraded as a novel idea.

In an effort by Robinson to gain the support of the electorate in Caroni, he published his manifesto in the daily press. Robinson claimed that he had achieved more for the working class than his rival Teelucksingh and that the latter was not officially endorsed by the TWA:

> You will observe with a great deal of caution and query that my opponent represents none other than a particular few. This is borne out by the fact that he is not supported by his own party – The Trinidad Workingmen's Association – the members of which constitute the majority of the working people of the colony … As an employer of

> labour, my duty necessarily brings me into more intimate and constant contact with the worker, and, consequently, I am better positioned to interpret his true feelings and aspirations than one whose knowledge of labour conditions is merely theoretical and therefore impractical.[37]

Robinson's statements in his manifesto were an attempt to erode the support base of the incumbent Teelucksingh in Central Trinidad . However, the electorate was not swayed by the claims of Robinson.

In the 1938 elections, Teelucksingh proposed a programme which was labour-oriented. This included the establishment of an Old Age Pension scheme, the provision of higher salaries for assistant teachers, the creation of Industrial and Trade Union Courts, the creation of a better system of arbitration between capital and labour and the protection of farmers' interests due to the restricted quota system.[38] His rival, Abidh, also devised a plan which dealt mainly with labour issues, such as the need for government subsidies to encourage minor industries, better cane prices, full pensions for teachers, reduction of taxation and improvement of labour conditions.

In South Trinidad, an electioneering meeting for Harold Piper was held at Princes Town. Mentor, one of the supporting speakers, enumerated some of the interests of the candidate which included the reinstitution of competitive examinations for entry into the Civil Services and a land settlement scheme to help the peasantry.[39] It is obvious that rival candidates had a common perspective on certain electoral issues, and this was certainly of benefit to the colony. In 1925, Stollmeyer and Cory-Davies shared similar views on the manner in which Canadian reciprocity could affect the colony's trade. Similarly, in 1933, both Teelucksingh and Robinson championed the case for a better and more efficient water supply for the colony. Whether labour-supported or independent, the candidates' concerns enunciated on the platform or media reiterated matters for consideration by the colonial government.

Interestingly, in 1938, Rienzi, as did Roodal in 1928, also presented eleven objectives in his programme with the first being the reduction of taxation. Other initiatives included a proper road-building scheme, unemployment insurance, government control of the price of food, equitable price for farmers' case and the reduction of the price of petrol.[40]

The editorial of the *Trinidad Guardian* launched a scathing attack on Rienzi who suggested the tax burden be reduced, "On analysis of his plan we find, however, that what he really desires is a lightening of the load in one, and its increase in another."[41] In addition, the editor noted the apparent contradiction as Rienzi advocated an export duty on petrol whilst seeking to reduce the price of petrol. Not surprisingly, the editor praised Piper's five-plank programme as being "moderate" and noted that it included a comprehensive agricultural scheme with an emphasis on peasant proprietors.[42]

On 10 January at the Indian Walk Friendly Society Lodge Room, Piper sought to reveal the flaws in Rienzi's promises. First, Piper claimed, "we cannot have reduction of taxation for this would mean depriving ourselves of many of the things we need. I say re-adjust the taxes by placing them upon the shoulders of those who are better able to carry them after relieving the weaker ones."[43] Piper sought to defend the tax on petrol, by stating it was for the development of the nation's roads. Furthermore, Piper claimed that Rienzi, who owned a car, attacked the price of petrol because he wanted to operate the car for free. This was a ludicrous accusation by Piper because Rienzi could afford the price of petrol and was not the only person on the island who owned a vehicle.

Second, on Rienzi's promise of unemployment insurance, Piper felt it was not needed and that Trinidad needed "a state of trade where there will be work for all."[44] Piper argued that Rienzi's planks did not deal with agriculture. However, this is not accurate because Rienzi did mention the need for an equitable price for the farmers' canes. And, Rienzi's promise to reduce taxes and the price of petrol would mean lower transportation costs for farmers and allow for lower prices of foodstuffs.

The concerns about the provision and improvement of social services were common among candidates during the early elections. Undoubtedly, the issues affecting the daily lives of the colony's citizens, such as better roads and provision of water supply, impacted voting patterns. Promises of a better standard of living and working conditions coupled with the discussion of social concerns on the political platform struck a chord and proved to be a subject that future politicians would see as an essential component of their manifesto and agenda.

The great divide: class and ideology

> Ganesh called a Press conference at the end of the week ... He warned that the labour movement in Trinidad was dominated by communists and he had often unwittingly been made their tool. "From now on," he said, "I pledge my life to the fight against communism in Trinidad and the rest of the free world."[45]

This statement by a fictional character in Naipaul's *The Mystic Masseur* captured the stigma of labour in the Caribbean during the early decades of the twentieth century. Labour leaders were usually associated with anti-capitalist and radical ideologies.

The racial division of political parties in Trinidad and Tobago in 2010, with Indo-Trinidadians supporting the UNC and Afro-Trinidadians voting for the PNM, also existed during the 1920s and 1930s. In the colony's early elections, "class" was also an important topic among candidates. There was an obvious dichotomy between labour candidates and their electoral opponents. The groupings were loosely defined as being "labour" and "capital." Interestingly, both groups were class-based and ideologically polarized.

Persons representing the "capitalist class" were either aligned to or belonged to the ruling elite (upper class). Also, persons belonging to the "capital" were usually white and against the colony's working class, which comprised mostly Africans and Indians. Both ideological/class camps attracted considerable support from and exerted an influence on the electorate. The schism between labour and capital was obvious, as illustrated in an editorial of the *Labour Leader*: "Part of the dope with which this Ruling Class has kept the people in subjection has been the spreading of the idea that government is a very difficult and very mysterious business."[46]

At his election meeting in Woodbrook on 7 January, Rust criticized articles published in the *Port-of-Spain Gazette* by Gaston Johnston (his rival in Port-of-Spain) as "incoherent and unconvincing."[47] Rust told the electors that it was their duty to ensure that they returned men to the Legislative Council who would ensure their money was used "economically and properly." In response, Johnston did not believe Rust would be a suitable candidate because the latter was involved in the oil and asphalt industries.[48] This was one of the instances in which involvement in business was considered a determinant against effective representation of the citizenry.

During the 1920s and 1930s, a candidate associated with labour, particularly from the TWA/TLP, was identified in the media and public as "socialist" or "labourite." Roodal (contesting in St Patrick) published his manifesto (see Appendix 9) in the *Labour Leader* pledging to be a labourite:

> I shall always uphold, and be true and loyal to, the great traditions of Labour and socialism, based as they are on the great fundament of the Fatherhood of God and the brotherhood of man, a fair day's wage for a fair day's work and a square deal for the underdog. As Labour is built on this firm and steady foundation, as she is advancing onward and upward, not destroying but constructing, adjusting and consolidating her position, – and as she is on the eve of returning into power to guide the destinies of this great and mighty Empire, of which we form an integral factor it is incumbent on you to return only those who could conform to the Labour and Socialist platform.[49]

In 1933, one of the daily newspapers reinforced the stereotype of labour with the headline "Socialist Rally Broken Up."[50] In 1933, the editorial of the *Trinidad Guardian* noted the failure of socialism to appeal to the electorate:

> Mr. Mahabir was the official Socialist candidate, backed by all the resources of Captain Cipriani and the fact that the combined vote was split reveals, if it reveals nothing else, that the official Socialist policy was rejected by hundreds of its former supporters ... the brand of Socialism as presented by Captain Cipriani, with its vituperation and attacks on everybody who does not see eye to eye with him, is out of political fashion once and for all.[51]

Apart from a few independent candidates, both labour and capital sought to exhort the virtues of their philosophy. For instance, at an electioneering meeting in July 1924, one of Cipriani's reasons for not supporting Robinson was that the candidate for Caroni stood for capital, and capitalists were his friends.[52] Despite criticisms, labour did not outrightly condemn capitalists. At the first of a series of electioneering meetings to endorse the candidature of Gobin, at Theatre Hall, Chaguanas, Howard-Bishop praised Gobin as being a "consummate man of business." Howard-Bishop further claimed that the candidate's business ability would be an asset to the Legislative Council.[53] By 1929, the TWA seemed to have adopted a mature approach as one of its banner headlines in the *Labour Leader* stated "Labour and Capital Must Agree."[54]

The TWA regularly refuted statements and allegations emanating from the opposing candidates who often projected a distorted image of labour's representatives. At a meeting at Liberty Street in January 1925, Vivian Henry informed the gathering that the opposition was spreading rumours that Cipriani was a Bolshevist and a Communist.[55] Stollmeyer, another labour candidate, told supporters at Tunapuna that one of his friends called him a Bolshevik.[56] In 1928, at Sobrian's meeting in Siparia, one of the speakers, Rust, asked the gathering whether any member of the TWA had been communicating with the Soviets in Moscow. Though some members of the crowd disagreed, this did not deter Rust from warning them that Communism in the colony was unsafe because starving workingmen in Communist Russia were eating cats and dogs.[57] Rust sought to instil fear among the working class that Communism would lead to poverty and hardship.

Other categories of allegiances were highlighted during the election. For instance, Mrs F. Adams, a platform speaker at a political meeting, identified the ideological affiliation of the candidates: Rust as conservative, Johnston as liberal and Cipriani as being both a labourite and socialist.[58] However, Adams did not elaborate on the philosophy or beliefs of being a conservative or liberal. It was apparent that labour was ambivalent in classifying a person as "capitalist." Both Vice Presidents of the TWA, Roodal and Teelucksingh, were wealthy middle-class Indians who could be easily classified as capitalists. Likewise, in 1925, at one of Teelucksingh's meetings, a platform speaker, C. C. Abidh, claimed that because Teelucksingh was neutral, the candidate would be able to mediate between the two groups – labour and capital.[59] However, as a wealthy Indian, Teelucksingh would have been seen as belonging to the capital.

C. H. Pierre (formerly a planter), the labour candidate in 1925, was a lawyer, which meant he could also have easily been branded a capitalist. It is ironical that even Cipriani's status, race and wealth would have placed him in the same category as labour's opponents – Robinson and Cory-Davies. The obscure boundary between a "capitalist" and a "socialist" was determined by who was able to identify more with the struggles of the working class. The main reason for the middle- and upper-class status of the labour representatives was the high income and property qualifications for electoral candidates.

In 1938, the electorate in Caroni would have been confused because both Teelucksingh and Abidh were claiming to be representatives of labour. Teelucksingh was identified as "independent labour," and Abidh was the "unionist" candidate in Rienzi's Unionist Party. The familiarity of Teelucksingh among the residents of Caroni and his achievements from 1925 to 1937 would have given him an advantage over the newcomer. In addition to individuals purporting to be labour representatives, by 1938, two major groups were claiming to represent labour: the TLP and the Unionist Party. As a result, the public, particularly the working class, would have been confused as to who genuinely represented labour.

On 10 January 1925, the editorial of the TWA's newspaper accused the "Goliaths of local journalism" – the *Trinidad Guardian* and *Port-of-Spain Gazette* – of refusing to objectively report the activities of Cipriani. The editor clamoured for the daily press to give a true account of the events in which labour was involved during the elections.[60] There was a definite bias among the two daily newspapers in the colony. The editorial of the *Port-of-Spain Gazette*, on 18 January 1928, noted the general feeling of apathy regarding the upcoming general elections. The opinion expressed in the editorial was an indicator of the polarization between labour and capitalist representatives: "The suggestion has been thrown out that possibly the present attitude of aloofness on the part of certain sections of the community is due to the certainty of defeat should they place their own candidates in the field against such forces as are represented by the so-called 'labour socialists.'"[61] A decade later, the view of the *Port-of-Spain-Gazette* had not changed. In January 1938, the newspaper questioned the extent of Rienzi's support, "Mr. Rienzi … by his efforts for the down-trodden workers before and after the industrial disturbances of June last, and his masterly representation of their case before the commission, has become immensely popular, but it remains to be seen whether that popularity extends beyond San Fernando and to places where vested interests exercise no little influence."[62] The bias was also evident in the aftermath of the 1938 elections. The *Sunday Guardian* reported that Rienzi "scored a surprisingly overwhelming victory over Harold Piper."[63] The use of the word "surprisingly" suggested that the newspaper doubted Rienzi's popularity.

The success of labour in the 1925 elections coupled with forceful contributions to the Legislative Council would have prompted such a response. Labour responded to the biased reporting and sought to enlighten the public about the underlying tension. In early 1928, the TWA drew attention to the incompatibility of the two classes in Trinidad – the working class and the capitalist class:

> Between these two there is an irreconcilable antagonism of interests. We do not like this class antagonism, this class struggle, but there it is. The Workingmen's Association has come into prominence as a result of this class struggle and the workers are now fully alive to the fact that in by-gone days the employing Capitalist class had its interests exclusively represented in the Legislative Council; and at the back of it all the machinery of Government was used to confirm and strengthen their position.[64]

This would have also been a subtle reminder to the working class of the importance and need to support labour candidates in the elections.

At Penal, on 9 January 1928 at one of labour's national election meetings, Cipriani sought to clarify Radcliffe-Clarke's inaccurate public statements that the TWA was neither the accredited representative of labour in the colony nor affiliated to the BLP. Furthermore, Cipriani felt that Radcliffe-Clarke's address which was directed to workers in the colony was an insult to their intelligence, "If Radcliffe-Clarke wanted to address people of his class it would have been better if he spoke to the employers and capitalists – the class which he belonged."[65]

A significant feature of the 1933 elections was the addition of the ideological affiliation next to the names of candidates. For instance, Timothy Roodal (socialist), S. Teelucksingh (independent socialist), Cipriani (socialist), C. H. Pierre (independent), Harold Mahabir (socialist) and Isaac Hope (independent). The newspapers were believed to be responsible for using such descriptions for the candidates[66] (see Appendix 7). In the 1938 elections, candidates were represented in a similar manner: Rienzi and C. C. Abidh were identified as "labour" belonging to the Unionist Party whilst Teelucksingh was considered as "independent labour."

In 1933, the controversy over the worthiness or advantage of being a capitalist or labourite remained a divisive issue, especially in the battle for

Caroni. The ongoing struggle of Robinson to unseat Teelucksingh by appealing to the working class was evident in the former's manifesto: "As an employer of labour, my duty necessarily brings me into more intimate and constant contact with the worker, and, consequently, I am better positioned to interpret his true feelings and aspirations than one whose knowledge of labour conditions is merely theoretical and therefore impractical."[67]

At a political meeting in Mamoral, Robinson refuted allegations that he was incapable of assisting the poor because he was a capitalist. Robinson defended his status, "The difference between my opponent and myself is that I have made capital and he has lost it. I utilise my capital to bring relief by providing employment to hundreds of the poor of this country. Isn't that better than taking it and frittering it away."[68] Thus efforts were made to remove the distorted images of capitalists. At a meeting in Tabaquite, Robinson told 600 supporters that they should not heed the allegations of Teelucksingh who wanted to alienate and ostracize capitalists. Robinson claimed that "capital" had assisted the colony's economy.[69] On 19 January at Couva, Robinson once again sought to dispel the fears surrounding capitalists, "Mr. Teelucksingh tells you not to vote for me as I am a capitalist. In these times no one knows whether he is a capitalist or not."[70] Despite Robinson's valiant efforts, he failed to achieve the intended results and was again soundly defeated by Teelucksingh.

In addition to the socialist philosophy of the BLP (to which the TWA was affiliated), Cipriani's ideology was also influenced by another British socialist organization, namely, the Fabian Society. This group was founded by Edward Pease and his friends on 4 January 1884. The objective of the Fabian Society was "to help on the reconstruction of society in accordance with the highest moral possibilities." The membership usually discussed social problems and delegated members to attend meetings on relevant social issues. In 1926, a branch of the Fabian Society was established in Port-of-Spain, Trinidad. Two prominent members of the TWA spearheaded the local arm of the Society: Cipriani was elected temporary President and Howard-Bishop was temporary Secretary.[71] In 1933, the return of only Cipriani and Roodal, coupled with the loss of the labour candidates who contested, was seen by the *Sunday Guardian* as a major blow to socialism in the colony:

> Captain A. –, the dictator of the Trinidad Workingmen's Association suffered the greatest reverse in his political career in yesterday's General Election in Trinidad and Tobago. Regular Socialist candidates, supported by the T. W. A. met with defeat wherever they opposed Independent candidates. The Hon'ble T. M. Kelshall (Ind.) Defeated the Cipriani "Socialist" in Victoria, and more than 500 votes were polled by Mr. Harold Piper, the Cipriani "rebel" candidate. In Tobago Mr. Isaac A. Hope overwhelmed his Socialist opponent. In Caroni, Mr. Sarran Teelucksingh, Capt. Cipriani's bitterest political foe, was returned at the head of the poll.[72]

The link between labour and socialism would be further solidified when Rienzi founded the Trinidad and Tobago Socialist Party in 1941.

The class and ideological differences were further accentuated at political meetings in which support for labour was visibly displayed. Labour publicly used the colour "red" as a symbol among its supporters and to promote labour's general show of solidarity. On 19 February 1925, to celebrate Cipriani's electoral victory, a "Red Button Night" was held at the Princes Building.[73] A similar situation was reported in February 1928 in St Patrick:

> The whole county was red. Men and women wore bits of red ribbon on their breasts or as armlets and epaulets and little girls and boys sported the same colour. One woman wore a whole blouse of it. Lorries and cars had red flags stuck all over them, and hundreds carried on their hats red cards with a photograph of the successful candidate on each. Along the roads leading to the polls there were men of the red brigade going about from house to house like census takers.[74]

Cipriani is reported to have worn a red badge on his shirt and encouraged supporters to wear red buttons as a symbol of their support for working-class candidates.[75]

The colour red, which was associated with the Communists in Russia and the rest of Europe, was proudly and boldly utilized in labour's involvement in Trinidad and Tobago's party politics. Samaroo noted, "Cipriani wore a red button on his lapel and many of his followers wore red shirts in imitation of the participants of the Bolshevik Revolution of 1917."[76] Indeed, the links between the BLP, with its socialist ideology, and the TWA led to labour supporters and candidates being referred to as "Reds." The bold headline after the 1928 elections was "Reds Return Roodal."[77] The use of red by labour candidates as a defining symbol was unique during this early electoral period.

The supporters of labour not only wore red but also sometimes challenged others who did not conform to the colour scheme. For instance, on 7 February 1925, at the Town Hall, Port-of-Spain, a supporter of Rust wearing a "Rust rosette" on the lapel of his coat was accosted by a female labour supporter. The woman wearing "a red frock, red tie, red pair of stockings and red button" confronted the man who eventually removed and destroyed the offending rosette.[78] This spectacle was witnessed by an apparently pro-labour crowd who did not intervene. There is little evidence to suggest the regular use of a distinctive logo, emblem or symbol among the non-labour candidates. Godfrey Teelucksingh recalls that his father (Sarran) wore a green rosette whilst his rival, Robinson, wore a red rosette at meetings. Robinson's use of red would have been an attempt to identify with the working class whilst Teelucksingh's display of green would have occurred during the 1933 and 1938 elections after his acrimonious break with the TWA.[79] Despite the use of a different colour, Teelucksingh was still successful in convincing the electorate that he was the representative of labour.

During the campaign for the 1933 elections, the supporters of labour continued to use red as an indicator of their loyalty and support to candidates. An illustration is at an election rally for Harold Piper on 21 December 1932, "Socialistic Rebels from six leading Branches of the Trinidad Workingmen's Association, flaunted broad scarlet sashes and huge scarlet rosettes, encamped in the Town Hall in open defiance of the "expulsion" threat of Captain the Hon'ble Cipriani, and in proud support of their new Leader, Mr. Harold Piper."[80] Interestingly, Piper, the "independent socialist" candidate contesting Victoria, though not endorsed by the TWA and Cipriani, used the colour red to attract support from the working class.

In November 1937, a contributor to *The People* unfavourably assessed Cipriani's effort to be re-elected as Mayor of Port-of-Spain and replace Mayor A. Richards. The author of the article, who used the pseudonym "A Special Representative," noted thus: "No person is so looked down upon in Port-of-Spain today as a 'Red.' "[81] Furthermore, the writer dismissed the propaganda of the "Reds" by claiming that the Port-of-Spain Corporation "needed a strong Mayor to stand up to Government."

By 1938, the use of colours other than red to represent labour continued. Rienzi advised his supporters that their election wear should be "blue shirt, blue tie and grey flannel trousers."[82] Thereafter, supporters of Rienzi would be identified by their blue clothes. This would have been to distinguish themselves from TLP supporters who adhered to red. On 22 January, election day, the Unionist Party supporters were described in animated terms, "Sporting their blue shirts and blue ties, Unionist were to be seen on every side ... Blue-shirts were at all the polling stations and their presence was felt."[83] Piper, the challenger for the Victoria seat, had yellow as his colour. In addition, *The People* reported that, on the day of the election, Piper's sister had a yellow rosette and Councillor Audrey Jeffers also sported the colour of Piper's supporters.[84]

As President General of OWTU and the ATSE+FWTU, Rienzi received unwavering support from the members of these two vibrant unions. Smaller unions based in Port-of-Spain openly endorsed the candidacy of Rienzi. After his victory in Victoria, he gave a speech to his supporters, and among the audience were delegates from the Public Works Workers' Trade Union (PWWTU) and the Amalgamated Building and Woodworkers' Union.[85] Such support would explain the ability of Rienzi to garner 2,003 votes whilst his opponent mustered only 547 votes.

The Second World War

The Second World War has an impact on the trade unions and working class in the Caribbean and the rest of the world. On 3 September 1939, France and Britain declared war on Germany. One year later, Britain's military defeats prompted closer ties with the United States.[86] In 1940, Winston Churchill, Prime Minister of Britain, leased areas in the British West Indies to the United States for the construction of naval bases. The lease was valid for ninety-nine years and the agreement, signed on 27 March 1941, was in exchange for fifty old US destroyers. Rienzi was critical of the secrecy surrounding the lease. The outspoken trade unionist said that the colony's Court of Justice should have jurisdiction over foreigners employed in the leased areas.[87] Chaguaramas, on the north-western peninsula of Trinidad, was selected as the site for one of the US naval bases. In 1945, in a letter to the editor of *Trinidad Guardian*, a citizen using the nom de plume "West Indian" hoped that after the war ended, the peninsula would be returned to Trinidad.[88]

It was obvious that during the Second World War, the British West Indies attained greater significance to both the United States and Britain. The strategic location of the region was vital in thwarting the threat of German submarine invasion in the Caribbean.[89] The bombing of Pearl Harbour on 7 December 1941 meant an increased need to defend the Panama Canal. The fears of the Allies were intensified in February 1942 when two ships were torpedoed by German submarines in the Gulf of Paria, near Port-of-Spain, Trinidad. Added to the US and British concerns was the discovery of a spy ring in Rio de Janeiro. Among the seized documents was correspondence that mentioned "Trinidad."[90] This would have certainly created concern because of Trinidad's close proximity to South America. The economic importance of Trinidad and other neighbouring colonies was essential in aiding the war effort. For example, Suriname and British Guiana were producers of bauxite used for the manufacture of aluminium.[91]

In 1938 and 1939, there was widespread poverty, inflation, burdensome foreign debts and a low standard of living in the British colonies. During 1939–1945 in Trinidad and Tobago, the price of iron and steel increased by 45 per cent. In Jamaica, the cost of footwear increased by 373 per cent, and there was an increase in the price of flour by 119 per cent.[92]

On 1 September 1939, Britain enforced the Defence Regulations, under Section 1 of the Emergency (Defence) Act 1939. This legislation which was applicable in any British colony allowed detention without trial of persons suspected of being a threat to national security. Accordingly, in November 1939, T. U. Butler was imprisoned at Nelson Island in the Internment Camp for Enemy Aliens. Interestingly, the *Barbados Herald* reported that the government's reason was that Butler attempted to organize an oilfield strike.[93] Subsequently, there were responses in *The People* citing a different reason for his arrest. An eye witness reported that, on the night of 28 November 1939, while accompanying Butler, the car in which they were travelling was stopped, and Butler was escorted away by the police.[94] Furthermore, while imprisoned, Butler's relatives were denied visitation.[95] Unfortunately, there was no public condemnation of his arrest from labour.

On 8 November 1939, the government curtailed unionism by prohibiting public demonstrations, meetings and any assembly of more than ten persons.[96] On 1 February 1940, May McClean, General Secretary of the Public Works & Public Workers Service Union, requested permission to march in Port-of-Spain on 11 February. However, the Commissioner of Police, without a valid reason, rejected the union's request.[97] On 5 February, three people (Quintin O'Connor, Alexander Duke and Alroy Donawa) were arrested due to violation of the public meeting regulations. They were convicted and fined but eventually won their appeals.[98]

In the Legislative Council, Cipriani opposed the war bonus to civil servants. Cipriani's action prompted a critical response from the editor of *The Vanguard* who questioned the sincerity of Cipriani's interest in the working class.[99]

The portrayal of the unions by the media was a setback for trade unionism. For instance, a public meeting of the PW&PWSU was held on 9 December 1940, at Prince's Building, to discuss the issue of a government subsidy to offset the high cost of living. One of the editors of *New Dawn* noted that the press table at the meeting was "significantly vacant" and yet the press extensively covered the plight of the cocoa farmers.[100] At the same venue, another meeting of the PW&PWSU was planned for 14 February 1941. The evening edition of the *Trinidad Guardian* (on 12 February) mentioned the meeting as well as the topics to be discussed: namely, food subsidy, war bonus, land for the landless and Legislative Council elections. The *New Dawn* highlighted the *Trinidad Guardian*'s grave omission of two topics which were debated: (1) wages paid to American workers in Trinidad and (2) territorial concessions to the Americans and plans for importing labour into the colony.[101]

The editorial of *The People*, in March 1940, observed that the most serious error of the trade union movement, since its inception, was to passively allow the arrest of Butler.[102] Later, at a meeting organized by the Negro Welfare Cultural and Social Association (NWCSA), two members of Butler's British Empire Workers' and Citizens' Home Rule Party

(BEW+CHRP) also echoed their disappointment as they chastised the unions for their general apathy regarding Butler's arrest.[103]

In November 1940, the Commissioner of Police refused the NWCSA's request to use Woodford Square to host a meeting. The Commissioner informed the representatives of the NWCSA that at their last gathering, O'Connor (Secretary of the Union of Shop Assistants and Clerks) read passages from the pamphlet *Your Freedom Is in Danger*.[104] This was a publication of the National Council for Civil Liberties based in the United States. Even though there was no disorder due to O'Connor's statements, the police were intent on using the slightest incident as an excuse to reduce the influence of trade unionism.

The suppression of critics of official policies, especially by labour leaders, extended to other British colonies. Among those imprisoned for this reason were Alexander Bustamante, W. A. Domingo and Richard Hart of Jamaica, Michael Imodu of Nigeria and Otto Huiswood of Dutch Guiana.[105] In 1941, in India, Jawaharlal Nehru was sentenced to four-year imprisonment because of his anti-war speech which was in contravention of the Defence of India Act.[106]

On 22 February 1945, the Port-of-Spain City Council unanimously accepted a motion by Councillor E. M. Mitchell seeking the release of Butler.[107] A few weeks later, the colonial authorities decided to release Butler.[108] On 27 April, in the Legislative Council, Roy Joseph (representative for Victoria) asked about Butler being banned from the Victoria, St Patrick and Mayaro counties. On 18 May, the government replied that as a result of the repeal of certain Defence Regulations, the restrictions on Butler were no longer enforced.[109]

Notes

1. *TG* 3 January 1925.
2. *TG* 15 January 1925.
3. *TG* 20 January 1925.
4. *TG* 21 January 1925.

5. *TG* 21 January 1925.
6. *TG* 20 January 1925.
7. *TG* 20 January 1925.
8. *POSG* 12 January 1928.
9. *TG* 15 January 1933.
10. *TG* 19 January 1933.
11. *TG* 19 January 1933.
12. *Labour Leader* 11 August 1924.
13. *Labour Leader* 14 January 1925.
14. *TG* 20 January 1925.
15. *TG* 20 January 1925.
16. *TG* 17 January 1925.
17. *TG* 20 January 1925.
18. *TG* 21 January 1925.
19. *TG* 8 January 1925.
20. *TG* 15 January 1925. Also Ince, "Politics before the People's National Movement," 48.
21. *TG* 24 January 1925.
22. *Labour Leader* 19 March 1927.
23. It was reported in the press that voices from the crowd responded with "That is true!" and "That is quite true!" *POSG* 14 January 1928.
24. Singh, *Race and Class*, 135.
25. *Labour Leader* 4, 31, December 1927. Also *Labour Leader* 5, 8, 15 January 1928.
26. *POSG* 14 January 1928.
27. *POSG* 14 January 1928.
28. Singh, *Race and Class*, 134–135.
29. *POSG* 10 January 1928.
30. *POSG* 12 January 1928.
31. *POSG* 20 January 1928 (the letter was dated 18 January 1928).
32. *POSG* 25 January 1928 (the letter was dated 24 January 1928).
33. *POSG* 29 January 1928.
34. *POSG* 31 January 1928. Support for Sobrian was obvious in the poem "To the Electorate of St. Patrick" published in *POSG* 3 February 1928:

    They tell me he's been there before
    And proved he was no cheat!
    He treats both poor and rich alike!

35. *TG* 8 January 1933.
36. *TG* 8 January 1933.
37. *TG* 11 January 1933.
38. *POSG* 14 January 1938.
39. *POSG* 4 January 1933.

40. *TG* 6 January 1938.
41. *TG* 8 January 1938.
42. *TG* 8 January 1938.
43. *TG* 13 January 1938.
44. *TG* 13 January 1938.
45. V.S. *Naipaul, Three Novels: The Mystic Masseur, The Suffrage of Elvira, Miguel Street* (New York: Alfred A. Knopf, 1982).
46. *Labour Leader* 9 September 1924.
47. *TG* 8 January 1925.
48. This statement by Johnston was mentioned by Rust in his meeting at Belmont E. C. School on 14 January 1925. *TG* 15 January 1925.
49. *Labour Leader* 24, 31 December 1927, 21 January 1928.
50. *TG* 19 January 1933.
51. *TG* 2 February 1933.
52. *Labour Leader* 26 July 1924.
53. *Labour Leader* 27 August 1924.
54. *Labour Leader* 6 July 1929.
55. *Labour Leader* 20 January 1925.
56. *TG* 20 January 1925.
57. *POSG* 31 January 1928.
58. *Labour Leader* 27 August 1924.
59. *POSG* 11 January 1925. Also Singh, *Race and Class*, 128.
60. *Labour Leader* 10 January 1925.
61. *POSG* 18 January 1928.
62. *POSG* 8 January 1938.
63. *Sunday Guardian* 23 January 1938.
64. *Labour Leader* 10 March 1928.
65. *POSG* 14 January 1928.
66. Ince, "Politics before the People's National Movement," 99–100.
67. *TG* 11 January 1933.
68. *TG* 14 January 1933.
69. *TG* 18 January 1933.
70. *TG* 22 January 1933.
71. Rhoda Reddock, *Women, Labour and Politics in Trinidad and Tobago: A History* (London: Zed Books, 1994), 125.
72. *Sunday Guardian* 29 January 1933.
73. *Labour Leader* 21 February 1925.
74. *TG* 12 February 1928.
75. See Ince, "Politics before the People's National Movement," 48. Samaroo, "Constitutional and Political Development," 191.
76. Samaroo, "Constitutional and Political Development," 219.

77. *TG* 12 February 1928.
78. *Labour Leader* 14 February 1925.
79. Teelucksingh, personal interview, 27 April 2001.
80. *TG* 28 December 1932.
81. *The People* 13 November 1937.
82. *TG* 6 January 1938.
83. *The People* 29 January 1938.
84. *The People* 29 January 1938.
85. *The People* 29 January 1938.
86. See Paul Knaplund, *Britain Commonwealth and Empire 1901–1955* (Connecticut: Greenwood Press, 1974), 270.
87. Letter to the editor, *New Dawn* February 1941, 29.
88. *TG* 2 February 1945.
89. Harriet Edwards, "The Decline of British and the Rise of American influence in Trinidad 1939–1962," PhD dissertation, University of the West Indies, St Augustine, Trinidad and Tobago 1997, 121. See also Fitzroy A. Baptiste, *War, Cooperation and Conflict: The European Possessions in the Caribbean, 1939–1945* (Connecticut: Greenwood Press, 1988), 23–24.
90. *Sunday Guardian* 29 March 1942.
91. Edwards, "The Decline of British and the Rise of American Influence," 122.
92. Michael Havinden and David Meredith, *Colonialism and Development: Britain and Its Tropical Colonies 1850–1960* (London: Routledge, 1993), 207.
93. This was reprinted in *The People* 2 March 1940.
94. *The People* 6 April 1940.
95. *The People* 23 March 1940.
96. *The People* 11 May 1940.
97. *The People* 2 March 1940.
98. *The People* 11 May 1940.
99. *The Vanguard* 3 January 1942.
100. *New Dawn* January 1941.
101. *New Dawn* March 1941.
102. *The People* 16 March 1940.
103. *The People* 30 March 1940.
104. *New Dawn* November 1940.
105. *The Vanguard* 14 February 1942, *New Dawn* November 1940.
106. *New Dawn* April 1941.
107. *TG* 24 February 1945.
108. *West India Committee Circular (WICC)* April 1945, 68.
109. *Hansard* 27 April, 18 May 1945.

Bibliography

Baptiste, Fitzroy. *War, Cooperation and Conflict: The European Possessions in the Caribbean, 1939–1945* (Connecticut: Greenwood Press, 1988).

Edwards, Harriet. "The Decline of British and the Rise of American Influence in Trinidad 1939–1962," PhD dissertation, University of the West Indies, St Augustine, Trinidad and Tobago.

Havinden, Michael, and Meredith, David. *Colonialism and Development: Britain and Its Tropical Colonies 1850–1960* (London: Routledge, 1993).

Knaplund, Paul. *Britain Commonwealth and Empire 1901–1955* (Connecticut: Greenwood Press, 1974).

Reddock, Rhoda. *Women, Labour and Politics in Trinidad and Tobago: A History* (London: Zed Books, 1994).

CHAPTER 6

Consolidation of Trade Unions, 1937–1946

The Trade Union Ordinance (1932) provided little incentive for workers' organizations particularly since peaceful picketing was deemed illegal and unions were not protected, as in the British law, from prosecution for damages due to strike action. Even Cipriani's legal and reformist convictions refused to accommodate this major anti-labour restriction in the Ordinance. Subsequently, he modified his position indicating that he was against strikes. Trade unionism remained in the doldrums between 1932 and the labour revolt of 1937. In the absence of institutional machinery to resolve disputes between labour and management, there was little to protect the working-class employees from ruthless domination by capitalist investors in agriculture and mineral exploitation. Governmental apathy provided no protection for the working class not only from injustices by employers but also from the harsh conditions created by the Depression. The strikes and demonstrations of June 1937 gave an unmistakable signal both to employers and the government that labour was determined to resume direct action against employers and the ruling class.

That the strike movement quickly became Caribbean-wide was symptomatic of a profound crisis in both the colonial order and the global capitalist system in which it was embedded. In the midst of the crisis, colonial and local government officials anxiously searched for alternative solutions to labour-related disputes. Governor Fletcher and Acting Colonial Secretary Howard Nankivell supported the oilfield workers in the formation of their union, and in quick succession, a series of commissions, despatched by the Colonial Office, enquired into the causes of the widespread unrest and related issues in the British West Indian colonies. Among their diverse recommendations, there was unanimous agreement on the need for the promotion of trade unionism with supporting legislative and supervisory mechanisms. The Forster Report revealed that trade unions were "the surest means of securing industrial stability and the removal of extremist tendencies." It further suggested that "the workpeople appear to be realizing the necessity of establishing constitutional Trade Unions ... Such a movement, given sympathetic guidance by Government and a tolerant encouragement on the part of employers during the transitional stage of its development, is the surest means of securing industrial stability and the removal of extremist tendencies."[1]

The West India Royal Commission (1938) submitted proposals for a Wages Board, a Labour Department and a Labour Advisory Committee in all the West Indian colonies.[2] Also, it recommended that the formation of unions be encouraged and legislation enacted to allow for peaceful picketing, protection of unions from actions for damages due to strikes, the compulsory registration of unions and the audit of their funds.[3] The Orde-Browne Report (1938), which considered labour conditions in the West Indies, recognized the inadequacies of the existing labour regulations and recommended governmental intervention in setting up machinery "for regulating conditions by negotiation,"[4] including a well-staffed Labour Department, comprising an Industrial Adviser, Labour Officer and a Statistical Officer. In addition, trade union legislation ought to provide for the regulation of the election of officers and the general administration of labour organizations.

Although capitalist interests opposed unionization, it remained the most viable option for dialogue and negotiation and was eagerly promoted by the working-class leaders who recognized that strike action had its limitations against employers who were historically supported by imperial military power. The stage was therefore set for the transition from the unilateralism preferred by the capitalist class in resolving labour issues to the insistence on a bipartisan approach which included labour representation.

In mid-1937, unionization was vigorously pursued by labour leaders in the critical oil and sugar industries in South and Central Trinidad. With equal urgency, labour leaders outside these two sectors formed a plethora of small unions comprising clerks and shop assistants, printers, railwaymen, tailors, stevedores and sanitation workers, particularly in urban areas. Although ten unions were formed by the end of 1938, agricultural workers outside the sugar industry were not unionized.[5] Among the large agricultural holdings, non-unionized workers included 17,523 labourers on cocoa estates and 2,751 on coconut plantations.[6] The Taussig Commission investigated the non-unionization of so many workers and observed the difficulties within the agricultural sector, particularly employers' opposition to unionization and their determination to be the sole decisive force in labour relations: "They are frank to admit that agricultural labor is difficult to organize. They blame it largely on illiteracy, apathy and general lack of education … The planter instinctively opposes labor organizations and because of his power to dispossess the labor that is tenanted on his lands he is able to exert considerable influence in holding down agricultural organization."[7]

Extant records are bereft of much information on the administration and activities of several unions. Organizations were cautious with their membership registers; the recording of resolutions and other union data were not made public due to fear of victimization by employers or intimidation by the government.

Amalgamated Building and Woodworkers' Union

The Amalgamated Building and Woodworkers' Union, consisting primarily of carpenters, masons and other construction workers, was registered on 30 March 1936, and it was thus the first legally constituted trade union in Trinidad and Tobago. In 1933, Charles Atkinson organized a loose association of building workers who met at Unity Hall in the St Joseph-San Juan area. He sought guidance for the formation of a union, and in November 1933, he requested from the BLP a copy of the rules and constitution of the four British unions representing masons, fitters, carpenters and painters.[8] Atkinson's letter was forwarded to the General Secretary of the Trades Union Congress (TUC), Walter Citrine, who subsequently advised him thus: "In order, therefore, to avoid overlapping we think it advisable for you to get into (sic) touch with Captain Cipriani with a view to his assisting you to form the Trade Unions which you it (sic) is necessary to set up."[9]

There is no evidence to suggest that Atkinson sought Cipriani's advice. In any case, Cipriani would not have approved the existence of any labour group outside his TLP. Atkinson proceeded to form "The Amalgamated Building and Woodworkers' Union" which was registered in 1936 under the Trade Union Ordinance (1932). However, the union was neither recognized by the TLP nor affiliated with any international labour organization.

Some concerns were raised in England about Atkinson's union. In March 1936, Captain W. H. Coombs of the Officers Federation Limited (Merchant Navy) in England wrote to W. J. Bolton, Secretary of the TUC's International Department, enquiring as to the status of Atkinson's Amalgamated Building and Woodworkers' Union.[10] Bolton indicated that the department was unable to provide an update on Atkinson's union.[11]

Atkinson was determined to pursue the matter of recognition, and therefore subsequent to registration, he wrote to Citrine in May 1936 on behalf of "The Amalgamated Building and Woodworkers' Union, National Centre," advising him "I have been able to establish the first trade union in the West Indies."[12] There was cause for further frustration for Atkinson because of Citrine's insistence that Cipriani's TLP was the only labour entity with the authority to provide the required advice and guidance. Determined to avoid dealing with Atkinson's request, Citrine suggested that assistance be sought from the Amalgamated Society of Woodworkers in Manchester.[13] In 1937, Atkinson communicated with the BLP and this prompted Mary E. Sutherland, Chief Woman Officer of the BLP, to contact Cipriani, seeking information on Atkinson's union. In October 1937, Cipriani advised Sutherland that she should entertain correspondence only through the TLP as this was the only accredited entity to deal with such labour issues in the British West Indies.[14] Apparently, no further efforts were taken by Atkinson for international recognition nor attempts made to seek guidance from Cipriani. Atkinson was reluctant to seek Cipriani's advice since there were indications that Cipriani was losing the confidence and support of the more radical members of the TLP, namely, Butler and Rienzi. Citrine visited Trinidad in February 1939 and addressed the TLP as well as the Amalgamated Building and Woodworkers' Union.[15] Atkinson's union did not survive too long beyond 1939, and its workers were subsequently absorbed into other unions which catered to various occupations.[16]

Oilfield Workers' Trade Union

After the oil workers' strike and the subsequent island-wide social unrest of June 1937, it was not unexpected that the first major industrial union was formed in the oil belt. Although the birth of the Oilfield Workers' Trade Union (OWTU) "was directly facilitated by the strikes and disturbances,"[17] oil workers brought experiences of co-operation from an existing welfare organization they formed in 1935 to their newly established trade union. The United Workers' Trading Association (UWTA) was a sort of "co-operative" venture formed in 1935 which subsequently constituted the nucleus of the OWTU.[18] Although the Manager of Leaseholds refused to assist in the formation of a workers' trading store, a group of oil workers, under the leadership of E. R. Blades, established the UWTA to provide cheaper foodstuffs and other commodities. This was a workers' initiative in response to the consequences of the Depression and also the inflated cost of living associated with oil-producing districts. Though not a trade union, the UWTA also served as a working-class organization concerned with labour issues.

Due to the strike in 1937, registration of the UWTA was deferred to January 1939. Its office was located at 21 Coffee Street, San Fernando, and its share capital ($48,000) was valued at $1.00 each.[19] There is no evidence to suggest that the association functioned beyond 1940, but oilfield workers shared membership in both OWTU and UWTA during the period between 1937 and 1940. In preparation for the launch of an oil workers' union, Blades, through the use of handbills, mobilized the district committees of the UWTA and canvassed other workers, especially in the Forest Reserve field.

The initial meeting proposing the formation of a union for oilfield workers was held on 15 July 1937 at the home of Cecil Williams at Coon's Town, Fyzabad, with Governor Murchison Fletcher and Acting Colonial

Secretary Nankivell in attendance.[20] Blades, who chaired the meeting, addressed the workers and appealed for their support of the proposed union:

> We have in hand a very important undertaking, that is, the formation of a trade union which to my mind calls for much wit and forethought for plain sailing is not to be expected as difficulties will crop up even among the workers themselves, and as for the capitalists, one must remember that they are always determined to hold their capital … Therefore the only right and natural thing for any conscious workers to do is to organise in order to defend their labour but as long as the workers fail to organise, so long they will suffer and be disunited, they will always be, industrial serfs.[21]

The second of the preparatory meetings was held on 17 July 1937 at "The Club" on Butcher's Stall Road, Fyzabad, where decisions were finalized for the formation of the new union. At the founding conference on 25 July 1937 when officers were elected to the OWTU, Blades was instrumental in the election of Rienzi as its first President General.[22] He had invited Rienzi to address the meeting and subsequently nominated him as a candidate for the presidency. E. F. Shuffer, an oil worker, objected to Rienzi's nomination on the grounds that the position should be filled by an oil worker and not "an outside barrister-at-law." Blades disagreed with Shuffer and after a lengthy address, the two other candidates, Caleb Roach and Leslie Nelson, withdrew from the contest.[23] At this historic conference, there were 150 delegates from fifteen districts in the oil belt.

Blades would have recognized in Rienzi those radical leadership qualities required to maintain the momentum established by oil workers for better working conditions. Rienzi's identification with the oil workers and Butler's approval of his role as his mediator during the strike won him the confidence of oil workers. There is no doubt that Blades would have also acknowledged the value of his legal background and his social standing for dialogue with government officials and the employer class. The race question would have been minimal since Rienzi was emerging as a leader of the working class rather than merely an influential Indian leader. The enthusiasm for trade union formation after the 1937 riots could not be curtailed or diminished by the local government or even the Colonial Office. The initial response from Fletcher and other colonialists was the urgency of having responsible trade union leadership to avert future labour disturbances.[24]

The six-year presidency of Rienzi in the OWTU (1937–1943) began with a struggle for official recognition of the union as the legitimate bargaining unit for oil workers as there was no automatic acceptance by the Petroleum Association. In addition to the support of UWTA branches, the Executive of the OWTU embarked on a membership campaign and conducted a series of public meetings throughout the oil belt. During the first three weeks, membership reached 1,350 workers with good attendance at public meetings such as the one at Barrackpore where there were over 600 men and women.[25] Branches of the union were formed at Pointe-a-Pierre, Point Fortin, Palo Seco, Fyzabad and Guayaguyare.

A well-organized union developed with sectional units representing the Machine Shop Department, Salvage Department, Field Engineering, Garage and Transport Department, painters and gaugers. The union maintained administrative efficiency, control and discipline through the inclusion of branch representatives in the Executive and the submission of duplicate copies of minutes of the branches' weekly meetings to the Central Office. The onerous responsibilities of the union included its concern for 13,568 workers: both union members and those non-unionized in ten oil companies. Members of the OWTU could be easily recognized with their blue shirts and were referred to as the "blue shirt army."

Since its inception, the OWTU has included women in its membership – while some of them were relatives of oil workers, others were domestic workers and former members of the TLP.[26] In 1944, there was an article in the union's publication, *The Vanguard*, entitled "Special Appeal to Women" which championed their cause, "Thousands of women are employed here in various spheres and they do not possess that talent to understand that they too must be organized to bring about a united front to assist the men in the industries, etc."[27]

The official recognition of the OWTU helped defuse the tensions generated by the strikes and demonstrations of June 1937 and set the stage for the implementation of modern methods of collective bargaining in the colony. The failure of the Forster Commission to make recommendations on the wage issue, which was one of the major causes of industrial unrest, exposed the limitations of certain British-based enquiries and the imperial unwillingness to attribute responsibility for such social unrest to metropolitan capitalist interests, as in the case of the 1937 unrest.

It was, therefore, left to the workers and their newly recognized OWTU to deal with the wage issue. The threat of further disturbances in 1938 was minimized by Rienzi who, through his astute leadership, advised both oil and sugar workers that a negotiated settlement by way of collective agreement was preferable while confrontation with the police ought to be avoided.[28] The decision of the Petroleum Association to recognize the OWTU in negotiations under the guidance of A. V. Lindon, Industrial Adviser, was a major achievement for unionism both in the colony and also in the British West Indies. But concessions in these negotiations were disappointing for oil workers since the Petroleum Association merely upgraded certain workers to a minimum of nine cents per hour comparable to what is paid to government employees in the Public Works Department.

Although capitalist interests were unwilling to fully accommodate the union's demands, the OWTU initiated a new era in industrial relations, and when the Lindon arbitration failed, a special tribunal was commissioned. The new tribunal consisted of five persons from London, two from the Petroleum Association and two from the OWTU. The Executive members of the OWTU led by Rienzi were among those who testified before the tribunal which met from 5 December 1938 to 13 January 1939. The traditional obstinacy of the employer class towards the needs of workers produced a deadlock in the tribunal, which was resolved only when the Chairman made the historic arbitration award on 21 January 1939, the first in Caribbean labour relations. The OWTU was awarded 50 per cent of its demands inclusive of a wage increase of one cent an hour, retroactive to February 1938 with an additional one cent from February 1939.[29] Although both sides agreed to the award for at least a one-year period, the OWTU was disappointed, but the union was also triumphant in the struggle with monopolistic employers whose unilateralism in labour relations had hitherto excluded workers' representation.

The first major difficulty of the new union came in 1939 when Butler left the OWTU's special position as General Organizer. Kambon believes that when "Rienzi assumed the leadership of the OWTU as its first

President, it was widely understood that he was acting for Butler. His credibility with the oil workers was enhanced by his association with Butler."[30] Prior to his exit from the union, Butler commended Rienzi for his leadership role in the OWTU, "You praise and honour me for what I have done, but I assure you that you owe more praise to Bonnie Prince, the Honourable Adrian Cola Rienzi, your President and Leader, who risked his profession, his life in building a solid structure on the foundation I so humbly laid."[31] Butler's departure and that of several hundred members of the OWTU created a serious schism among oil workers and temporarily impeded the expansion of the union with a loss of $7,000 in membership fees.

Between 1939 and 1942, the OWTU emerged as an exemplary labour organization in the colony. The union was represented on the Joint Conciliation Board which was established in 1940 for the oil industry. By January 1942 the union had established a bereavement fund which provided $100 in death benefits on behalf of financial members and $35 for dependents.[32] In May 1942, in consultation with the board, strategies were initiated for unemployment relief to oil workers and for the introduction of Unemployment Insurance legislation.[33]

Responsible leadership

Government officials were impressed with the operations of the OWTU: "This Trade Union has developed on a very sound and responsible basis and is well maintained by an efficient leadership and a solid nucleus of trade unionists by conviction."[34] The Taussig Commission also recognized the quality of leadership within the union, "Ralph Mentor, who is second to Rienzi, is a mulatto, sullen, suspicious and sarcastic, but obviously a man of power and mentality … McDonald Moses of the same labor organization is a young man of intellectual attainment, who has come into the good graces of the government."[35] This was not a casual observation but based on their service in different capacities. Mentor was General Secretary of the OWTU and editor of *The Vanguard*. He toured Britain, with other West Indian editors, where he met other labour leaders and the Prime Minister.[36] Mentor was also a Trustee of the

All Trinidad Transport and General Workers' Union, Secretary of the Trinidad and Tobago Trades Union Council (TTTUC) and General Secretary of the Cane Farmers' Section of the ATSE+FWTU. He was also elected to the Borough Council in 1940, 1942 and 1945, and he filled the roles of Deputy Mayor and Mayor of San Fernando. His comrade, Moses, served on the Price Control Committee, Poor Relief Board, Unemployment and Health Insurance Committee and the Labour Recruitment Committee.

The concept of "responsible" trade union leadership has come under attack in some of the post-independence scholarship dealing with the events of the late 1930s.[37] Rienzi was criticized for adopting what is deemed an imperialist concept of leadership by breaking with Butler and discouraging confrontation with management. However, the issue has to be put in context. Rienzi was not opposed to confrontation but felt it should not be used indiscriminately. He helped mobilize oil and sugar workers in 1938 and threatened to resort to renewed strike action if employers adopted an intransigent position. Rienzi was aware, however, that strike action had its practical limits. It could disrupt production and create a climate of industrial instability which employers knew could reduce the profitability of their operations. But once the armed forces of the state were mobilized against strikers, as in December 1919 and June 1937, strikers and their leaders faced arrest and imprisonment or would be on the run, as Butler was in the immediate aftermath of June 1937.

Responsible leaders like Rienzi understood that strikes and demonstrations were part of a dialectic process and that, instead of attempting a revolutionary overthrow of the existing power structure, the workers' best hope was in securing progressive, incremental concessions from management. This could be achieved by collective bargaining when the state was prepared to lend its weight in support of that process, as evidenced in 1937 under Governor Fletcher and Colonial Secretary Nankivell.

There were labour disturbances in the post-1937 era, and the emergence of responsible leadership promoted collective bargaining as a concomitant to militancy. This was the preferred strategy adopted by Rienzi and some of the unions based in Port-of-Spain, "The UK preferred to deal with those leaders it defined as responsible rather than those who were more political and militant, and the leaders who were favoured by the authorities tended to have an advantage over others when the political system became more democratised."[38] The dilemma of "militancy as against responsibility" polarized union leadership in the post-First World War era particularly since the failure to be militant was being questioned.[39] Although militancy was not abandoned, it was to be used tactically. Indeed, war conditions (1939–1945) gave the government greater military and police power.

Indeed, the OWTU provided responsible leadership beyond the oil belt and introduced trade unionism to other occupational groups in the colony. Rienzi, Blades, Moses and Mentor were instrumental in taking trade unionism to the sugar workers while Rienzi served as President of the OWTU and ATSE+FWTU. Under the leadership of Rienzi and the Executive of the OWTU, the Committee for Industrial Organization (CIO) was formed.[40] The organization submitted a major memorandum from labour to the West India Royal Commission in 1938, which included, among its recommendations, the nationalization of the oil and sugar industries. Implementation of this proposal, they suggested, should begin with the imposition of a tax on petroleum products and the acquisition of the Ste Madeleine Sugar Company Limited, which was the best-organized factory in the colony.[41] The CIO also recommended that a minimum wage be established for the sugar industry in an attempt to end the deplorable housing, poverty, misery and squalor in the estates. The West India Royal Commission was informed of the need for legislation to provide unemployment insurance and workmen's compensation for the working class throughout the colony.[42]

Perhaps one of the finest gestures of the OWTU towards the unionization of Indians in the sugar industry was *The Vanguard*'s contribution as an agency for the promotion of the work of the fledgling ATSE+FWTU. This publication of the OWTU gave "more attention than *The People* to the struggle of the Indians."[43] In his 1940 New Year's message, Rienzi said that the intensification of the class struggle in South and Central Trinidad in the two major industries (oil and sugar) required an organ in these areas to supplement the work of *The People* which he praised.[44] Although *The Vanguard* gave weekly updates on the work of the OWTU and dealt with issues pertaining to oil workers, there were extensive reports of labour-related issues affecting sugar workers and cane farmers. It also gave greater coverage of the struggle for India's independence.

Involvement in politics

Despite Rienzi's Socialist persuasions, the OWTU developed without a radical flavour under his leadership. Nevertheless, it was through the influence of both Rienzi and Mentor that the OWTU became politically oriented. The active engagement of the union's officials in politics was a source of controversy, which led to the unfortunate dismissal of Blades, one of the pioneers of the union. Rienzi and Mentor served both on the union's Executive and also on the San Fernando Borough Council in 1937–1939, and in 1938, Rienzi won the Victoria seat in the Legislative Council. Under the leadership of Rienzi, Mentor, Moses and Rojas, the OWTU's political interests were crystallized in 1941 with the formation of the Socialist Party of Trinidad and Tobago (SPTT), which became the unofficial "political arm" of the OWTU. In Rienzi's address to the Third Annual Conference of the OWTU delegates, he implored the workers to organize themselves in trade unionism and support the SPTT.[45]

Moses and Rojas subsequently requested the union to increase their salaries as this would enable them to contest the general elections, but Blades objected on the grounds that labour would suffer if its members were involved in politics. The ensuing conflict led to Blades' dismissal when the new General Secretary, Mentor, accused him of embezzlement of the union's funds.[46] The conflict between Blades and other members of the Executive of the OWTU over the issue of political unionization indicates that within labour there were concerns that opportunistic politicians would exploit trade unions for personal political advancement. Furthermore, conservative unionists feared that political trade unionism would have diverted the attention of labour from "bread and butter issues" to wider political and social concerns which may not directly affect the working class.[47]

Labour leaders from Cipriani to Rienzi, and later Butler, recognized that political power was one of the major instruments to counteract the apathy of the political directorate and the flagrant disregard for working-class issues by the officials in the Legislative Council. Involvement in municipal politics was regarded merely as a preparatory step to the legislature. Both Cipriani and later the Executive of the OWTU appreciated the need to win seats in the council in which the employer class was always well-represented. The plantocracy dominated the colonial legislatures, but in the early twentieth century, agricultural and merchant capitalists were joined by representatives of petroleum interests in the Legislative Council. The omission of labour representation among the Governor's unofficial members made it imperative for labour's involvement in electoral politics.

Labour's involvement in politics aimed to advocate for the working class on economic and political matters that affected them. In the context of a limited franchise and executive authority as the arbiter of legislation, labour's views and interests needed to be publicly expressed at the level of the Legislative Council. Indeed, the greater objective was to neutralize the alliance between the colonial government and the metropolitan capitalist class which constituted a formidable bastion of oppression against labour.

During the period 1943–1946, the OWTU was severely tested as it expanded its programme of political unionization. Sponsored by the union and supported by Rienzi, Moses contested the San Fernando Borough Council elections in 1943.[48] Unfortunately, the electoral campaign produced disastrous results both for the OWTU and for the labour movement. Individualism, petty jealousy and rivalry dominated the campaign in which the efforts of the OWTU were undermined by the combined forces of Dr David Pitt (West Indian National Party, WINP) and Roy Joseph in San Fernando, aided by Albert Gomes in Port-of-Spain. These forces agitated for Butler's release from detention and seemed determined to capitalize on the hostilities which hitherto existed between Butler and the Executive of the OWTU. Roy Joseph conducted the lobby in the Legislative Council for Butler's release while Gomes, writing in the *Sunday Guardian* under the nom de plume "Ubiquitous" supported the "Free Butler" campaign.[49] Pitt's WINP, Trinidad's new political party, also agitated for Butler's release; therefore, against such a formidable coalition of Pitt, Joseph, Gomes and the Butlerites, there was little hope for Moses, the OWTU candidate who was defeated in the elections.[50] In the call for Butler's release, these political aspirants expected to benefit by utilizing his martyr image as the rallying symbol to challenge the Rienzi-led group. In the Borough Council electoral campaign, Gomes launched a bitter attack on Rienzi's leadership of the southern and central unions as he intensified his animosity and jealousy which became evident since Rienzi's appointment to the Executive Council in 1943. There is no doubt that Rienzi's earlier involvement in the franchise controversy in defence of Indians[51] as well as the subsequent emergence of Indian mobilization and his withdrawal from labour leadership contributed to the weakening of the labour movement in the colony.

The events of 1943 militated against Rienzi's efforts and that of the OWTU Executive for a united labour movement. The hope that the OWTU's SPTT would have served as the catalyst for the creation of an integrated labour organization in the colony did not materialize because of the isolationist tendencies of northern unions, particularly the Seamen and Waterfront Workers' Trade Union (SWWTU), the Union of Shop Assistants and Clerks and Gomes' FWTU.

In May 1943, Rienzi was recommended by the TTTUC to the colony's Executive Council. He decided to relinquish the posts of President General of the ATSE+FWTU and OWTU that he held for six years. The leadership of the OWTU was passed on to John Rojas (President General) and Ralph Mentor (General Secretary). On 19 February 1944, Rienzi wrote to the General Council of the OWTU and informed them of his resignation from the Legislative and Executive Council "with a view to filling a legal post which has been created in the Government of the Colony."[52] Rienzi's decision to accept the post of Second Crown Counsel meant severing his political and trade union connections.

Although there were modest wage increases under Rienzi's leadership, the period was relatively free from major industrial unrest in the oil belt. This was so because, during the war years, the colonial government had emergency powers. Under the presidency of Rojas, workers' restlessness was more obvious with frequent wage-related disturbances beginning in 1944. Bolland sees in Rojas' leadership a spirit of "compromise and co-operation"[53] with colonial authorities and employers. However, also obvious was some measure of defiance of the employer class as well as the denunciation of British capitalism and its exploitation of the working class.

The agreement reached in February 1944, negotiated by Butler's union for workers at the Van Leer West Indian Steel Works, paved the way for the agitation of oil workers demanding more urgency in wage-related negotiations. Although there was an absence of extreme militancy, Rojas supported a series of street demonstrations for wage increases. On 22 February 1944, hundreds of workers joined in an OWTU march at Point Fortin, and on 26 March, there was another demonstration at Palo Seco with 4,000 workers. Rojas denounced capitalist exploitation in the oil belt and appealed to workers to unite and work for the emancipation of the working class.[54] Mass protests were organized among La Brea's asphalt workers and among oil workers at Fyzabad and Guayaguyare. Butlerites joined the OWTU when employers persisted in the non-recognition of the BEWP+RU (Ratepayers Union).

In his address at the first World Federation of Trade Union (WFTU) Conference in 1945, Rojas denounced British racism and imperialism, "The wealth and material resources of Trinidad have been taken to the United Kingdom ... In our colony a white boy and a black boy may finish the same college with the same marks, but the white boy is started off on a job at $1.30 a day and the black boy is started at forty cents."[55]

The SPTT contested the 1946 general elections on a joint platform with the TTTUC. The SPTT candidates were all OWTU officials: John Rojas (St Patrick) and McDonald Moses (Victoria). Released from detention, Butler contested the elections and conducted a bitter campaign against OWTU-connected candidates. Although Rojas, Mentor and Moses retaliated in kind, the rift with the Butlerites was a major contributory factor in the defeat of the SPTT candidates. Although the race factor was crucial in previous elections in Victoria, it is more than likely that Moses lost because of the overall successful campaign of Butlerism against the OWTU which Moses represented. His defeat by Ranjit Kumar added to the overall humiliation of the OWTU and TTTUC in the elections. Kumar was an independent candidate, but he was also pro-Butler, and therefore supported the anti-OWTU campaign in Victoria and St Patrick. In addition to the influence of Butler in the elections, the union failed because the "OWTU was regarded ... as an Oilfield Union"[56] and was bereft of the appropriate universal appeal, hence its inability to capture support outside the oil belt from that portion of the electorate with non-oil interests.

There is no evidence of the continuing activity of the SPTT after the defeat of its candidates in the 1946 elections. It may have been dissolved since John Rojas, President of the OWTU, subsequently formed a new organization, the West Indian Independence Party (WIIP), in collaboration with the Workers' Freedom Movement.[57] The party, with its socialist and nationalist outlook, was intended to be a labour-oriented political force in the colony. Because of its association with Marxist leaders such as Lennox Pierre (Chairman) and Rojas (First Vice Chairman), the party failed to attract membership in a society that was suspicious of Communism.

Both the *Trinidad Guardian* and *Port-of-Spain Gazette* were openly critical of Rojas' alleged subversive, Communist-inspired utterances, particularly his anti-capitalist denunciation of British investors in Trinidad: "The powerful Oilfields Worker's Trade Union was being exposed to "communist" influence. The OWTU's official organ, *The Vanguard*, reprinted numerous articles from the British Communist Press."[58] In 1945, the government maintained its ban on the importation of Communist publications such as *Russia Today*, *Soviet Weekly* and the *Daily Worker*. This prompted Gomes, in the Legislative Council, to appeal for the government's cancellation of such prohibitions in lieu of the principle of freedom of information as espoused by the Allied powers.[59]

The Federated Workers Trade Union

The Federated Workers Trade Union (FWTU), formed in July 1937 and registered on 21 September 1937, was one of the earliest attempts to form an omnibus union to represent various categories of workers outside the oil and sugar industries.[60] Rienzi, who initiated the drive for the unionization of oil and sugar workers, advised other workers in the colony to unite in an umbrella organization and he prepared "their first constitution and saw them through the difficult process of obtaining recognition at a time when trade unionism was being actively discouraged both by state and big business."[61]

The union's head office was located at 66 George Street, Port-of-Spain. In August 1937, the FWTU submitted a memorandum to Ormsby-Gore commending the prompt action of Governor Fletcher in handling the June strikes. The union applauded Fletcher's appeals to the citizens for peace, the creation of an emergency Mediation Committee, the establishment of dialogues with stevedores, longshoremen and lightermen, an increase of police force personnel to protect life and property as well as his personal tour of the country districts.[62] Sylvester Patrick (Secretary) commended the FWTU as "a labour organisation of usefulness and one that will obtain the recognition and fair comment of all concerned."[63] He added that the Executive of the FWTU was intent on acquiring international laws relevant to trade unionism and using it to improve the working conditions of labour in the colony.

Clement Payne, a member of the NWCSA, was one of the founders of the FWTU.[64] Under its first leaders, Alfred Richards[65] (Honorary President), Sylvester Patrick (Secretary) and Gaskynd Granger (Organizer), there were efforts by the FWTU to be affiliated with the British TUC. Patrick in his correspondence to Citrine not only requested affiliation for the union but also added some concerns of the FWTU such as the absence of provisions for peaceful picketing in the Trade Union Ordinance. He added his union's interest in the "wages question," which was the "chief bone of contention" not considered by the Forster Commission in its enquiry into the 1937 labour unrest. Other concerns of the FWTU were the "insufficient employment of the masses" and "a greater measure of representation in our legislature."[66]

In late 1937, the union established contacts with the pro-Ethiopian and London-based International African Service Bureau (IASB)[67] and on 22 November, the union informed the IASB of the inadequacy of wages of railway workers: "The Railway branch of the Federated Workers Trade Union, has long been promised an increase of wages because of the sudden rise in the cost of living which even highly-paid men find it difficult to cope with."[68] The FWTU also expressed concern over the "electoral irregularity" concerning the election of Cipriani as Mayor of Port-of-Spain in November 1937.[69]

In July 1938, after a joint meeting with the Superintendent of Railways and A. G. V. Lindon (Industrial Adviser), the union was granted full recognition to represent the Plate-layers Section and the Signal-men of the Trinidad Government Railways. Furthermore, a southern branch was formed to represent Pilot Guards and Porters. The union functioned as the chief intermediary between railway employees and the Superintendent of Railways, discussing matters such as wages or extended working hours during harvest time. Selwyn John, a former trade union leader, recalls the early operations of the FWTU:

> The Union comprised mainly daily paid manual labourers such as carpenters, construction workers, plumbers and sanitation workers who were employed in the Port-of-City Corporation. Also represented were various occupational groups connected with the Trinidad Government Railways, Department of Health, Department of Agriculture inclusive of Government Farm and Dairy Workers, and the Local Road Board. There were several branches of the Union and its only competing union was the Public Works Workers Union.[70]

The FWTU lost a major section of its membership in 1939 when workers with the Trinidad Government Railways joined the Railway Workers' Trade Union. Members disclosed that they would be better represented by a union which dealt specifically with labour in the railway system. This loss in membership seriously affected the union, and when Albert Gomes and Quintin O'Connor became its leaders by 1943, the organization was on the brink of collapse:

> When Quintin and I took over the Federated Workers Trade Union, its total membership was eleven. Our office was the kitchen of an old building in one of the slum headquarters of Port-of-Spain. I particularly remember those early efforts to organise shop clerks. Quintin and I held our meetings in Woodford Square, a park in the heart of the shopping district of Port-of-Spain … our aim was to capture their attention as they passed through the Square. We hoped this way to begin our indoctrination … more often we were addressing the grass and trees, and a few vagrants.[71]

After his failure to attract the clerical workers, Gomes used his influence as a member of the City Council in 1938 to successfully incorporate the municipal workers into a renewed FWTU:

> We began to organise municipal workers into the Federated Workers Trade Union and were very successful, especially among the scavenger gangs, the street-sweepers

> and those who burrow, often on their bellies, into the dark and malodorous labyrinth of underground drains beneath the surface of Port of Spain's streets to wage war unendingly with their brooms against the ceaseless slime and debris. These workers, the vast majority of them Indians, took to tuberculosis and died with a truly remarkable ease and celerity. Little persuasion was required to arouse them to united action against their employers.[72]

Gomes and O'Connor led a campaign against Cipriani, the Mayor of Port-of-Spain, and the City Council, and the FWTU was successful in negotiations for increased wages and improved working conditions for scavengers. This victory was primarily through the efforts of both union leaders who inspired a scavenger strike in the city which lasted for several days. In the aftermath, the FWTU worked in collaboration with Butler's British Empire Workers and Citizens Hope Rule Party as Gomes promoted co-operative efforts between both unions: "I have great sympathy with and respect for the Home Rule Movement and for Butler and Ramsarran and for those members of the Negro Welfare who had been consistent in the struggle."[73] Gomes developed a close relationship with Butler's allies in the NWCSA and also with Butlerites in La Brea and Point Fortin, where at least 140 workers of the La Brea branch of the FWTU together with officers of the BEW+CHRP worked together in mobilizing workers of the asphalt industry as they pledged to struggle for "the emancipation of the Asphalt industry."[74]

In February 1946, Gomes successfully led the FWTU through a seventeen-day strike which involved 1,522 municipal workers engaged in building, construction, transport, electricity and sanitation.[75] The strike was initiated by twenty lorry loaders who refused to work when the Planning Housing Commission reduced their wages from twenty cents to sixteen cents per hour. Sympathy strikers included 200 workers of the Reclamation Department and employees of the Port-of-Spain Electricity Board.[76] Led by Dudley Mahon (President General), A. Gomes (Vice President) and Quintin O'Connor (General Secretary), the union's Executive met with the Governor for consultations on arbitration; however, this effort failed to elicit support from the Governor. Therefore, the union sent Gomes to England to seek the support of George Hall, Secretary of State for the Colonies.[77] With the failure of this mission, the strike ended on 18 February

1946 and four workers employed with the Port-of-Spain Corporation Electricity Board and the Trinidad and Tobago Electricity Commission (T&TEC) were found guilty in court of breaking their job contracts.[78]

Supported by the French Creole and business community who ensured his success in the 1946 general election, Gomes remained with the FWTU in order to bolster his political career. Later, in 1946, Gomes resigned as President of the FWTU when he accepted membership in the Executive Council.[79] By then, he felt strong enough politically to do without the support of the union, and this hastened his alienation from the working class.

The Seamen and Waterfront Workers' Trade Union

The majority of workers employed on the Port-of-Spain docks were members of both the Workingmen's Reform Club of the late nineteenth century and its successor the TWA.[80] At the waterfront, workers toiled under difficult and sometimes unbearable conditions, and with no job security, they could be fired without explanation by employers. The dock workers laboured under unsafe conditions, particularly when coal ships berthed at Port-of-Spain. Hundreds of Indian and African women were temporarily employed to transport coal blocks to the sheds at the port manually. Workers often protested and appealed for protective glasses particularly when temperatures were high and the excessive heat from coal stored in the ships' bunkers would "burn their eyes." Since wages were based on cargo tonnage, labourers were exploited through dishonest practices by the supervisors who falsely recorded the actual tonnage handled by workers.[81] The Shipping Association required a large number of workers to ensure speedy offloading of cargo which would have reduced costs for berthing. Since the wages of women in the colony were lower than that of their male counterparts, their employment was a cost-effective measure exploited by shipping merchants. After the containment of the dock workers strike of 1919–1920, the TWA came under the leadership of Cipriani, who eschewed strikes in favour of constitutional reform. However, the impact of the Great Depression began to erode the TWA/TLP's credibility, and stevedores began to regroup under new leaders.

In July 1934, Randolph Folkes presided over the first stevedores' meeting at Tamarind Square, Port-of-Spain.[82] Jim Barrette, a founding member of the NWCSA, recalled thus: "We held a meeting and we decided to form a union. Folkes came from the United States vibrating (sic) trade unionism and we held several meetings. I remember organising workers, getting them to join our group."[83]

A stevedores union was not formed until renewed efforts were made in 1937 when, at a public meeting of dock workers at the corner of Duncan Street and Independence Square, decisive action was taken for unionization.[84] Finally, on 19 November 1937, the Seamen and Waterfront Workers' Trade Union (SWWTU) was registered with Randolph Folkes as President, Reginald Baptiste as Secretary and Christopher Carrington as Union Organizer. The SWWTU, an urban-based union with its headquarters and membership in Port-of-Spain, represented boatmen, launchmen, lightermen, baggage porters and waterfront workers, and it eventually developed into one of the most vibrant and powerful unions.

The first significant achievement of the union was its representation of dock workers who, in June 1938, protested that they were paid less than the agreed wages by the contractor of Alston and Company for their work on the Danish steamer *Lundby*. Subsequently, six representatives of the SWWTU held discussions with Alston and Company, which then agreed with the union, compensated the workers and dismissed the offending contractor.[85] On 15 July 1938, the SWWTU courageously challenged the power of the Trinidad Shipping Association (representing Trinidad Shipping Agencies) which requested the names of union members who were employed by the shipping agencies. The union's officers, after discussion with its members, promptly refused to submit the requested names to the association, anticipating that such a list would facilitate the victimization of workers.[86]

In its first year of operation, the SWWTU entered into major negotiations with the Trinidad Shipping Association. These discussions conducted from 30 September to 11 October 1938, under the chairmanship of Industrial Adviser A. V. Lindon, produced an agreement which specified working conditions and wage rates for lightermen, stevedores and launchmen. The settlement also considered travelling allowances, medical treatment costs, compensation for injured workers and an assurance of clean drinking water and lavatory accommodation for the workers. This historic agreement represented the first of its kind in the West Indies.[87] Orde-Browne acknowledged the significance of the settlement, "This detailed agreement deals with all aspects of work on the waterfront and clears up the situation which was previously most unsatisfactory. The agreement is a conspicuous example of the advantage of industrial negotiation between representative bodies working with an impartial and experienced chairman."[88]

The SWWTU was aware that some of its members were unable to afford membership dues. Therefore, on 1 June 1939, the entrance fee for longshoremen was reduced from $1.56 to $1.00. The extension of the work of the union included the formation of a Tobago branch under the guidance of Rupert Gittens, the union's Educational Director who visited the island and mobilized waterfront workers.[89] One of the main achievements of the union during the Second World War was its successful negotiations with the Trinidad Shipping Association for a temporary war allowance of two cents an hour for all workers. Furthermore, the wages of shipwrights were increased to thirty-one cents an hour.

After the pioneering work of Folkes, Carrington and Baptiste, other notable leaders continued to lead the SWWTU with the support of the veteran Jim Barrette. In 1939, C. Harper served as President, and Elton Alleyne succeeded him in 1940.[90] In 1941, C. P. Alexander, a former TWA member, was elected as President of the SWWTU and continued to serve in that office for the next fifteen years.

All Trinidad Sugar Estates and Factories Workers' Trade Union

Under the guidance of Rienzi, initial efforts were made in July–August 1937 for the unionization of sugar workers. The first sugar union was formed at the "Be-of-Good Cheer Lodge" in Ste Madeleine on 7 August 1937 where Louis A. Smart was elected President of the "Ste. Madeleine Sugar Workers Trade Union."[91] It was appropriate that the launch of a sugar workers' union should take place at Ste Madeleine since it was from there that two pan boilers had previously indicated to Blades their interest in joining the newly formed OWTU. Unfortunately, they were not eligible because the union had to restrict its membership only to oil-field workers as unions were recognized on the basis of occupation. In the earlier struggles of the oil workers, Blades was warmly received at Ste Madeleine as he enlisted the support of sugar workers. Reuben Drakes, the Vice President of the Ste Madeleine Sugar Workers Union, was present when fifty workers from Brechin Castle met at Yallery Street for the formation of a second union, the "Trinidad Sugar Workers Union."

The newly formed unions at Ste Madeleine in South Trinidad and the other at Brechin Castle in Central Trinidad were not registered, and therefore they were easily absorbed into an all-embracing union called the All Trinidad Sugar Estates and Factories Workers' Trade Union (ATSE+FWTU) formed in August 1937 (registered 24 November 1937) with its Central Office located at 16 Coffee Street, San Fernando. The leadership of the union came primarily from the OWTU: Rienzi (President General), A. M. Warner (General Secretary) and E. R. Blades (Trustee). Rienzi did not allow his social status as a lawyer to detract from his role in the sugar industry: "For although he had, by his education entered the ranks of the upper class, he was able to de-class himself and make common cause with true workers like Butler and Rojas and with thousands of sugar workers scattered all over the land."[92] One sugar worker recalled that Rienzi was "giving the workers a vision of betterment which they had never experienced."[93]

The expansion of the union included the formation of branches under the guidance of McDonald Moses, John Rojas and Ralph Mentor. Although there were approximately 34,000 sugar workers, only 2,000 joined the eighteen branches which were established between 1939 and 1940. Sugar workers, the majority of whom were illiterate, were yet to be convinced of the value of trade unionism. The Cane Farmers' Section was formed on 30 January 1938 at Ste Madeleine with 1,000 representatives from Reform, Penal, San Fernando, Princes Town, Tunapuna, Arouca, Lengua and Diamond Village.[94] With the focus on South Trinidad, branches of the Cane Farmers' Section were also established in Williamsville, Diamond Village, Barrackpore, Penal and Debe under the direction of a Central Committee which comprised Ralph Mentor (Secretary) and McDonald Moses (Trustee).[95]

During the war years, both the union and sugar companies were engaged in numerous wage-related disputes. In 1939, there were forty work stoppages in the colony: two in the Asphalt sector, four in the garment trade, and one each in the coconut, quarrying and printing industries; but there were thirty-one in the sugar industry. In 1940, out of the colony's fifty-nine work stoppages, forty-six occurred in the sugar industry.[96] It is evident that sugar workers, more than any other sector of labour, sustained the class revolt that had begun in 1937. Through labour disruption and persistent agitation, workers challenged the sugar manufacturers to consider better wages, reduced working hours and improved housing conditions for the working class. These were the principal social and economic causes of the labour rebellion in 1937. Governor Hubert Young responded with the formation of the Joint Sugar Board in September 1939 and, later, the Cane Farmers' Price Control Committee. The Taussig Commission observed the complaints of the ATSE+FWTU: "A.C. Rienzi complained, as did some of the labor leaders in other colonies, that labor was given no opportunity to check the plea of poverty made by the sugar companies; that they had no access to their books and that they were entitled to study the cost of producing sugar."[97]

The SMA expressed their inability to meet workers' demands because of the depressed state of the industry, but Rienzi responded that the sub-committee of the Joint Sugar Board, with no labour representatives, had access to the companies' books and were aware of the financial state of the industry.[98]

In the same year when the SMA finally recognized the ATSE+FWTU as the bargaining unit for sugar workers, a historic agreement was reached (5 December 1945) whereby the SMA approved an increase of $300,000 in wages for 20,000 workers.[99] In reality, each worker received a paltry sum of $15 per annum or merely four cents per day. Although these were small benefits for sugar workers, W. W. Burrows, Industrial Adviser, congratulated both the federation and union for their contribution to the formulation of the agreement. McDonald Moses, President of the ATSE+FWTU, was complimented for his "brave and courageous effort" in leading the union to procure such benefits for sugar workers.[100] *The Vanguard* appreciated the government's participation in the venture: "The Government is pledged to support the principle of collective agreements made between responsible, representative associations of employers and trade unions."[101]

The recognition of the ATSE+FWTU and the collective agreement of 1945 indicated that the union had won the legitimacy which it was denied since it was founded in 1937. However, this did not guarantee its primacy in the sugar industry, and the fragmentation of the unionization movement in the industry became apparent with the presence of competing unions.

The Soulbury Commission recognized that, among all the industries in the colony, it was in the sugar industry that the "most competing organizations" were to be found. Furthermore, they were not all committed to the welfare of the labour force on the plantation, "Our attention was drawn to the undesirable practice of certain individuals of collecting subscriptions from cane farmers and sugar workers under the pretext that an organisation was being formed to further their interests. The so-called promoters of such organisations issued no receipts or membership cards for subscriptions collected, kept no books of account and issued no statement of policy or rules."[102]

The entry of Butler into the sugar sector, where he was able to promote strikes, marked the emergence of the first of the major rivals of the ATSE+FWTU. Butler's success demonstrated the limited authority of the ATSE+FWTU. The SMA would have benefitted from a fragmented and thus weakened union movement, while the government made no effort to restrict the mushrooming of small unions in the colony.

The plantation provided attractive prospects for those who needed a platform to nurture their political ambitions. Southern-based Indian leaders, none with experience in unionism, eagerly exploited the deficiencies of the labour movement in the estates and created new workers' organizations. Mitra Sinanan's Sugar Industry Labour Union (SILU), Lionel Seukeran's Sugar Workers' Union (SWU), Ashford Sinanan's Cane Farmers and Sugar Workers' Association and the ATSE+FWTU perpetuated the chronic division in labour representation in the sugar belt. In addition, pseudo-unionists served for short periods using sugar workers to promote their political vision, which took precedence over serious working-class representation.[103]

The Public Works Workers' Trade Union

The Public Works Workers' Trade Union (PWWTU) was formed in August 1937, its rules were adopted on 1 November 1937, and the union was officially registered on 20 November 1937. Its primary objective was "to struggle for increased wages and better conditions for the workers in the Public Works."[104] The union represented various occupations in the government service, including laundresses and maids in nursing institutions, construction workers in the Public Works Department, government quarry operations as well as municipal sections in the Port-of-Spain City Council and the Borough Councils. PWWTU's membership, an estimated 800 employees of the Public Works Department, adopted the use of the colour "red" for buttons, badges and streamers at its rallies, meetings and public demonstrations.[105]

Although the union was based in Port-of-Spain, it expanded its influence through the formation of branches at Princes Town, Couva, La Brea, Talparo, San Fernando, Cedros, Carenage, Longdenville, Guaico, Manzanilla, Moruga, Cunupia and Tobago. In these communities, the PWWTU made representation to local officials on behalf of workers as well as for improved social services, particularly in rural villages. For instance, in August 1939, the Arima branch met with the Warden of Arima to discuss the unemployment situation, and also the need for resident medical officers in the rural areas such as Blanchisseuse, Talparo, and Four Roads, Tamana.[106] The various branches of the union organized programmes designed to improve the efficiency of workers in the municipalities. Classes in reading, writing and arithmetic were held on Fridays, and on Wednesday evenings, classes in Domestic Science were conducted by the Women's Section.[107] In 1939, the Castara branch forwarded a petition to Governor

Young appealing for improved telephone service in Tobago and better roads at Moriah. With branches at Charlotteville, Speyside, Castara and Roxborough, the PWWTU functioned in the 1940s as the only major union in Tobago which not only sought improvement in the island's social services but also addressed issues of unemployment on a regular basis.

At the World Trades Union Conference in Paris, France, in 1945, the union was represented by its General Secretary, Rupert Gittens. At the conference, Gittens referred to the instability in employment which resulted in the transient membership in trade unions, "The bulk of labour in the West Indies are casually employed – and it is very difficult with labour of that kind to retain any strong organization. Work people often join at times, and as soon as they are out of work, they cease being members of the organization."[108]

On 3 December 1946, the union wrote to the government seeking a meeting to discuss the issue of an all-round increase of wages for all government employees. In addition, the PWWTU petitioned the government for the appointment of an Arbitration Tribunal, and the union nominated C. Y. Shephard (Acting Principal of the Imperial College of Tropical Agriculture) as its Arbitrator. With no response from the government, the General Secretary of the union, R. J. Hulder, relayed the union's petition to Arthur Creech Jones, Secretary of State for the Colonies,[109] but unfortunately, here too the union failed to elicit official recognition for their concerns. By the 1950s, the membership of the union had declined despite which it remained as a registered union.

All Trinidad Transport General Workers' Union

John Rojas and Rienzi assisted in the formation of the All Trinidad Transport and General Workers' Union in 1938. They both served in the union's first Executive with Rojas as President and Rienzi as Vice President. Transport workers who joined this union belonged to an important cadre of public service employees in the government railway system, the tramway system in Port-of-Spain and the motor omnibus services.[110] McDonald Moses noted that both the FWTU and this new union competed for the membership of transport workers particularly in Port-of-Spain and that such competition among rival unions often created friction within the labour movement.[111]

When the union began its work in early 1938, Rienzi, invited tenants in San Fernando to be affiliated since their interests would be better served against landlords who made new proposals for rent increases. Tenants as well as domestic servants, who were subsequently affiliated, would have been accommodated in the General Workers' Section of the union. Taxi and bus workers belonged to the Chauffeurs Section while Overseers and Checkers of the Public Works formed another section. Rienzi also enlisted clerks in San Fernando, and in 1939, he made representations to merchants for improved working conditions in shops and stores in San Fernando. The union represented telephone operators and negotiated wage claims and working conditions for operators with the Trinidad Consolidated Telephone Company. Successes included a revised wage agreement in January 1940 on behalf of operators with the Trinidad Consolidated Telephones Limited and the roll-out of similar benefits for linesmen and officials in February 1940.[112] In its attempt to unionize domestic workers, tenants, clerks, transport workers, telephone and employees in the Public Works Department, the vision for this union transcended the limitation of specific occupational-related unions such as OWTU or ATSE+FWTU, "The intention was to make this an omnibus union that would serve to bridge the gap between the central-southern unions and those of the north, for the Transport and General Workers Union not only catered for workers throughout the colony but also associated itself with the co-ordinating movement in the north … But the attempt at co-ordination in the north petered out."[113]

Printers' Industrial Union

Employees engaged in printing, particularly those attached to Port-of-Spain-based newspapers, formed the Printers' Industrial Union in 1939 with M. Critchlow as President General and E. W. Bowen as General Secretary. Membership included workers at the *Trinidad Guardian*, *Evening News*, *Port-of-Spain Gazette* and *The People*. In March 1939, at one of its earliest meetings at the Court of Lily in Port-of-Spain, the union agreed to petition the Industrial Adviser for a revision of the low wages for apprentices and female compositors. Possibly the first serious encounter between this fledgling union and management came on 4 October 1939, when the steno typists and compositors employed at the *Trinidad Guardian* and *Evening News* abandoned their jobs. This was in solidarity with Bowen who was suspended for his activities as a trade unionist, being charged for the forceful manner in which he presented workers' grievances at a meeting with the colony's Industrial Adviser.[114] The incident not only illustrated workers' defiance but also portrayed the determination of employers to suppress and impede the work of unions.

After a period of dormancy due to limited membership in the 1940s, the union was revived in May 1949 primarily by printers in North Trinidad. *The Vanguard* reported that the revival received an enthusiastic response from printers "Their membership has already gone into three figures and the Executive Committee of the Union are planning to stabilize their efforts in order to make this organization a powerful unit of the trade union movement in this Colony."[115] The Secretary of the union indicated that their aims and objectives were similar to those of other unions and that they would serve members without creating conflict with employers.[116]

The Trinidad and Tobago Union of Shop Assistants and Clerks

In August 1938, a section of the TLP's Clerk Union broke ties with the TLP and formed a new union called the Trinidad and Tobago Union of Shop Assistants and Clerks. Led by Quintin O'Connor, Albert Gomes and Rupert Gittens, the union's membership comprised primarily women employed as store clerks in Port-of-Spain.[117] The struggle of this union on behalf of workers who laboured in shops and small garment factories brought into focus employment practices and conditions under which women worked in the city's small businesses.

One of the early achievements of the union was its support of a strike by the female employees of the Renown Shirt and Pyjama Factory Limited located on Queen Street, Port-of-Spain.[118] Negotiations broke down between the factory and the union, strike action ensued on 22 June 1939 and the union responded through the collection of funds to assist the women on strike. Eventually, under the guidance of A. V. Lindon, the Industrial Adviser, a provisional settlement was reached regarding wages and working conditions. Similarly, in August 1939, the union organized a boycott of another Syrian store, Gabriel and Company, for unfair treatment of two girls who were fired from their jobs.[119]

The Tailors and Garment Workers Section of the union also represented two female employees who were suspended at the garment factory of Jang Bahadursingh because they did not work during the Christmas holidays. Furthermore, the factory refused to pay compensation to one of the suspended girls who was injured while at her job.

Under the guidance of O'Connor,[120] attempts were made to enhance the efficiency of the union by establishing links with the Garment Workers' Union of Britain. The Union of Shop Assistants and Clerks sought to protect its members at the outbreak of the Second World War. In November 1939, the Tailors and Garment Workers Section petitioned the local government to ban the importation of shirts made in Hong Kong. Further action was taken in 1941 when the Japanese bombed Pearl Harbour. The Garment Workers Section launched a campaign to boycott Japanese garments and textiles.

The Union of Shop Assistants and Clerks was one of the few labour organizations which publicly denounced the incarceration of Butler in 1939. At a specially convened meeting on 24 July 1940, the union accepted a resolution to petition the Governor for the release of Butler. In response, J. Nicholls, the Acting Colonial Secretary, informed the union that the government was not prepared to institute an enquiry into Butler's case.[121]

Tailors' Industrial Union

Tailors and garment workers in Port-of-Spain were members of either the Trinidad and Tobago Union of Shop Assistants and Clerks or the Tailors' Industrial Union.[122] Rienzi presided at the inaugural meeting of the Tailors' Industrial Union which was held at the Trinidad Co-operative Bank Hall in June 1939.[123]

The union received support from the SWWTU whose President, Randolph Folkes, encouraged tailors to co-operate with one another even though they were members of rival unions, "He deplored the fact that it was the custom of local tailors to criticize one another and they should bear in mind that if they were to continue in that strain they would suffer materially and the net result would be that the Jews would be permitted to dominate the situation."[124] Folkes advised tailors to unite for the protection of the local garment industry against the "Jews" (Syrians) who dominated the trade in imported textiles as well as garments tailored in the Far East. In addition to self-employed tailors, Folkes appealed to those who operated tailoring establishments to consolidate under the Tailors' Industrial Union. These small businessmen included tailors of African descent such as Julian Hinds and Fitz Clarence-Spencer of Frederick Street, Port-of-Spain.

The small urban union experienced difficulties because tailors belonged to competing labour organizations. In addition, several tailors were self-employed tradesmen who preferred to manage their private tailoring establishments, while there were others whose labour could easily be exploited when private jobs were scarce. Given the high degree of individualism in this occupation, the union failed to mobilize the requisite proletarian mass to make a serious impact on industrial relations.

Overview

Occupational differentiation, which was the basis of trade unionism in capitalist societies, provided leverage for the employer class to surreptitiously exploit divisions in the labour movement. Employers promoted rivalry within the labour movement and manipulated unions whenever possible. This was most evident in the sugar industry as alluded to by Ranjit Kumar, who informed the Legislative Council that in the industry there were several trade unions "but none with a membership of more than a few hundred and the membership of them all would not amount to 1,000. It is impossible … for any single trade union to come forward to negotiate on behalf of workers with the employers."[125] In general, fragmentation within the labour movement was reflected in the existence of three unions which represented railway workers, two unions which represented domestic workers, two others that competed in the oil belt and four in the sugar industry. *The People* succinctly expressed its dismay with regard to the diversity in the trade union movement, particularly the rivalry, duplication of efforts and contradiction which impeded effective worker representation, "There exist too many workers Trade Unions, consequently there exist competition and confusion among the Unions that should never have existed in such a small community. Different Unions catering for the same industry act independently of one another thereby causing confusion and they thus become an easy prey to any employer who undoubtedly will realise their stupidity and therefore be able to make most of this weakness."[126]

Union leaders were aware of the inherent disadvantages and dangers of independent unionism, particularly for small organizations. In the campaign against competitive unionism, working-class leaders focused on unity in labour to ensure better opportunities for commanding greater advantages in industrial relations. The pioneers in the campaign were Rienzi, Moses, Blades and Mentor of the southern and central unions. In addition to forging links between the OWTU and the ATSE+FWTU in South and Central Trinidad, Rienzi, in July 1937, took the unity movement to Port-of-Spain where he inspired the formation of the Federated Workers Trade Union (FWTU) which comprised a variety of occupations. Subsequent efforts led to the formation of a general union, the All Trinidad Transport and General Workers' Union, which extended membership to all categories of workers except those in the oil and sugar industries. The union was expected to function as a unifying force among several workers' organizations "to bridge the gap between central-southern unions and those of the north."[127] One of the most significant platforms for labour collaboration came with the formation of the Committee for Industrial Organization (CIO) in 1938. Although the CIO was unsuccessful in its co-ordination with northern unions, further efforts at labour unity led to the formation of the Trinidad and Tobago Trade Union Congress (TTTUC) in 1939. This body embraced unions in North, Central and South Trinidad.[128]

Unfortunately, the diversity within trade unionism was further complicated by antagonism and rivalry which hindered efforts for co-operation. In his analysis of the challenges facing the TTTUC, Albert Gomes observed that "severe internecine strife" made the congress "more of a battleground for the warring factions than a means of achieving increased influence and viability through united action."[129] It is obvious that one of the major contributing factors to the crisis within the congress was the influence of certain leaders who were "pathetically inexperienced ... opinionated, assertive and chauvinistic." Such instability in trade unionism subsequently militated against successful industrial negotiation making the first unions vulnerable in their encounter between labour and management.[130]

The Industrial Adviser's Report (1938–1940) identified the weak organizational structure of unions and their rivalry as contributory factors for their inability to attract a substantial membership:

> Membership of the trade unions is yet very unstable and fluctuates considerably both in numbers and in financial support. Two of the Unions, the Oilfields Workers' Trade Union and the Public Works and Public Service Workers' Union, have outstripped the others in size and substance but even these organizations seem to pass through periods of depression and disinterest, chiefly because the majority of members are not yet trade unionists by conviction. It would appear that local trade union propaganda, which usually consists of an uninspiring appeal to class distinction and bitterness, suspicion and political enmity, is partly responsible for this.[131]

The splintering of the trade union movement took its toll as early as 1944 when at least five small organizations had ceased to function. Among the inactive unions were the Tobago Industrial Trade Union, the Amalgamated Building and Woodworkers' Union, the Trinidad and Tobago Union of Shop Assistants and Clerks, the Railway Workers' Trade Union and the Printers' Industrial Trade Union. The small membership in these unions would have been absorbed by larger organizations such as the PWWTU which gradually accommodated the railway employees and other government workers.

Trade unions were plagued by internal conflicts, but the state served as another formidable opponent of unionism during its formative years. Although the BLP was traditionally associated with trade unionism, colonial policy preferred a non-political labour movement in the Caribbean: "A great deal of British thinking before 1950 about colonial affairs was dominated by the conception of social advance through voluntary association of a non-political character ... hence the emphasis on trades unions."[132]

In pursuit of its mission and understanding of Caribbean development, labour made a radical departure from metropolitan expectations of labour organizations in the colonies. When trade unionism was conceded to the Caribbean's non-white workers, it came only in the context of crisis within the West Indian economy and social structure. Subsequently, adult franchises and other constitutional concessions were granted within the context of the anti-imperial movement which was led by labour in the colonies.

Imperial policy was determined to maintain white elite domination. The state therefore sought to curtail the political inclination and radicalism in the labour movement, as evident in 1937, but more decisively during the Second World War with the harassment of union leaders who were accused of corruption and subversion. The employer class benefitted from police surveillance of union activities because management considered trade unionism as a threat to their traditional control of labour. Furthermore, employers regarded trade unions "with mistrust or suspicion and relations between capital and labour were thus characterised by antagonism rather than co-operation."[133]

George Padmore denounced state repression of the strike movement and the government's policy of press censorship. He also criticized both the introduction of a special middle-class volunteer force to protect vested interests and the state approbation of door-to-door searches by police in several villages.[134] Britain's Defence Regulations of 1 September 1939, applicable to any British colony, made provisions for the detention without trial of persons considered a threat to security. Accordingly, in November 1939, Uriah Butler was detained in the Internment Camp for Enemy Aliens at Nelson

Island. The severity of colonial repression was felt by trade unionists and supporters whose activities were not as pronounced as Butler's militancy. On 7 March 1941, Dudley Mahon (of the NWCSA and PWWTU) and Irish school teachers Kathleen Donellan and Francis Cahill were detained at an internment camp near the St James Barracks for alleged "anti-British and anti-war propaganda."[135]

Both Donellan and Cahill taught at the St Joseph's Convent and also at the Catholic Women's Teachers College in Port-of-Spain. However, the contracts of both teachers were terminated in May 1940 after they delivered a series of educational lectures to members of the PWWTU. The Executive of the TTTUC contacted the Mother Superior of St Joseph Convent requesting a meeting between her and trade union representatives regarding the firing of Donellan and Cahill. The Superior responded that she was not accountable to any unions.[136] Both teachers expressed concerns that the convent had not acted independently but on instructions from another "authority":

> Evidently, the trouble started with our appearing and speaking on Trade Union platforms. We were glad to avail ourselves of a platform from which we could disseminate our ideas on the necessity for a greater demand for and interest in education on the part of the masses. Naturally, in view of the present colonial and government policy of encouraging Trade Unionism in the West Indies we had no idea that anybody could object to our appearing on responsible Trade Union platforms.[137]

Donellan served as the editor of *New Dawn*, a working-class publication which first appeared in November 1940. Both women who were detained for appearing on trade union platforms admitted that their concern was for the education of the masses.[138] Donellan refused to leave the colony despite local authorities' promise to release her from detention if she agreed to return to Ireland. On 3 June 1941, she escaped from the detention camp and was later found dead. The inquest concluded that she committed suicide by drowning since she had attempted to end her life twice during her three-month detention.[139]

The state made no concessions for workers engaging in public protests, and on 8 November 1939, the government prohibited street demonstrations and any assembly of more than ten persons. In February 1940, the PWWTU was denied permission for a workers' march in Port-of-Spain; later Quintin O'Connor, Alexander Duke and Delroy Donawa were arrested, convicted and fined for organizing a protest march.[140] The NWCSA was not allowed to conduct a meeting at Woodford Square because O'Connor read passages from "Your Freedom is in Danger," a pamphlet issued by the United States-based National Council for Civil Liberties, on a previous occasion.[141] The resolution of the SWWTU in 1940 to march to Government House in support of unemployed seamen led to the arrest of leaders who were interrogated by the Commissioner of Police and warned to desist from any public demonstration.[142]

The police were used by the state as one of its major agencies to monitor and repress working-class organizations. Calder-Marshall reported that trade union leaders were under constant surveillance: "With their elaborate system of spies, informers and plainclothes detectives, the police have fallen victim to their own fantasies ... The unions they regard as potential centres of sedition. They never meet the union leaders personally unless they rope them in on a sedition charge. They see labour problems through the eyes of those spies and detectives whose main stock-in-trade is the peddling of sinister rumours."[143]

John Jagger, a visiting MP from England, observed two policemen taking notes at the opening of a new branch of the PWWTU in April 1940.[144] Also, policemen were present at BEWP+RU meetings in Fyzabad and at FWTU meetings chaired by Gomes and O'Connor in Port-of-Spain.[145] The homes of Jim Barrette and Bertie Percival of the NWCSA were searched by police and on at least two occasions, the Gomes' residence was ransacked as police seized insignificant personal letters and other literature, which were eventually returned.[146]

The government infiltrated unions through fickle workers who functioned as agents of the security forces, "The Government kept a watchful eye on all we did ... We discovered that workers were paid by the security branch to spy on us. The shadow was with us everywhere we went."[147] Such workers served as spies and informers or "bosses' agents" for both police and employers. Percy Mullin did not conceal his suspicion that certain members of the ATSE+FWTU who attended the meeting at St John village on 11 January 1942 functioned as informers of estate managers.[148]

The negativism and suspicion of the police towards the trade union movement were reflected in their general hostility towards the masses. Corporal Charles John, in a sworn statement, said, "I have observed that the attitude of ignorant members of the labouring class is the same today as it was in the early part of 1937."[149] The police were under the control of an officer of the white elite. Moreover, many members of the police constabulary were Barbadians, recruited because they would not identify themselves with the local population. The Royal Commission (1938) was advised thus: "There is need for a very full investigation, it is felt that there has been, almost a system of irregularities and terrorism. It is safe to say that this is the most hated of any department."[150]

State repression targeted local working-class publications and included regular scrutiny of correspondence to *The People* before delivery to its office in Port-of-Spain. Even the office was ransacked by the police in August 1940.[151] Censorship by the government included restrictions on the publication of articles covering matters affecting the working class but viewed as subversive to governance. Ralph Mentor, editor of *The Vanguard*, received a letter from the Colonial Secretary warning him against publishing such articles as "News From Tobago: Coloured Survivor Complains of Discrimination." The Colonial Secretary threatened to invoke the Defence Regulation if such articles continued to be published.[152] In addition, five members of the *Civil Service Review*, a working-class newsletter, were charged for publishing an article titled "African Methods in a Government Department" in October 1943. These persons were threatened with dismissal by the Governor, but they defiantly refused to apologize and were subsequently reprimanded.[153]

Towards the end of 1946, trade unionism had survived the perils of internal disunity and fragmentation; the deliberate delay on the part of the employer class in conceding union recognition; the tardy response of workers to membership; repressive state policies; and the defection of experienced leaders to political enterprise. Working-class unity and cooperation, which constituted the best survival mechanism of trade unions, were yet to be fully developed. Fortunately, foundations were already laid for collaborative unionism through Rienzi's CIO and later the TTTUC. Fraternal relations were also promoted through experimentation with the unification of occupational groups in the FWTU and the All Trinidad Transport and General Workers' Union. The next decade produced the most resolute efforts at unification through the formation of omnibus unions and the promotion of inter-union solidarity.

Notes

1. *Forster Report*, 81. Report of the Commission on Trinidad and Tobago Disturbances. 1937 (London: HMSO, 1937). Also known as the Forster Report.
2. *West India Royal Commission Report* (London: HMSO, 1945), 51.
3. *West India Royal Commission Report*, 49.
4. *Labour Conditions in the West Indies, Report by Major St. J. Orde-Browne* (London: HMSO, 1939) (hereafter cited as the *Orde-Browne Report*), 119. During 1909–1931, Orde-Browne served as an Administrative Officer in East Africa. During 1930, he served as a member of the International Labour Office Committee of Experts on Native Labour. Basdeo, *Labour Organization and Labour Reform*, 229.
5. By December 1938, there were ten registered unions operating in Trinidad and Tobago: Amalgamated Building and Woodworkers' Union, Oilfield Workers' Trade Union, Federated Workers Trade Union, Seamen and Waterfront Workers' Trade Union, All Trinidad Sugar Estates and Factories Workers' Trade Union, Public Works Workers' Trade Union, All Trinidad Transport and General Workers' Union, Railway Workers' Trade Union, Trinidad and Tobago Union of Shop Assistants and Clerks, and Printers' Industrial Union.
   Orde-Browne Report, 126.
6. *Orde-Browne Report*, 126.
7. *Taussig Report*, 51. Charles Taussig was the chairman of the United States Commission to study Social and Economic Conditions in the British West Indies., He also served as the co-chairman of the Anglo-American Commission.
8. Letter from Charles Atkinson to the Secretary of the BLP, 18 November 1933. Modern Records Centre, University of Warwick. Another prominent member of the union was George Bostic. Basdeo, *Labour Organization and Labour Reform*, 217.
9. Letter from Citrine to Atkinson, 11 December 1933. TUC Library, University of North London.
10. Letter from Captain W. H. Coombs to W. J. Bolton, 25 March 1936. Modern Records Centre, University of Warwick.
11. Letter from W. J. Bolton to Coombs, 26 March 1936. Modern Records Centre, University of Warwick. In the letter, Bolton indicated there were no recent reports of

the TWA: "Our records are somewhat out of date, and we know of no one in Trinidad who could give us a truly independent account of the situation. Consequently, we have to rely upon reports, and many of them are probably tendencious (sic)." TUC Library, University of North London.

12. Letter from Atkinson to Citrine, 9 May 1936. Modern Records Centre, University of Warwick.
13. Letter from Citrine to Atkinson, 29 May 1936. Modern Records Centre, University of Warwick.
14. Letter from Cipriani to Sutherland, 13 October 1937. Modern Records Centre, University of Warwick.
15. Basdeo, *Labour Organization and Labour Reform*, 223.
16. Selwyn John, personal interview, 10 June 2002. John served the trade union movement for fifty years (1951–2001). He served as General Secretary of the National Union of Government and Federated Workers (NUGFW) from 1965 to 1986; and President General of NUGFW from 1986 to 2001.
17. Jacobs, *Butler versus the King*, 22.
18. There were similar welfare organizations which were not directly linked to the formation of trade unions. These include the NWCSA and the Penal East Indian Friendly Society.
19. *The People* 7 January 1939.
20. Interview with E. R. Blades in John M. Hackshaw, *One Hundred Years of Trade Unionism* (Diego Martin: Citadel Publishing Sservice,1997), 28.
21. *60 and Going Strong*, Oilfield Workers' Trade Union anniversary brochure (San Fernando: Syncreators, 1997), 2.
22. The meeting was held at the Union Diamond Friendly Society Hall, Mucurapo Street, San Fernando.
23. Nelson was a former member of the TLP. Hackshaw, *One Hundred Years of Trade Unionism*, 26. Officers elected were A. Rienzi (President General), E. R. Blades (General Secretary), Caleb Roach (Assistant General Secretary), J. F. Morgan (Treasurer), Ramrattan Madoo, Arthur McNish and James Hall (Trustees).
24. Bolland, *Politics of Labour*, 271.
25. *The People* 14 August 1937.
26. Reddock, *Women, Labour and Politics*, 144.
27. *The Vanguard* 15 April 1944.
28. See Singh, "Adrian Cola Rienzi and the Labour Movement," 24–25.
29. Singh, "Adrian Cola Rienzi and the Labour Movement," 26. Also Basdeo, *Labour Organization and Labour Reform*, 213.
30. Khafra Kambon, *For Bread, Justice and Freedom: A political biography of George Weekes* (London: New Beacon Books, 1988).
31. *The People* 13 May 1939. Also cited in Brinsley Samaroo, "The Contribution of Adrian Cola Rienzi to the National Labour Movement," in *A Tribute to Rienzi: A Collection*

of Speeches Delivered at the Opening of the Rienzi Complex (San Fernando: Battlefront Publications, 1982), 25. See Ramdin, *Chattel Slave to Wage Earner*, 145. Singh, "Adrian Cola Rienzi and the Labour Movement," 28; Bolland, *Politics of Labour*, 277. An editorial in *The People* praising Rienzi was entitled "The Triumph of Bonnie Prince Cola," *The People* 29 January 1938.

32. *The Vanguard* 3 January 1942.
33. *The Vanguard* 16 May 1942.
34. "Administrative Report for the Year 1944," *Council Paper* no. 46 of 1944, 8.
35. *Taussig Report*, 75.
36. *The Vanguard* 17 January 1942.
37. See Jacobs, *Butler versus the King*, 23–24. Obika, *An Introduction to the Life and Times of Tubal Uriah Butler*, 122–123.
38. Bolland, *Politics of Labour*, 660.
39. Teresa Cardinez, "Politics in Trinidad and Tobago 1946–1956: From Personal Politics to Ethnic-based Parties," MPhil thesis, University of the West Indies, St Augustine, 1990, 34.
40. Although there were ten members of the CIO, the majority of officers belonged to the OWTU: Rienzi (President), Mentor (First Vice President), Blades (Second Vice President), John F. Rojas (Secretary-Treasurer) and McDonald Moses (Assistant Treasurer). Other members were John Allen, Caleb Roach, Frank D. Allen, Durham Maharaj and Clarence C. Abidh.
41. *Memorandum from the Committee for Industrial Organization*, 5–6 (hereafter cited as *Memo from the CIO*).
42. *Memo from the CIO*, 7–8.
43. Bolland, *Politics of Labour*, 457.
44. *The Vanguard* 6 January 1940.
45. *The Vanguard* 19 December 1942.
46. Bolland, *Politics of Labour*, 417.
47. Cardinez, "Politics in Trinidad and Tobago 1946–1956," 32–33.
48. *POSG* 31 October 1943.
49. *Sunday Guardian* 25 October 1943.
50. *POSG* 2 November 1943. Dr Pitt's party won all three seats in the San Fernando Borough Council elections (Dr D. Pitt, Dr E. A. Lee and G. A. Richards).
51. Rienzi's most significant contribution on the Franchise Committee (1941) was his campaign against the language qualification which would have disenfranchised several Indians.
52. *The Vanguard* 26 February 1944.
53. Bolland, *Politics of Labour*, 566.
54. *The Vanguard* 1 April 1944.
55. *The Vanguard* 8 December 1945. After the WFTU Conference, Rojas attended the international Pan-African Conference in Manchester, England, in October 1945.

56. John La Guerre, "The General Elections of 1946 in Trinidad and Tobago," Social and Economic Studies 21 (1972), 196.
57. The Workers Freedom Movement was formed in 1948 and based in Port-of-Spain.
58. La Guerre, "Elections of 1946," 188. Mentor served as editor of *The Vanguard* from 1941. William Gallaher (MP in Britain) praised the USSR: "In the Soviet Union whose democracy our pundits so volubly criticize, there is government for a great mass of people, workers, collective farmers and professional people, all united against the remnants of Czarism, the wrecker and agents outside capitalism." *The Vanguard* 15 December 1945.
59. *Hansard* 30 November 1945.
60. Williams inaccurately stated that the FWTU was registered before July 1937. See Williams, *History of the People of Trinidad and Tobago*, 231.
61. Samaroo, "Contribution of Adrian Cola Rienzi," 24. For further evidence of Rienzi's role in the FWTU's formation, see also Lewis, *Labour in the West Indies*, 32; Singh, "Adrian Cola Rienzi and the Labour Movement," 27; Calder-Marshall, *Glory Dead*, 234.
62. Memorandum of the Federated Workers' Trade Union on the Strike Situation in Trinidad to Ormsby-Gore, 5 August 1937. CO 295/599.
63. *The People* 14 August 1937.
64. See Bolland, *Politics of Labour*, 213, 270–271, 275. Payne was a main figure in the labour rebellion in Barbados in 1937 and was deported to Trinidad on 26 July 1937.
65. Richards was also the Mayor of Port-of-Spain. Other members included Fitz Clarence-Spencer (Treasurer) and J. M. T. Roberts (President General).
66. Letter from Sylvester Patrick (Secretary) to Walter Citrine, 11 October 1937. TUC Library, University of North London.
67. James and George Padmore, two Trinidadians, were members of the IASB.
68. Abstracts from the FWTU's communication were cited in a letter from Wallace Johnson (General Secretary of the IASB) to the Under Secretary of State for the Colonies, 7 December 1937.CO 295/600.
69. Letter from Wallace Johnson (IASB) to the Under Secretary of State for the Colonies, 23 December 1937. CO 295/599.
70. John, personal interview, 10 June 2002.
71. Gomes, *Through a Maze of Colour*, 38. Singh mentions that by 1943, Gomes was President of the FWTU. Singh, *Race and Class*, 217.
72. Gomes, *Through a Maze of Colour*, 40.
73. *The People* 13 July 1940.
74. *The People* 20 September 1940.
75. *Report by F.W. Dalley, Trade union organization and industrial relations in Trinidad*, 1947. Available in Alma Jordan Library, University of the West Indies, St. Augustine.

76. Dudley Mahon told the protestors that "we must act together and fight for our common rights, and if we have to fall on our knees let us fight like men for the good and welfare of our wives and our children." *POSG* 5 February 1946.
77. *POSG* 10 February 1946.
78. *POSG* 20 February 1946.
79. Gomes, *Through a Maze of Colour*, 47.
80. Rennie, *History of the Working Class*, 18.
81. Rennie, *History of the Working Class*, 18–20.
82. Folkes served as a member of the Maritimes Union of North America. He was a Trinidadian who had returned from the United States.
83. *Anniversary Brochure of the SWWTU*, 35.
84. Among the persons attending were Randolph Folkes, James Wallace, Jim Barrette, Errol Cunliffe, Alan Walker, Bertie Antoine, Alexander Carter, A. Dopwell and James Taylor. *Anniversary Brochure of the SWWTU*, 29.
85. *The People* 11 June 1938.
86. *The People* 6 August 1938.
87. *The Vanguard* 13 January 1940. Also Campbell, "'En'less Pressure,"' 250. Basdeo, *Labour Organization and Labour Reform*, 214.
88. *Orde-Browne Report*, 119.
89. *The People* 29 April 1939.
90. Other officers serving in 1939 were Rupert Gittens (Educational Director) and Christopher Harper (Financial Secretary). Reddock, *Women, Labour and Politics*, 280.
91. Other elected officers were Harold Bryant (First Vice President), Reuben Drakes (Second Vice President), Vernon Trotman (Secretary), Albert Duval (Assistant Secretary), J. Arthur (Treasurer), N. Padmore and A. Friday (Trustees). The members of the committee were Blaize [*sic*] of the OWTU, N. Rouse, C. Philip, H. Bourne and Mrs C. Steele. *The People* 14 August 1937.
92. Samaroo, "Contribution of Adrian Cola Rienzi," 26.
93. Interview with Mahabir Bahadur (in 1977) conducted by Brinsley Samaroo. Bahadur worked at Ste Madeleine during the 1930s, cited in Samaroo, "Contribution of Adrian Cola Rienzi," 26.
94. *The People* 12 February 1938. In 1937, farmers supplied 629,881 tons of canes to the factories from a total supply of 1,442,910. There were approximately 20,705 cane farmers of which 13,822 were East Indians and 6,833 were Africans. *Council Paper* no. 50 of 1938, 4.
95. Other officers of the Central Committee were C. C. Abidh (President), W. G. Culverhouse (First Vice President), Joseph Assiz (Assistant Secretary), B. Gobin (Trustee) and E. Lucky (Treasurer). *The People* 12 February 1938.

96. "Administrative Report of the Industrial Adviser for the Year 1938–1940," *Council Paper* no. 25 of 1941, 7 (the Industrial Adviser was A. G. V. Lindon). By 1938, the sugar companies were Ste Madeleine Sugar Company, Caroni Estates Limited, Woodford Lodge Sugar Estates Limited, Trinidad Sugar Estates Limited, Gordon Grant and Company Limited and Reform Estates Limited.
97. *Taussig Report*, 53.
98. *Taussig Report*, 54.
99. *TG* 5 January 1945. The agreement provided for 15% increase in basic wage rates, fixed overtime rates and holiday remuneration for all factory and field workers. See also *The Vanguard* 6 January 1945.
100. Letter from D. Maharaj, San Fernando *TG* 12 January 1945.
101. *The Vanguard* 13 January 1945.
102. *Soulbury Report*, 117.
103. See Bolland, *Politics of Labour*, 571–572.
104. See *Rules of the Public Works Workers' Trade Union*. Clause 2, 1–2. The "Public Works Workers Trade Union" was the official title of this union as listed with the Registrar of Trade Unions. The union was sometimes referred to as "The Public Works and Public Services Trade Union." The founding members of the PWWTU were Caesar Ashby (Chairman), Edmund John, Lionel D. Mitchell, G. S. Franklin (Financial Secretary), Leonardo Jordan, Emanuel de Lande, Dudley Mahon, Alexander Duke, Stephen Lyons, James A. Corbin and Gaskynd A. Granger (Organizing Secretary).
105. *Rules of the Public Works Workers' Trade Union*, 12.
106. *The People* 9 September 1939.
107. *The People* 31 August 1940.
108. *The Vanguard* 24 November 1945.
109. *POSG* 18 December 1946.
110. The railway system which covered 188 miles of tracks was the most extensive form of public transport in the colony. The tramway cars were owned by the Port-of-Spain City Corporation and operated by the Trinidad Electricity Boards. Buses were privately owned.
111. McDonald Moses, personal interview, 1 January 2001.
112. *The Vanguard* 3 February 1940. The officials representing the union were McDonald Moses, Rienzi and Miss Vera Trotman. The two members of the Telephone Company were George de Nobriga and R. A. Berry-Hart.
113. Singh, "Adrian Cola Rienzi and the Labour Movement," 27.
114. *The People* 7 October 1939.
115. *The Vanguard* 21 May 1949.
116. *The Vanguard* 21 May 1949.
117. Bolland, *Politics of Labour*, 275.
118. *The People* 1 July 1939. The owner of the store was Joseph Sabga (a Syrian).
119. *The People* 26 August, 23 September 1939.

120. O'Connor was a store clerk who later went into full-time trade unionism. John, personal interview, 10 June 2002. During the 1920s and 1930s, O'Connor was a member of the Clerks Union of the TWA.
121. *The People* 7 September 1940.
122. Moses, personal interview, 1 January 2001.
123. The President of the Tailors' Industrial Union was R. C. Maundy; E. Harlequin was the Organizing Secretary and B. Forde was the Treasurer.
124. *The People* 5 August 1939.
125. *Hansard* 6 May 1947.
126. *The People* 13 July 1940.
127. Singh, "Adrian Cola Rienzi and the Labour Movement," 27.
128. Unions in the TTTUC included the following: OWTU, All Trinidad Sugar Estates and Factories Workers' Trade Union, PW&PWSU, SWWTU, Printers' Industrial Union, Tailors' Industrial Union, Trinidad and Tobago Union of Shop Assistants and Clerks, Amalgamated Building and Woodworkers' Union, All Trinidad Transport and General Workers' Union. "Administrative Report of the Industrial Adviser," *Council Paper* no. 25 of 1941, 12.
129. Gomes, *Through a Maze of Colour*, 46.
130. *Orde-Browne Report*, 43.
131. "Administrative Report of the Industrial Adviser," *Council Paper* no. 25 of 1941, 12.
132. J. M. Lee, *Colonial Development and Good Government: A Study of the Ideas Expressed by the British Official Classes in Planning Decolonization 1939–1964* (Oxford: Clarendon Press, 1967), 157.
133. *Orde-Browne Report*, 44.
134. *The People* 21 May 1938. See also Jerome Teelucksingh, "The Immortal Batsman: George Padmore the Revolutionary Writer and Activist," in Fitzroy Baptiste and Rupert Lewis, eds, *George Padmore: Pan-African Revolutionary* (Jamaica: Ian Randle Publishers, 2009), 1–20.
135. In the labour historiography of this era, Cahill is referred to as "Frank Cahill" but Campbell identifies her as "Francis Cahill." Campbell, "'En'less Pressure,'" 252. Cahill, who served on the editorial board of *New Dawn*, was referred to as "Francis Cahill" in its first issue of November 1940. The camp at St James could accommodate 300 persons. See *New Dawn* April 1941, 3.
136. *The People* 20 July 1940.
137. *The People* 20 July 1940.
138. *The People* 20 July 1940.
139. This was disclosed in the House of Commons by George Hall, Under Secretary of State for the Colonies, *WICC* 24 July 1941. At the time of her death, Donellan was pregnant. In 1945, Cahill was released from detention and returned to England but remained emotionally traumatized. Campbell, "'En'less Pressure,'" 259.
140. *The Vanguard* 24 February 1940.

141. *New Dawn* November 1940, 3. The NWCSA attracted activists who supported the association, but subsequently became leaders of other organizations in Port-of-Spain. Among these were O'Connor and Gomes who together led the FWTU. Gomes said that he served his "political apprenticeship" with the NWCSA. Gomes, *Through a Maze of Colour*, 161. Prior to his involvement in the FWTU, O'Connor would have been also associated with the NWCSA.
142. *The People* 27 April 1940.
143. Calder-Marshall, *Glory Dead*, 215. In de Boissiere's novels set in this era, there is mention of a detective taking notes at a union meeting and an incident of police dispersing a gathering of unionists. See de Boissiere, *Rum and Coca Cola*, 129 also *Crown Jewel*, 96. Ralph De Boissiere *Rum and Coca Cola: A novel* (London: Allison & Busby, 1984)
144. *The People* 1 June 1940.
145. Gomes, *Through a Maze of Colour*, 39.
146. Gomes, *Through a Maze of Colour*, 63.
147. Gomes, *Through a Maze of Colour*, 39.
148. *The Vanguard* 17 January 1942.
149. Sworn statement at the Port-of-Spain Police Court by Charles John, Corporal of Police, 27 November 1939. Confidential Despatches from Governor to Secretary of State 1939, National Archives, Trinidad.
150. Submission of Trinidad Citizen's League, 31 January 1939. *Memo from the CIO.*
151. *The People* 17 August 1940.
152. *The Vanguard* 9 January 1943.
153. *The Vanguard* 12 February 1944.

CHAPTER 7

Radical but not Progressive: The 1950s and 1960s

The suffering of the working class during the 1920s to 1940s continued during the 1950s and 1960s. The socio-economic conditions during the 1950s contributed to the agitation among the working class. In May 1951, the cost of living index was 235 points, and a few months later in August, it had risen to 240. The employees' wages were linked to the cost of living index and as a result, the workers would benefit from a pay increase.[1]

Britain had puppet leaders and administrators in the Caribbean colonies. For instance, the Leeward Islands Governor, Earl Baldwin of Bewdley, was speedily summoned to London and later dismissed. The reason was that his bold presentation entitled "Talk, Talk, but No Money for the West Indies" offended the political status quo. *The Clarion* gave an ominous warning: "It is time that the people of these Colonies wake up to the fact that BIG BUSINESS is vitally interested in Government's WHITE ELEPHANTS as a major part of these squandered funds finds its way directly or indirectly into their pockets."[2]

The local leadership also had shortcomings. In 1956, the Consulate General, in Port-of-Spain, dubbed Eric Williams "as cocky as ever" and was aware that politicians in the colony were "individualists first and foremost."[3] Jack Kelshall, a local lawyer and politician, was forthright in condemning the governance of the 1950s, "We must shake off the present Colonial administration and create at the same time a democratic society with sufficient stability to survive and to govern effectively."[4] His political views stemmed from his ideology of Democratic Socialism.

The problems of internal squabbling among unions and lack of proper leadership were two problems plaguing unionism in the colony of Trinidad and Tobago. The editorial of *The Clarion* in June 1951 contended that one of the major causes of disunity was "the absence of a vigorous and effective trade union movement." The editorial was also critical of leaders, "Leadership has become concentrated in the hands of a few selected men who change from one executive post to the other and seem to accomplish little for the worker."[5] Arthur Lewis, Professor of Political Economy at Manchester University, in 1956, noted the problem of colonial labour, "Unions fight not only employers but each other, and Colonies must expect to have their share of such disputes."[6] Disunity among unions in Trinidad and Tobago was the norm. The paternal role of Britain continued, as noted by Herbert Tracy in his article on the TUC in Britain: "Real help from Britain's trade union movement and the international Confederation" assisted the trade union movement.[7]

The problems would be further compounded by the inability to fully report on labour issues. By 1951, *The Vanguard* and *The People* were no longer in circulation, and *The Clarion* reported on the need for "a weekly organ of informed opinion" with "a progressive labour outlook on current topics"; the article lamented, "For us the freedom of the press is still a somewhat meaningless and empty phrase."[8] The OWTU had a regular column in *The Clarion* entitled "Current Notes" or "Current News." The column's writer Cyril Gonzales, who was Assistant General Secretary of the union in 1956, wrote of trade unions becoming "effective agents of democracy" and being able to "vitalize" the working class. However, Gonzales bemoaned the fact that "Trade Unionism in Trinidad has not yet reached this needed standard of consistency, unity and ideal purpose."

Opportunists and weak opposition

The lack of loyalty to an ideology affected the membership of political parties. Some individuals were opportunistic and joined a Labour Party only if they felt it helped them succeed in elections. Jack Kelshall was critical of local politicians, "It is also necessary for the opposition to be effective. And this means that the opposition must be able to get the ear of the electorate."[9] In a letter to *The Clarion*, James Isaac, an oil worker of Forest Reserve, condemned the deception by politicians, "Hon. Roy

Joseph some years ago took on a Labour label climbed on the backs of the Oilfields Workers' Trade Union and got into the Legislature and subsequently denounced the Oil workers Union."[10] A similar scenario unfolded, in June 1956, when the Minister for Health and Local Government Norman Tang, an independent candidate in the last election, was contemplating joining the TLP. The Mayor of Arima Raphael Chinaleong, initially a member of TLP, resigned from the Party of Political Progressive Groups (POPPG) and returned to the TLP. Likewise, Victor Bryan, a member of the Caribbean Socialist Party (CSP), had won the elections and was appointed Minister of Agriculture and Lands; Bryan left the CSP and joined the TLP.

Obstacles to unity

By 1950, the ideologies of Butlerism and Garveyism were no longer as prominent as they were during the 1920s and 1930s. However, the issue of race/ethnicity was unavoidable; as Arthur Lewis noted: "Even where there is no industrial colour bar, racial prejudice plays havoc with industrial relations because it stands in the way of mutual respect and good personal relations."[11] On 16 August 1955, at a lecture at Woodford Square entitled "Historical Background of Race Relations in the Caribbean," Williams identified the cause of the race problem as being imperialism and economic in nature. He added that the racial problems in the Caribbean stemmed from one ethnic group attempting to dominate whilst "everyone is struggling for a greater share of a small cake." In offering a solution, Williams deemed it necessary that the rights of others be respected and a climate of harmony be created to ensure religious and racial groups felt secure.[12] However, this contradicts the view of Colin Palmer whose biographical study of Williams revealed, "he opposed the teaching of Hindi in the schools" and that "he wondered whether the teaching of Hindi might lead to requests for the introduction of African languages."[13] Interestingly, the Prime Minister "blamed the desire for teaching Hindi on Outside interference"[14]

In 1951, Bhadase Maraj was selected as a delegate to represent Trinidad at the Festival of Britain. *The Clarion* questioned his qualifications and the government's choice, "Is he being rewarded for faithful service? Or is this merely a token of greater things to come if Mr. Mahraj (sic) continues to be a good boy."[15] The editorial of *The Clarion* carried a warning to Maraj that "the use of religious organisations for political purposes would be a disastrously dangerous course. In the case of the Maha Sabha the dangers are even greater because in that organisation religion can so easily become confused and identified with race."[16] Dennis Mahabir, in June 1956, championed political unity but lamented, "A pity it is that the leader of the P.D.P. Bhadase Maraj cannot as yet be visualised on such a platform, but his influence on a large number of people must not be ignored."[17] Mahabir was the editor and associate editor of two Indian literary magazines (*The Spectator* and *The Observer*), and he later served as Mayor of Port-of-Spain between 1957 and 1960.

The issue of race also affected the federation. In March 1954, a confidential despatch from William Maddox, the American Consul General, in Port-of-Spain, to Washington noted the Indian factor:

> Victor BRYAN, the Colonial Secretary said, was all for postponement, and this was difficult to understand since the Africans of Trinidad have much to gain in consolidating their position in what would be a predominantly African federal legislature to protect themselves against the rapidly-growing East Indian population of this Colony. In this connection, it is also difficult to understand the apparently favourable disposition towards federation manifested by Sinanan, an East Indian leader. The East Indian group of politicians, in general, have been lukewarm, if not hostile. The Consul General suspects that Sinanan's gesture was more for the purpose of embarrassing the Government than for promoting the cause of federation.[18]

The Indian influence would again be noted by Maddox who mocked Maraj's letter to the *Trinidad Guardian* on the federation. Maddox said it demonstrated "little of intellectual coherence" and further added:

> Another important personality who has proclaimed his opposition to federation is Bhadore (sic) S. MARAJ, East Indian legislator, leader of the largest Hindu society, and founder of his own Peoples' Democratic Party, which he is presenting as a thinly-veiled racial threat in the coming campaign … The position of the East Indian in

> Trinidad (nearly 40% of the population) would also be weakened by unrestricted immigration of Africans from the neighboring islands.[19]

The American Consul General sought to identify those who were responsible for intensifying racial tension in 1955, "certain East Indians, including the Indian Commissioner, Bhadase Maraj, and the editor of the *Observer* must bear a large share of the responsibility. For in seeking to strengthen East Indian sentiment and solidarity, they have aroused the deep-seated distrust of the Indian among negroes and whites alike, who, incidentally, are not aware of the rate of population growth of the Indian element."[20]

Colonial officials had scant respect for local politicians. In 1955, the Consul General believed Mitra Sinanan, the MP for Caroni South, and a barrister from San Fernando, was an "aspiring political leader" of the Indians in Trinidad. The Consul General noted, "Within Government circles, he is regarded as crafty, untrustworthy, and unpredictable."[21] This contempt for locals was the norm for officials from Britain and the United States.

On 22 February 1956, Maraj convened a meeting of heads of political parties in the colony. The parties that attended were the People's Democratic Party (PDP), Trinidad Labour Party (TLP), National Democratic Party, West Indian Independence Party (WIIP) and Butler Party. The American Consul General identified these parties as "socialist" and felt Maraj wanted to form a "socialist bloc." This was an unsubstantiated claim from the Consul General who was also aware of Maraj's political acumen:

> Since the political parties in Trinidad are personally controlled organizations for the most part, Maraj, with his increasing power and influence, should have no difficulty in dominating the WIIP and TLP leaders in the event of a coalition … There are no indications that the more influential parties are prepared to cooperate with Maraj. The Butler Party has demonstrated no willingness to enter into an alliance with Maraj at this time (T.U.B. Butler, Chief Servant is still in England) and Dr. Eric Williams, political leader of the new People's National Movement, although invited to the meeting called by Maraj, is said to have declined participation on the pretext of having a prior engagement.[22]

The American Consul General, Douglas Jenkins, in June 1956, made condescending remarks about Maraj's "swashbuckling campaign" in the northern Caroni district, "His speeches are interlarded with threats and boasts and consist primarily of a recital of what he has done for the sugar workers and cane farmers with frequent references to the fact that he financed the sugar strike of 1954."[23] There was a concern that the divisiveness among the political parties could lead to a fragile and weak government in which Maraj and the Hindu-dominated PDP would have political dominance.[24] One writer in the *Trinidad Chronicle* believed that a coalition between the POPPG and the PNM was necessary to prevent PDP from gaining political power.[25] This reflected the fears among a segment of the population that political power among Indians/Hindus would have a disastrous effect on the colony.

Selwyn Ryan claimed that Williams promoted polarization among Muslims, Christian Indians, progressive/reformist Hindus and orthodox Hindus. Williams achieved this by first branding the Maha Sabha in Trinidad as being linked to the fanatical Hindu Maha Sabha based in India. Further, he stereotyped the PDP as the "political voice of the Maha Sabha."[26] Maraj helped promote secular and religious education and was considered the "Nehru of Trinidad" primarily because he helped fund the building of temples and Hindu schools.

In 1956, Maraj had served three and one-half years as the head of the Maha Sabha. During this time, thirty-one primary schools were built and ten more were under construction. Douglas Jenkins, American Consul General, analysed Maraj's character and influence within the Maha Sabha:

> Maraj is well able to take advantage of the credit given to him for being the driving force behind the building program and the mainspring of the effort to make the organization the important, closely-knit society it now is. Maraj, undoubtedly, finds the organization a convenient vehicle to increase popularity. He also uses to good advantage the gratitude of the underprivileged members whom he helps with personal loans and other hand-outs in the true manner of the lower level party politician.[27]

In March 1956, the American Consul also revealed the private discussions with another diplomat who was in contact with Maraj:

> It has been learned from the Acting Commissioner for India, who, incidentally, does not pride himself on his acquaintanceship with Maraj, that the ego of the creator

> of the PDP has become so inflated by his various successes of late that he is now openly boasting that he will organize a panel of East Indian candidates who, with his support, will sweep the polls in the next general elections for the Legislative Council ... Moreover, according to the Indian Commissioner, Maraj in working toward the election to the Legislative Council of a majority of East Indian representatives will surely concentrate on those who will look to him as their acknowledged leader and do his bidding.[28]

Despite contesting fourteen of twenty-four seats, Maraj felt the PDP would win the majority of seats in the Legislative Council. The confidence was also due to the fact that he funded the Butlerites.[29]

The anti-Indian views of Williams prevailed in 1958 when the PNM was defeated in the federal elections. Williams, who was the leader of the PNM, penned an article entitled "The Danger facing Trinidad, Tobago and the WI. Nation" which was published in the party newspaper *PNM Weekly* (later to be re-named *The Nation*). He did not fully appreciate the Indian identity:

> PNM's decimation in areas with a preponderance of Indian votes reflects the DLP campaign and the DLP's appeal that Indians should vote for Governor and DLP so as to ensure an Indian Prime Minister. Religion figured prominently in their campaign ... The Indian nation is in India. It is a respectable, reputable nation ... It would repudiate any such divisive attempts as are being made in Trinidad.[30]

Williams was bitter when he wrote of "the recalcitrant and hostile minority of the West Indian nation masquerading as 'the Indian nation' and prostituting the name of India for its selfish, reactionary political ideals."[31] Williams also expressed sentiments to a large crowd at the University of Woodford Square whilst Winston Mahabir, an Indo-Trinidadian and a member of the PNM, was in attendance. Mahabir was horrified and in his autobiography highlighted the impact of the presentation, which

> contained generous ingredients of abuse of the Indian community which was deemed to be a "hostile and recalcitrant minority." The Indian community represented the greatest danger facing the country. It was an impediment to West Indian progress. It had caused P.N.M. to lose the federal elections. There were savagely contemptuous

> references to the Indian illiterates of the country areas who were threatening to submerge the masses whom Williams had enlightened.[32]

This speech by Williams seemed to prove that all citizens were not viewed equally by the beloved "Father of the Nation." This blunder by Williams further polarized the colony's two major ethnic groups. Brinsley Samaroo believed the Indians in Trinidad and Tobago have never forgiven Williams for making this statement.[33]

In retrospect, the statement by Williams was aimed at those who did not support him in the federal elections. It should not be interpreted that Williams and the PNM were always anti-Indian. A considerable number of Indians belonging to the Islamic faith, particularly those residing in the areas of San Juan and St Joseph in North Trinidad, were staunch supporters of the PNM. This was largely attributed to the influence of Kamaluddin Mohammed, Minister in the government and parliamentary representative, of the PNM. Thus, it was no surprise when *The Nation* published Ramadan greetings from Williams and Eid messages.[34] In addition to the support of Muslims, the Vedic and Christian Indians supported the PNM rather than the PDP, which comprised mostly Hindus.[35]

In 1958, Williams boasted of the "solidly inter-racial" face of his party's legislative team that had two Mayors and Ministers of Indian ancestry, one Parliamentary Secretary and one Federal Legislator-elect of Chinese ancestry. Williams believed, "And it is better a hundred times for them to have lost on the PNM ticket of inter-racial solidarity than to have won on the DLP ticket of racial chauvinism."[36]

Many persons continue to question the supposedly equal treatment that Williams displayed to all citizens of Trinidad and Tobago whilst he was Prime Minister. In 1996, at an Eric Williams conference, Kenneth Parmasad, a Black Power activist and university lecturer, argued that for Williams "recalcitrant" signified "any person or group who went against the grain of what he perceived to be the working-out of his nationalist project."[37] Parmasad noted that creolization was the main agenda of Williams and the Prime Minister sought to implement "a cultural system with specific intention of achieving his nationalist agenda in a society noted for its cultural diversity."[38]

Municipal elections

Representatives of labour also contested the local elections. Some were fortunate whilst others were unable to attract the electorate. On 22 May 1956, the failure to win a by-election for a seat on the Port-of-Spain City Council reflected the lack of support for parties considered Communist. The seat was won by Joseph Castillo of the POPPG, who earned 646 votes. One of the unsuccessful candidates, Lennox Pierre, who was head of the WIIP, received 239 votes. In the by-election campaign, Pierre was publicly endorsed by John Rojas, head of the Caribbean National Labour Party (CNLP).[39] The POPPG comprised one-third of the City Council but could be outvoted by the labour representatives.

Civil Service Association

The Civil Service Association was one of the most powerful unions during the 1950s. In 1956, the headline of *The Clarion* was "HANDS OFF THE CIVIL SERVICE: Political Meddling Must Stop." The writer noted Cecil Kelsick was to act as Attorney General of Trinidad and Tobago whilst the Acting Attorney General Ellis Clarke attended a conference in Barbados. The article questioned Kelsick's ability and experience since he arrived in Trinidad less than three years ago to fill the post of assistant legal draughtsman. That the post of Assistant to the Attorney General was created for Wilfred Ferguson was also mentioned.[40]

In a letter to the editor of *The Clarion*, E. R. L. Ward attempted to explain the reason for the existence of foreigners in senior posts in the Civil Services in Trinidad. Ward's assumption was that Trinidadians were not willing to accept posts outside of Trinidad.[41] In November 1954, the Acting General Manager of the Port invited government employees, including Albert Gomes, to the annual Christmas banquet. Staff employees of the Port Services Department threatened to boycott the event claiming, "Other people dined, wined and abused them but we will not have them at all."[42] The letter urging employees of the Port Services Department to boycott the banquet was not supported by the Civil Service Association. The CSA stated its "disapproval" and referred to it as a "most inappropriate, inelegant and discourteous gesture towards our Government."[43] The origin of the dissatisfaction of the employees was the recommendation to have them placed under the control of an Executive Board. This would result in the workers being deprived of the "security of tenure" and their "civil service status."

The CSA and Legal Officers disapproved the recommendation by the government that Ellis Clarke be appointed as Solicitor General as C. V. Archer was being promoted to the Judiciary. The CSA protested against the principle involved, and consequently, the Secretary of State for the Colonies rejected the recommendation.[44] James Millette, a lecturer at the University of the West Indies, noted that the problems facing the Civil Services in the era of independence were due to "attitudes," "relationships" and "skills" that were inherited from the "old colonial system."[45] The CSA was one of the prominent voices that aired their grievances whenever they saw injustices.

Federated Workers Trade Union and Trinidad and Tobago Electricity Commission

The Federated Workers Trade Union (FWTU) was able to effectively deal with some of the unruly employers who ignored the plight of workers. On 2 February 1953, Balocco, Manager of the Tavern on the Green, dismissed seven employees who were members of the FWTU and two were eventually re-hired. Among those fired union workers were Abraham Daniel, Ali Mohammed and Chas Seaton. Dudley Mahon, President of FWTU, sought to meet with the Manager who refused to meet with the union. Subsequently, on 3 February, the FWTU wrote to the Commissioner of Labour complaining of the Manager's behaviour. This resulted in talks between the union and Balocco, with the meeting chaired by the Chief Labour Officer.[46] The four-day strike, which ended on 15 July, resulted in the management reinstating the five dismissed workers, without any salary loss.[47] The saga did not end and on 14 September, the FWTU met with the Manager to discuss working conditions and salaries. He walked off and refused to continue any dialogue with the union.[48]

The proactive union had a presence on the island's major estates. The FWTU had an agreement with respect to the working conditions and wages of workers on estates in Icacos and Cedros, Columbia, St Andrew, St Quentin, Perseverance, Constance and St Marie. The managers and representatives of the FWTU met to discuss the regular employment of workers. During negotiations, this issue was left "in abeyance to be discussed at some future date."[49] On 4 January 1953, the Manager of the St Marie Estates published a list of workers to be retrenched. The FWTU's Shop Steward was also on the list of names, and he was refused an audience with the Manager of the estate. This unfair treatment did not go unnoticed. A month later, a peaceful strike commenced on the coconut estate of Ste Marie and a few weeks later, the strikes had spread to Icacos and Cedros Estates.[50] The striking workers were not paid during their protest action. Quintin O'Connor commented on the strike action in Icacos, "No Union can survive if the employer has the power to retrench workers active in the Union on the plausible excuse of seasonal decrease in the need for labour."[51]

The leaders of the strike, Manmohansingh and Bridgemohansingh, approached Butler for support in the strike. On 9 April, Butler went to Cedros where he held a meeting and distributed membership cards. Butler organized another meeting at Fullerton but faced hostility as missiles were thrown at him. O'Connor saw these meetings as failed efforts of the Butlerites to "stab" the FWTU.[52] This was not an isolated incident, and the union was soon faced with more challenges.

The FWTU was plagued by internal problems. In April 1953, FWTU workers employed with British West Indian Airways (BWIA) decided to leave the union and formed the Aero Services Union. This new union agreed not to discriminate against other union members at BWIA.[53] Such actions contributed to friction within the labour movement.

The workers employed with the Port-of-Spain Corporation Electricity Board decided to strike. In January 1955, Quintin O'Connor noted that this Electricity Board "lacked proper guidance and trade union leadership." He felt these workers should be organized as their comrades in the Trinidad and Tobago Electricity Commission (T&TEC). He added that the management of the Electrical Board "never loved trade unionism."[54]

The disunity never disappeared. In 1956, O'Connor accused the relatively small Works and Hydraulics Union (founded by C. P. Alexander) of luring members of the FWTU to their union. O'Connor also alleged that the Union of Commercial and Industrial Workers poached members of the FWTU employed at the Port-of-Spain Corporation Electricity Board. In addition, O'Connor also claimed that Butler attempted but failed to recruit members from the FWTU.[55]

Women

Women played a crucial role in trade unions during the 1950s and 1960s. During the 1949 municipal election campaign in Port-of-Spain and Borough of San Fernando and Arima, *The Clarion* noted, "The women of the movement are eager to play their part, and in a few weeks Sections, Federations and Advisory Councils will have information about plans for special women's activities, beginning with a series of Regional Women's Conferences in February and March."[56] In 1956, May Day celebrations were organized by the Trinidad and Tobago TUC in San Fernando. Resolutions were moved by Miss Christina F. Lewis and seconded by Miss Ursula Rodriguez. Both were females of the Caribbean Women's National Assembly. Resolutions were to establish Convalescent Homes for Adults in the northern and southern parts of the island.

During 1965 and 1966, the WFP had female members such as Mrs E. Gonzales of Palo Seco and Mrs C. Phil of Pleasantville. Unfortunately, there were no women in the Central Committee of the party.

Sugar and cocoa

Attempts were made by the government to prevent disruptions in the sugar industry in Trinidad and Tobago. In April 1951, the government appointed eight persons as members of the Sugar Industry Labour Welfare Fund Committee. Among the unionists appointed were Quintin O'Connor and L. S. Seukeran. In November 1954, there was a strike among workers at Usine Ste Madeleine Sugar Estate. As a result, the workers from Brechin Castle and Caroni Estates Limited "formed themselves into a union" and staged a strike. This was largely because the management ignored the grievances of workers. One employee at Brechin Castle declared, "Now we are united and even though we work every day we will just do nothing until the Management comes to our terms and conditions."[57]

In early 1955, O'Connor offered advice to workers in sugar unions after their successful strike, "They must leave politics out of the Union, this victory must not be used with the object of getting seats on the Legislative Council." He also advocated the need for two sugar unions and cane farmers association to "form proper executive committees and have proper rules." O'Connor sincerely believed that one of the first steps in achieving this was for workers to hold important posts on Executive Committees.[58]

On 5 January 1955, a strike of sugar workers began on the Palmiste Estate in San Fernando, in South Trinidad. The employers sought to end the strike by using other workers, but they were unsuccessful.[59] The grievances of the sugar workers were for recognition, better working conditions and higher wages. The FWTU asked the Labour Commissioner to appoint a Commission of Inquiry. Quintin O'Connor, in his column "Trade Union Notes," argued that normal trade union procedure was that the dispute should be sent to the Arbitration Tribunal and not to the Board of Inquiry.

In the early months of 1956, there was a strike in the sugar industry. The SMA rejected peaceful efforts to end the strike and refused to deal with the ATSE+FWTU as they stated it would "jeopardise the entire future of the Industry."[60] Furthermore, the Sugar Manufacturers issued a release that the strike was "uncalled for and in breach of the agreement."[61] An ad hoc group, the National Trade Union Delegation, was formed to facilitate a peaceful resolution to the standoff between the Sugar Manufacturers and ATSE+FWTU. However, the delegation failed, and the Sugar Manufacturers were victorious.

The defeat made the delegation (comprising representatives from TUC and Trinidad and Tobago Federation of Trade Unions) more aware of the need for labour unity. The delegation held a meeting and Sam Worrell (Secretary of SWWTU and President of Trinidad and Tobago Federation of Trade Unions) moved a resolution calling for "industrial unity of the Trade Union Movement."[62] The resolution received unanimous support. Subsequently, a meeting was organized on 10 June 1956 in Port-of-Spain, and representatives from twenty-four active unions in Trinidad and Tobago were invited to attend.[63] Almost a week later, O'Connor noted, in *The Clarion*, that trade unionism within the sugar industry needed to be "saved" and hoped the sugar strike would be a lesson for all leaders, "I am sincerely hoping that the trade union movement would be united and that in the future no union would go on strike without consulting the whole movement."[64] This plea would resonate among most unions but complete unity was elusive.

The American Consulate General, in 1956, noted Maraj's influence within the sugar industry:

> Also, he is reported to have been invited to be a patron of the recently organized Sugar Worker's Union, which (probably with the good wishes if not more substantial support from the sugar manufacturers) is seeking to supplant the All Trinidad Sugar Estate and Factory Workers Trade Union. Maraj, however, did not see fit to accept the invitation at this time. The USWU, weak in membership and torn with internal dissension, is far from a sure bet, which probably accounts for Maraj's reluctance to associate himself with it.[65]

And, in March 1956, the American Consul General noted that Maraj "is working overtime to bring sugar workers into his political camp."[66]

In 1952, the Trinidad government passed the Exportation of Cocoa Ordinance. This allowed the creation of the Cocoa Exporters Committee.[67] The power of this committee included providing permits to the Cocoa Planters Association and producers to export cocoa. In 1954, the Peasant

Cocoa Proprietors Limited was formed. It represented 120 peasant proprietors, and they produced approximately 400,000 lbs of cocoa.[68] However, in early 1955, the members of the Peasant Cocoa Proprietors Limited were denied a permit to export their produce. No action was taken even though an appeal was made to the colony's Governor. The Independent Labour Party (ILP) planned to address this issue of the Peasant Cocoa Proprietors Limited at a meeting at Sangre Grande and also in the Legislative Council.

More than a decade later, sugar remained a prominent national issue. In 1965, Ronald Hoolasie explained his concept of the modernization of sugar, "It means that Sugar will not be controlled by expatriates and the privileged Paternalism must cease and only then will Trinidadians feel that Sugar is theirs."[69] It was painfully obvious that even after independence had been achieved in 1962, citizens of Trinidad and Tobago did not have full control of this vital industry.

Seafarers Union, Seamen and Waterfront Workers' Trade Union and Teachers' Union

In February 1951, the newly established Seafarers Union accused Albert Gomes, the Minister of Labour, of ignoring their two letters which outlined their grievances. The union, with a membership of 450 seamen, indicated, via letters, that their members faced "discriminatory practices" by the shipping companies. The union stressed the need for legislation to rectify the situation in which less than 1 per cent of the Trinidad seamen were employed on ships entering the Port-of-Spain harbour. In addition, the union complained that the Seamen's Welfare Office had ignored their interests.[70] Gomes seemed incapable of resolving this situation.

In late 1951, the Trinidad and Tobago Seafarers Union, with a membership of approximately 600 persons, convened in Port-of-Spain and held its election. The union re-elected C. B. Mathura for another term as President. Mathura, a Port-of-Spain Councillor, in his message, thanked the members "for their struggle at sea in the common cause against Nazism and Fascism."[71] D. C. Allette, the Union Organizer, praised Mathura for his "dauntless fight for the Union" and praised him as "a true leader of the Working Class people, irrespective to race or creed."[72]

The united stance of the capitalist status quo was apparent during the protests. In May 1956, the negotiations between the SWWTU and the Port Authorities were stalled. This was because the SWWTU threatened to impose an embargo on sugar if the Sugar Manufacturers continued their negotiations with the ATSE+FWTU. The Shipping Federation also sided with Port Authorities.[73] All three establishments – Caroni Limited, Shipping Federation and Port Authority – did not want the sugar embargo.

Two rival unions representing teachers – the Teachers' Union and Teachers' Federation – became embroiled in politics. Albert Gomes (the Minister of Labour, Industry and Commerce) accepted an invitation by the Teachers' Union to speak on the federation. This resulted in the Teachers' Federation, favoured by Roy Joseph (Minister of Education and Social Services), to protest the invitation. The influence of government to divide the teachers is obvious, "Our high ranking Civil Servants, anxious to keep in good ministerial graces, have constantly favoured the Federation." Furthermore, *The Clarion* reported that "threats" and "blandishments" were used "to lure the teachers away from their longtime Teachers' Union … Teachers who would not join the Federation, were transferred, on grounds of administrative convenience, to distant and inconvenient schools. In one case increments were withheld."[74] In April 1956, the controversial headline in *The Clarion* was "Teachers Bribed with Discounts: Stooge Union Subsidised." The publication accused the Teachers' Federation of "vindictiveness" by seeking to attract teachers by providing a membership card with discounts from selected stores in Port-of-Spain, San Fernando and Couva.[75]

Laundry, postal service, railway workers

Smaller working-class bodies also voiced their concerns and protested. In 1949, nineteen signal men of Trinidad Government Railways and thirty-two men of the Kelly Village from the Works and Hydraulics Department were fired. The FWTU noted that this action created "considerable amount of bitterness among the workers and the various Trade Unions" and asked a pertinent question: "Why these two departments continue to be run in such an incompetent manner?"[76]

In 1951, workers of Trinidad Steam Laundry went on strike. John La Rose, Chairman of the Strike Action Committee, condemned the action of the Commissioner of Labour and Minister of Labour who sympathized with employers and sought to break the strike.[77]

In 1954, the General Manager of Trinidad Government Railways, Dennis Eyre, faced hostile workers who invaded his office. They demanded their four and a half cents per hour increase that was given by the government to all their daily paid workers.[78]

There were incidents that indicated workers were being ignored. An illustration is the closure of the Postal Agency at Blanchisseuse due to the postmistress striking for more wages. *The Clarion* referred to her meagre salary as "sweated labour" and "a disgrace to the Postal Authorities."[79] One officer in the Trinidad and Tobago Postmen's Union (TTPU), Yussuf Ali, was on the American Embassy's radar as a potential leader in Trinidad and Tobago. In 1966, Ali was a former student of the American Institute for Free Labor Development in Washington.[80]

In April 1956, approximately seventy-five workers of the City Council demonstrated through the streets of Port-of-Spain demanding increased wages and back pay.[81]

Credit unions and co-operative movements

The labour systems of slavery and indentureship generated forms of credit arrangements. During the nineteenth and twentieth centuries, the Africans had sou-sou, which was a rotating credit system, the Indians had chitty while the Chinese had hui. In 1916, the Agricultural Credit Societies Ordinance (Chapter 23, No. 4) was passed. This legislation legitimized co-operative activities as it allowed for the registration and control of these societies in Trinidad and Tobago.

Credit unions played an invaluable role in the Caribbean during the twentieth century. On 12 September 1941, as a result of the efforts of the Roman Catholic Church, the first Jamaican Credit Union was registered.[82] A few months later, in 1942, Solicitor Malcolm Milne and a team from Trinidad and Tobago made a trip to Jamaica to better understand the benefits of the credit union.

In October 1944, the Cathedral Union came into existence. Later, on 29 December 1945, credit unions became a legal entity after the passage of the Credit Union Co-operative Ordinance (No. 48 of 1945). On 6 August 1946, the Health Services Credit Union became the first registered credit union in Trinidad and Tobago. Thirty credit unions were registered between August and December 1946. The nurturing of the co-operative movement was largely due to the founding of the Co-operative Department in 1949.[83] This had a positive impact on society, and from 1946 to 1956, there were 236 registered credit societies.

The Credit Union League of Trinidad and Tobago held a public meeting on 30 April 1951 at the Public Library, in Port-of-Spain. The objective of the meeting was to address "the problems with which the movement is confronted and to consider ways and means to overcome them."[84] In 1956, delegates from the Friendly Societies and the Co-operative Movement brought greetings to the May Day observances in Tobago. In the same year, another major development was the creation of the Credit Union Cooperative Bank Limited of Trinidad and Tobago.

W. P. Watkins, in an article titled "Co-operative Movements in the Colonies," noted that the movement was vital to the colonies as "its principles of economy, democracy, and social justice make it one of the best instruments for assisting backward peoples through their transition into the modern world and educating them to become the architects of their own liberties."[85] This was an attempt to promote the co-operative movement, but it was a conservative view. Watkins contended that if the goal of the co-operative movement is to direct its own course, then it is time for the roles of supervision and control by the Registrar to be given to co-operative unions.[86]

Federation

Since the 1920s, the British West Indian labour leaders clamoured for federation and self-government. Their contributions were discernible at regional labour conferences, private discussions with colonial officials and occasional articles in the local newspapers. These strategies failed to change Britain's stubborn refusal to grant political independence to the region. The TWA's adherence to the concept of regional unity was obvious in its assistance to the embryonic working-class movement in such colonies as British Guiana, Barbados and Grenada.

By the 1950s, the trade unions were confronted with a working-class population that was already class-conscious and politically awakened. Union leaders were becoming more militant in their attacks on colonialism and demands for federation. The different nationalities of Trinidad and Tobago's working class seemed a microcosm of regional unity. In the oilfields in South Trinidad and parts of Port-of-Spain, there was a considerable presence of immigrant labour from the colonies of Grenada, St Vincent and Barbados. Also, foreign labourers from the nearby British West Indian colonies were employed on the American bases in Trinidad; these workers were able to peacefully coexist in Trinidad and did not precipitate into violence.

On 6 October 1952, Butler held a meeting at Woodford Square to demand "a free and equal status for a West Indian Federation within the British Commonwealth." Maddox, the American Consul General, did not see Butler as a threat, "The cause of a self-governing West Indian Federation has a pretty ring to it and may serve Butler a purpose for the moment, but self-governance for any such Federation is too remote from present-day political realities to satisfy for long his megalomanical (sic) cravings for action and power."[87]

The attraction of Trinidad has also been seen as one of the reasons for supporting federation, "And it is unrestricted opportunity to migrate to industrial Trinidad that has helped to bring some of these Colonies onto the Federation."[88] The issue of federation was occasionally discussed in *The Clarion*. An article entitled "West Indian Federation: A Forgotten

Dream" revealed there was "general apathy" and "little public opinion on the issue of federation." In addition, it was noted that "labour bodies have on the whole been silent," and that "a Federated West Indies should considerably increase the Labour say in the scheme of things."[89] This was an interesting observation that revealed the ignorance and lack of interest among the working class.

In June 1953, *The Clarion* began publishing an informative series of articles entitled "No Federation without Dominion Status." The first article called "Crown Colony Rule Must Go" summarized the recent effort. These included the 1932 conference of the Caribbean Labour Congress and the Standing Closer Association Committee of 1949.[90] The articles would have given the working class a better perspective of the evolution of the campaign for self-government. Interestingly, *The Clarion* sought views from persons such as H. P. Singh, editor of *The Observer*, and a merchant who said, "From the point of view of the workers, Federation would be an unwelcome guest for the worker would see Federation just as a ship conveying thousands of people from the other islands to this colony to compete with them for employment."[91] Quintin O'Connor, Secretary of the Federated Workers Trade Union and Secretary General of the TTTUC, stated that he was fully in support of federation with independence. O'Connor, a former city Councillor and an official of the WIIP, believed that the discussion of the free movement of peoples among the colonies depended on the impact of federation.[92] Lennox Pierre and John La Rose, Chairman and Provisional Secretary of the WIIP, respectively, claimed that the view of WIIP was that "any plans for Federation should not be put into effect without a Referendum."[93]

The Rance Committee recommended that Trinidad be the site of the federal capital; then, in April 1953, at the London Conference, British West Indian delegates voted that Grenada be the site. The contentious issue was not amicably resolved. The American Consul General noted thus: "The decision was not well received in Trinidad," and it was uncertain as to whether Gomes could influence fellow Executive Councillors to support federation.[94]

In November 1954, an article entitled "Dr. Eric Williams – Is he a Propagandist?" was published in *The Clarion*, the local working-class newspaper. The anonymous author was critical of a public lecture delivered by Williams who accused Indians in Trinidad and Tobago of opposing federation due to racial prejudice. It seemed that Williams used the Indian factor as a scapegoat instead of seeking to unearth the real reason for the general lack of interest in federation. In a defensive tone, the author of *The Clarion* article referred to Williams as "an intellectual snub" and argued that "Indians have always been in the forefront of the struggle against Imperialism and Colonialism wherever they have gone, and Trinidad is no exception … There can be no fear of Indians not integrating with the other races here."[95] There were other signs that federation would collapse due to the lack of unity among the political leaders in the Caribbean. Maddox, the American Consul General, in a despatch in 1954 noted thus:

> It is clear that the federation issue had become a political football being kicked back and forth among Trinidad, Jamaica and Barbados. None of them wishes to go on record as rejecting it, none appears to be an enthusiastic supporter of the London report, and each seems to be waiting for the others to act first. There is no telling how long this jockeying may continue. The danger for any one of them will remain that the other two will "gang up" in an agreement to act favourably, and leave that one "holding the bag."[96]

Two years later, the Consulate General in Trinidad felt something was amiss among the leaders, "It was a bit of a surprise, therefore, when the PNM was not included in the recently established West Indian Federation of Socialist Parties. Mr. Manley has indicated that the situation in Trinidad with its plethora of parties is so obscure at present that it was not possible for the founding group to settle on any individual party in the Colony."[97] This public view of Manley might not be accurate because Eric Gairy, one of the founding members of the West Indian Federation of Socialist Parties, was present on a PDP platform in 1956. To have a Caribbean leader at one of his political meetings was a major achievement for Maraj.

Notwithstanding the perception of harmony, there were concerns at the conference in London on the West Indian Federation held in 1956:

> Jamaica fears that with Customs Union its home markets will be thrown open to Trinidad manufacturers and that Jamaican industry with its relatively high costs will be unable to meet the competition … Trinidad had similar fears that its economy would be dislocated by an unregulated influx of hordes of neighbouring West Indians in the smaller islands.[98]

The view of *The Clarion* was that "moral leadership in the cause of West Indian nationhood has clearly passed on to Jamaica. Trinidad now commands no respect." The advice for Trinidadians to seek the federal capital seemed simplistic, "We must assert ourselves as the moral leaders, in the fight for freedom. We must harness our energies to organizing our political life."[99]

Trade union bodies

The protests erupting in Trinidad and Tobago were not isolated incidents. In 1955, in towns of Gold Coast (in Africa), teachers were striking for higher wages. In Johannesburg, in South Africa, workers launched a campaign to end victimization and retrenchment, and they demanded higher wages. Likewise in Singapore, due to the breakdown in bargaining with the bank's association, the workers of eleven banks opted to strike.

Workers at Godchaux Sugar Factory in Louisiana, United States, were on strike for seven months. This strike occurred amidst dismissals and arrests. And, in three states (Arkansas, Illinois and Missouri) in the United States, 29,000 workers from fifty-nine factories of the International Shoe Company and the Brown Shoe Company went on strike.[100] The close relationship with British unions meant that colonial unions lacked a unique identity. They were modelled on British unions, but, more importantly, these smaller unions were closely monitored.

Trades Union Congress and International Confederation of Free Trade Unions

The unions in the Caribbean colonies regularly sought guidance and advice from international bodies such as the Trades Union Congress (TUC) and the International Confederation of Free Trade Unions (ICFTU). By

1951, the TUC had a membership of 1,037 unions with more than 616,000 members. The TUC General Council in Britain, in 1947, established the Council Fund and was able to assist unions in the colonies. This included £500 to Jamaica TUC and £250 to the British Guiana Labour Union. In addition, the British TUC brought trade unionists from Kenya, Trinidad, Nigeria and British Guiana to be trained at Ruskin College, Oxford, and at the TUC headquarters.[101]

In May 1951, George Woodcock, Assistant General Secretary of the British TUC, visited Trinidad. Prior to his departure, he advised that leaders of trade unions should not have political ambitions because this would undermine the trade union movement. Woodcock cited the conflict between the local TUC and the ICFTU, which resulted in the departure of the SWWTU and Railway Union from the TUC. He said, "I hope that it will be possible to get all the organisations to fight under a common unified movement … I do not believe in a multiplicity of trade unions."[102]

On 26 January 1955, the TUC General Council held a meeting in London to discuss attempts by trade unions of the Soviet Union and other Iron Curtain countries to "penetrate" trade unions in Britain.[103] The ICFTU rejected efforts to establish good communications with the Communist-dominated WFTU.

The TUC in Britain communicated with trade unions in twenty-nine colonies. It provided scholarships for members of these unions and "made grants towards the cost of new office buildings for them or helped with their rent." The TUC also sent trained unionists to these territories "to advise Colonial Unions on the correct ways to negotiate in disputes and in other problems. Many of these missions were undertaken in conjunction with the ICFTU."[104] The TUC also advised representatives of colonial employers in Britain on workers' rights.

The Secretary of the TTTUC, Quinton O'Connor, had a regular column titled "Trade Union Notes" in *The Clarion*. The local arm of the TUC felt there should be a National Injuries Act, as the one in Britain, implemented in Trinidad and Tobago to protect workers.[105] O'Connor served on an apparently ineffective Sugar Wages Council and later appealed for the creation of a Wages Council to ensure salaries of unorganized workers would be "fixed by statutory machinery."[106] O'Connor also felt the poorly organized Industrial Relations Department of the government resulted in the delay in labour issues such as trade disputes being resolved.[107]

When there were employer-union disputes and negotiations failed, a tribunal was established under the Arbitration Ordinance. The Governor would appoint the Arbitrator or a Chairman to head the tribunal which comprised two other persons. It was often difficult to find relevant persons to be part of this tribunal. To avoid political interference, O'Connor publicly clamoured for an Industrial Court. This special court was not to be aligned or controlled by the government but established as part of the judicial system.[108]

From its formation in 1949, the ICFTU had an impressive growth. By 1951 the union boasted a membership of 52 million across sixty countries.[109] During the 1950s, the widening rift between the local branches of the TUC and ICFTU was public knowledge. Quintin O'Connor in his column argued that the TUC sought to promote unity in the trade union movement but some leaders within the ICFTU "are doing all in their power to split the movement."[110]

Conclusion

In the embryonic stage of his political ambitions, Williams was both a speaker and advisor for various workers and trade unions. He spoke to sugar workers, fishermen, stevedores, steelbandsmen and labourers in the coconut industry. Williams had links with the labour movement but he encouraged no political accommodation with trade unions. He steered clear of any political association with the island's trade union organizations. Williams understood the problems of interacting with the multiplicity of workers' unions, and, most significantly, he understood the dangers of courting the major unions in the sugar and oil industries with their different ethnic bases and their failed attempts at unity.

Notes

1. *The Clarion* 18 August 1951.
2. *The Clarion* 29 January 1949.
3. Despatch from American Consul to Department of State, Washington, 28 June 1956, National Archives, Maryland, United States (unless otherwise noted, all similar correspondences are part of this archival collection).
4. *The Clarion* 7 February 1953.
5. *The Clarion* 2 June 1951.
6. *The Clarion* 29 February 1956.
7. *The Clarion* 20 January 1951.
8. *The Clarion* 21 April 1951.
9. *The Clarion* 7 February 1953.
10. *The Clarion* 5 March 1955.
11. *The Clarion* 29 February 1956.
12. Paul Sutton, Forged from the Love of Liberty: Selected Speeches of Dr. Eric Williams (Port of Spain: Longman Caribbean), 208–209.
13. Colin Palmer, *Eric Williams and the Making of the Modern Caribbean* (Chapel Hill: University of North Carolina Press, 2008), 262.
14. Palmer, *Eric Williams and the Making of the Modern Caribbean*, 263.
15. *The Clarion* 10 March 1951.
16. *The Clarion* 19 June 1954.
17. *The Clarion* 16 June 1956.
18. Confidential despatch from William Maddox to Department of State, 16 March 1954.
19. Confidential despatch from American Consul General Port-of-Spain to Department of State, 14 May 1954.
20. Despatch from American Consul General to Department of State, 24 January 1955.
21. Despatch from American Consul General to Department of State, 24 January 1955.
22. Confidential despatch from American Consul General to Department of State, 2 March 1956.
23. Despatch from American Consul to Department of State, 28 June 1956.
24. *TG* 3 July 1956.
25. *Trinidad Chronicle* 11 July 1956.
26. Selwyn Ryan, *Eric Williams: The Myth and the Man* (Jamaica: University of the West Indies Press, 2009), 123–124.
27. Despatch from American Consul General to Department of State, 2 March 1956.
28. Despatch from American Consul General to Department of State, 2 March 1956.
29. Ryan, *Eric Williams*, 122.
30. *PNM Weekly* 21 April 1958.

31. *PNM Weekly* 21 April 1958.
32. Winston Mahabir, *In and Out of Politics* (Port-of-Spain: Inprint, 1975), 78.
33. Brinsley Samaroo, "The Race Factor in the Independence Discussions at Marlborough House, 1962," *Caribbean Issues* 8 (1) (March 1998), 127.
34. *The Nation* 27 December 1968, 12 December 1969.
35. Ryan, *Eric Williams*, 14.
36. *PNM Weekly* 21 April 1958.
37. Kenneth Parmasad, "Among a Recalcitrant People," *Caribbean Issues* 8 (2) (March 1999), 77.
38. Parmasad, "Among a Recalcitrant People," 79.
39. Despatch from Douglas Jenkins to Department of State, 25 May 1956.
40. *The Clarion* 26 May 1956.
41. *The Clarion* 19 June 1954.
42. *The Clarion* 20 November 1954.
43. *The Clarion* 4 December 1954.
44. *The Clarion* 18 September 1954.
45. *We The People* 6 August 1965.
46. *The Clarion* 14 February 1953.
47. *The Clarion* 18 July 1953.
48. *The Clarion* 19 September 1953.
49. *The Clarion* 28 February 1953.
50. *The Clarion* 7 March 1953.
51. *The Clarion* 14 March 1953.
52. *The Clarion* 18 April 1953.
53. *The Clarion* 25 April 1953.
54. *The Clarion* 15 January 1955.
55. *The Clarion* 11 February 1956.
56. *The Clarion* 29 January 1949.
57. *The Clarion* 20 November 1954.
58. *The Clarion* 15 January 1955.
59. *The Clarion* 5 March 1955.
60. *The Clarion* 12 May 1956.
61. *The Clarion* 12 May 1956.
62. The Chair of the meeting was John Rojas, President of the OWTU and President of the TUC.
63. *The Clarion* 19 May 1956. The headline of the article was "UNIONS SEEK UNITY."
64. *The Clarion* 26 May 1956.
65. Despatch from American Consul to Department of State, 28 June 1956.
66. Confidential despatch from American Consul to Department of State, 23 March 1956.
67. *The Clarion* 22 January 1955.

68. *The Clarion* 22 January 1955.
69. *We The People* 6 August 1965.
70. *The Clarion* 17 February 1951.
71. *The Clarion* 3 November 1951.
72. *The Clarion* 3 November 1951.
73. *The Clarion* 12 May 1956.
74. *The Clarion* 7 April 1956.
75. *The Clarion* 14 April 1956.
76. *The Clarion* 2 April 1951.
77. *The Clarion* 18 August 1951.
78. *The Clarion* 20 November 1954.
79. *The Clarion* 16 June 1951.
80. Secret telegram. American Embassy, Port-of-Spain, to Washington, 24 October 1967.
81. *The Clarion* 28 April 1956.
82. Glenn Khan, "The Credit Union Movement of Trinidad and Tobago: Its Origins, Present Status and Potential," MPhil thesis, University of the West Indies, St Augustine, 16.
83. This department was changed, in 1952, to Department of Co-operative Development and the title "Registrar of Co-operative" was changed "Commissioner of Co-operative Development."
84. *The Clarion* 21 April 1951.
85. *The Clarion* 21 March 1953.
86. *The Clarion* 21 March 1953.
87. Confidential despatch from William Maddox to Department of State, 6 October 1952.
88. Confidential despatch from American Consul General to Department of State, 14 May 1954.
89. *The Clarion* 29 January 1951.
90. *The Clarion* 20 June 1953.
91. *The Clarion* 11 July 1953.
92. *The Clarion* 11 July 1953.
93. *The Clarion* 11 July 1953.
94. Confidential despatch from American Consul General to Department of State, 14 May 1954.
95. *The Clarion* 13 November 1954.
96. Despatch from American Consul General to Department of State, 14 May 1954.
97. Despatch from American Consul General to Department of State, 28 June 1956.
98. *The Clarion* 3 March 1956.
99. *The Clarion* 10 March 1956.
100. *The Clarion* 10 December 1955.

101. *The Clarion* 14 April 1951.
102. *The Clarion* 19 May 1951.
103. *London Times* 27 January 1955.
104. *The Clarion* 12 March 1955.
105. *The Clarion* 28 March 1953.
106. *The Clarion* 9 May 1953.
107. *The Clarion* 16 May 1953.
108. *The Clarion* 23 May 1953.
109. *The Clarion* 7 July 1956.
110. *The Clarion* 11 February 1956.

Bibliography

Khan, Glenn. "The Credit Union Movement of Trinidad and Tobago: Its Origins, Present Status and Potential," MPhil thesis, University of the West Indies, St Augustine.

Palmer, Colin. *Eric Williams and the Making of the Modern Caribbean* (Chapel Hill: University of North Carolina Press, 2008).

Parmasad, Kenneth. "Among a Recalcitrant People," *Caribbean Issues* 8 (2) (March 1999).

Ryan, Selwyn. *Eric Williams: The Myth and the Man* (Jamaica: University of the West Indies Press, 2009).

CHAPTER 8

Stagnation and Progress

The Afrocentric nature of the PNM and the Indian/Hindu-based DLP were social indicators of a post-colonial plural society which was still racially and religiously polarized. The mutual distrust and fears exhibited by the two major ethnic groups, since indentureship in 1845, had not disappeared. The continuous quest for political power only served to perpetuate racism and hatred between these ethnic groups.

Political parties

During the 1950s, the continued involvement of trade unions in politics seemed unavoidable. Trinidad and Tobago was granted a new Constitution in 1950. After the results of the 1950 elections, a confidential despatch revealed the concerns of the United States, "British officials regard the inexperience and irresponsibility of many local politicians as their greatest problem in the operation of a government under the new Constitution, and their anxiety in this respect focuses largely on the work of the prospective Ministers."[1] In addition, their analysis of the election results was obvious, "The more radical vote was distributed through the agricultural and oil producing areas of the Colony."[2]

Trinidad Labour Party and Independent Labour Party

Smaller political parties made unsuccessful but valiant efforts to gain the full support of the electorate. In 1953, the opposition voices in the

Parliament were under scrutiny by working-class institutions. An illustration is the "Parliamentary Opposition Group" which was criticized by *The Clarion* for displaying its "futility" and "lack of sincerity." The opposition group no longer functioned, and its members joined the Trinidad Labour Party (TLP). The writer noted, "We believe that the Trinidad Labour Party could be a force for progress and honest administration in the present corrupt state of Trinidad Politics."[3] In 1956, the American Consul General noted that the General Secretary of the Amalgamated Engineering and General Workers' Trade Union "apparently remains loyal to the Trinidad Labour Party."[4]

In March 1955, the TLP submitted a memorandum to the Constitution Reform Committee. The party wanted "amendments to the constitution which would definitely give the people a dominant voice in the control of their affairs."[5] Among the recommendations was the establishment of a Legislative Council with twenty-eight members, eight additional seats for elected members and the Premier having the power to allocate portfolios.

In the months prior to the general elections of September 1956, the American Consul General noted the political alignment of the TLP:

> More recently it has been enjoying a rather precarious existence. With Victor Bryan and possibly Norman Tang within the fold, the TLP should take a new lease on life. Already there are rumours that the TLP and POPPG will establish a working arrangement not to cut each others (sic) throats at the election and to combine forces in the new Legislative Council to gain control of the Government.[6]

The divisions among trade unions and the emergence of opportunists were apparent in other correspondence from the American Consul General in 1956:

> Currently, there is a determined struggle for power going on among the labor leaders who are entering the political arena in greater numbers than ever before. Samuel F. Worrell, *General Secretary of the Seamen and Waterfront Workers Union*, and recently-elected President of the *Trinidad Federation of Trade Unions*, is an official of Dr. Eric Williams' *People's National Movement*. Ulric Lee, General Secretary of the *Union of Commercial and Industrial Workers*, is also understood to support Dr. Williams. John Rojas of the CNLP and Dr. Williams of the PNM are at swords' points.[7]

Such developments were a major hurdle for the labour movement in their quest for unity. This political involvement of trade unionists also weakened their ability to be an effective voice for the working class.

The Independent Labour Party (ILP) was launched at the Harris Promenade, San Fernando, in South Trinidad on 7 April 1954. The first speaker, P. T. Georges, emphasized that the goal of the party is "for a tight party organisation if the electorate was to make its wishes felt in the manner in which this country was governed."[8] Kelshall, another speaker, reassured the crowd that the party recognized democracy as "the right of every human being to have a say in the government of his affairs irrespective of race, religion, education or economic status." He also condemned the suspension of the British Guiana Constitution by the Colonial Office.

In early 1954, the ILP claimed its first electoral victory. This occurred in the by-election of the Arima Borough Council. Malcolm Nelson, the ILP candidate (with 378 votes) defeated the other two candidates – Farrier of the Tax-Payers Association and Sam Peertamsingh who had the support of two members of the Butler Party. Peertamsingh also had the unofficial support of the POPPG.[9] This signalled some working-class unity at the political level.

In 1954, the US authorities noted, "It is understood that Raymond Hamel-Smith, editor of the Clarion and spark-plug of the Socialist Independent Labour Party, intends to oppose 'Bertie' in whatever district the latter decides to stand."[10] The ILP was short-lived and eventually merged in 1956 with the TTTUC to form the CNLP.

Butlerites

The government benefitted from the schisms within the political landscape. Ellis Bonnet, American Consul in Trinidad and Tobago, acknowledged this division in 1947: "Butler's demands on Government have the forced the more conservative Labor Union leaders, willingly or unwillingly, to aline [sic] themselves openly with Government against the 'Butlerites.'"[11] Bonnet also identified the fading support of Butler:

> Butler, and his followers, must make some definite action or surrender the leadership to their discontented followers. It is doubtful if Butler will have the courage to call a general strike or any strike in the knowledge that most of the leaders of organized labor in Trinidad will instruct their followers to ignore any strike announcement he may make but Butler may be willing to challenge the effectiveness of the leadership of those Union officials.[12]

At a campaign meeting held in January 1949, Councillor C. B. Mathura predicted that the Butler Union would capture fourteen seats in general elections.[13] Unfortunately, Butler remained a threat to British rule and was under constant surveillance:

> Butler is certain to demand substantial representation on the Executive Council, and the more conservative members are equally certain to oppose him. Both will compete for the support of the other members, who will of course have aspirations of their own. Unless a series of "deals" is worked out during the next month, a stalemate is not out of the question.[14]

The divisions continued, and during the early 1950s, the apparent lack of unity among the Butlerites was often displayed. In the Legislative Council, the government-sponsored Five Year Economic Programme was debated. Members discussed whether money should be derived from "ordinary revenue by increased taxation." Among the sixteen MPs who voted to support the programme were two Butlerites: Ashford Sinanan and Mitra Sinanan. Those against were Butler, Stephen Maharaj, Ranjit Kumar and Aubrey James. Pope McClean, a Butlerite, abstained from voting.[15]

In April 1951, in an unexpected move, Mitra Sinanan, a member contesting for the seat in Caroni South, resigned from the Butler Party. Sinanan accused Butler of being "reactionary" and "anti-labour." This was a result of Butler's perspective in the debate on the Cuban pact protest.[16] *The Clarion* noted that the exit of Sinanan "will considerably weaken the strength of the Butler opposition."[17] It was the view of this working-class newspaper that Sinanan was now "freed from the stigma of irresponsibility which has attached itself to the Butler Bloc."[18]

In April 1951, Butler was suspended for eight days from the legislature for responding "That is a lie" to a statement made by Albert Gomes. After his suspension from the legislature, Butler headed to Woodford Square and held a meeting with some of his supporters.[19] Robert Hale, the American Consul General, described the trade unionist/politician as having "his usual marathon of oratory" and further made a cautious evaluation:

> Butler's and McClean's defeats in the Council, Butler's hollow threat, the resignations of Sinanan and De Freitas, and failure of the asphalt strike – justify an assumption that Butler is on the downgrade *at the present time*. But he is by no means finished as a political leader or as a threat to the Colony's stability, and it cannot yet be assumed that he has lost his ability to inflame a mob at the right moment over the right issue.[20]

In June 1956, a few months before the general elections, the party seemed in a state of disarray. A report from the American Consul General revealed that "the Butler group are floundering a bit." Further, in reference to Butler, the Consul General further noted, "The Chief's whereabouts is still shrouded in mystery and the date of his return uncertain."[21]

Liberal Party and Party of Political Progress Groups

Farquar was an MP for the DLP, but he left the party to form the Liberal Party in 1966. The party's publication, the *Liberal Standard*, was short-lived and ended in 1968. Peter Farquar was the leader of the Liberal Party when he participated in the Transport Industrial Workers Union's (TIWU) illegal bus strike for which he was sentenced to jail. He continued to serve as the political leader of the Liberal Party; however, on 23 November 1969, Henry Pain was chosen as the new President of the party. Pain was described as a "local entrepreneur and self-styled gadfly" whilst the party was referred to as "middle-class and business oriented."[22]

The American Consul General was aware of the political nuances. In 1954, he noted the impact of Gomes being re-admitted to the Party of Political Progress Groups (POPPG), "He has thus made enemies of other pretending political groups in Trinidad, each of which strives to be more 'socialistic' than the others; at the same time, some P.O.P.P.G-ites, remembering that Gomes got into office in 1950 with their support and then went "independent," are not too happy about the reassociation."[23]

The American Embassy also noted that the POPPG "is being increasingly torn by internal wrangles and dissension."[24] On 24 November 1956, the POPPG held a special convention in which Albert Gomes was elected as the party's leader. Gomes had previously served as Minister of Labour, Industry and Commerce. He felt that the party's predicament of low membership and failure to win widespread public support was due to procrastination their policy of delaying and "putting things off."[25] Gomes also said the POPPG would revive its newspaper, *Progress*. Despite being unable to win a seat in the Legislative Council and Port-of-Spain Council elections, the POPPG refused to form any alliances with parties in the opposition. Whilst Gairy seemed supportive of Gomes, the POPPG wanted an alliance with Bustamante, a Jamaican who visited Trinidad in December 1956 to consider the formation of a Federal Liberal Party. The American Embassy mentioned the entity's progress:

> The success or failure of the POPPG to rebuild itself and again to become a force in politics, local or federal, is dependent primarily on how the PNM Government carries out its mandate. The POPPG has little hope of drawing any real measure of support from the predominantly East Indian agricultural districts and must look for adherents primarily to the urban areas where it previously found strength and which are now solidly PNM.[26]

Selwyn Ryan noted the dilemma that the POPPG faced prior to the 1956 general elections as the party "had become associated in the public mind with the old regime."[27] Undoubtedly, the POPPG was losing supporters who were attracted to the PNM.

After the failure to win a seat in the 1956 elections, Gomes abandoned the POPPG. In 1957, Carlton Achong was at the helm of the party. On 2 June 1957, Achong, the new leader, met with nineteen representatives from the party's groups. At the meeting, which was held in Port-of-Spain, Achong spoke about the party's programme. He claimed the party would develop the tourist potential of the country and improve the agricultural sector. He claimed that the POPPG would introduce legislation to ensure health and safety measures in factories, reform pension schemes, enhance family allowances and also revise the Workmen's Compensation Bill. The American Consul General did not see any hope for the party's revival:

> While the POPPG includes within its ranks a number of capable and conscientious individuals, it is cursed with the stigma of being known as the Party of the Chamber of Commerce. It has lost of the PNM its principal following which was among the professional classes, white collar workers and government servants ... Its recent demonstration of its willingness to prostitute itself by joining with such strange associates as the East Indian People's Democratic Party, which is dominated by the unsavory Bhadase Maraj, and the avowedly socialist Trinidad Labour Party, to support Bustamante's Federal Democratic Labor Party, is an indication of the straits to which it was come.[28]

In January 1955, two former members of the POPPG, Romalho Gomes (a Port-of-Spain Alderman) and Joseph Foster (Port-of-Spain Councillor), formed the short-lived National Democratic Party. This further weakened the POPPG's image.

Caribbean National Labour Party and West Indian Independence Party

In February 1956, there was an article in *The Clarion* entitled "A United Labour Party" by Dennis Mahabir. The writer appealed for unity among the political parties and other groups to "unite with a single purpose" and noted, "A United Labour front can give numerical strength sufficient to form a government even though such a front may not be united in support of a policy but in opposition to one."[29] The launch of the Caribbean National Labour Party (CNLP), on 23 March 1956, at Palms Club in San Fernando signalled a sign of unity as trade union leaders joined with political elements to further the achievements of the working class.

The genesis of the CNLP began when John Rojas (President of TUC and President General of OWTU) received a mandate from the TTTUC to request a meeting with the ILP and join forces. The CNLP was described by Rojas as "dedicated to the cause of honest and efficient self-government for the people of Trinidad and Tobago, and nationhood for the British Caribbean Peoples."[30] O'Connor stated that the purpose of CNLP was to ensure that "gains won by Trade Unions in the industrial front would be maintained."[31]

Among the officers of the CNLP were John Rojas as President, Simeon Alexander of the FWTU as Second Vice President; Bruce Procope (former ILP member); P. T. Georges (former ILP member) as First Assistant Secretary; Quinton O'Connor (Secretary of the FWTU) as Treasurer; and Norman Girwar, formerly of ILP, as Assistant Treasurer. Two posts were not filled: First Vice President and Second Assistant Secretary. The American Consul General hinted that Adrian Cola Rienzi might be willing to compromise his status within the labour movement:

> It has been learned that one of the vacant positions may be filled with a Government official. This report may refer to Mr. A.C. Rienzi who is presently serving as a Crown Counsel and is a former President of the Oilfield Workers Trade Union. According to James A. Bain, Acting Permanent Secretary of the Ministry of Industry, Labour and Commerce, he was given his official job to keep him from being a nuisance to the government.[32]

This suggested that Rienzi was not deserving of his job as Crown Counsel but more importantly was evidence that the British officials and government were willing to divide the labour movement and neutralize radical voices. The US official suggested that the CNLP should be closely watched because of their "proximity to the communist line" and the "questionable political reputations of Rojas and O'Connor."[33]

The CNLP noted previous developments as the colony's rising middle class tended to "dissociate itself from working class movements." Furthermore, the CNLP acknowledged the lack of genuine interest, "Middle class political leaders have in the past interested themselves in the workers, only to attain their own ends on their own terms."[34] In May 1956, O'Connor in a speech appealed to citizens to unite "for the political and industrial emancipation of the workers of Trinidad and Tobago." He outlined the rationale for the birth of a labour party:

> We here in Trinidad have formed the Caribbean National Party so that the trade union movement could play its full part in the political movement as the British

> Trade Union Movement ... We are going forward as the workers in the other Islands of the West Indies who lead a combined labour and trade union movement.[35]

The TTTUC and the ILP submitted a joint memorandum. On 23 May 1956, Quinton O'Connor's speech to the Caribbean National Labour Party in Marabella in South Trinidad reflected the belief of most members of his party, "Progressive leaders of thought and eminent men all agree that trade unions and trade unionists should enter the political field."[36]

Dennis Mahabir made a strident appeal in a column entitled "Unity Now!" prior to the 1956 elections. He offered a glimpse of the disunity, "Already an avalanche of criticism is pouring down from many quarters on the People's National Movement so much of it being irrelevant and unjustified. Then this party in turn ventures to criticize the doings of the Caribbean National Labour Party as far as its relations with the Trade Unions are concerned. And the Butler Party denounces one or the other at various times."[37] Whilst this appeared positive, the American Consul General contended, "The Caribbean National Labor Party of John F. Rojas did itself no good by coming out strongly against the sale of the Trinidad Oil Company to the Texas Company ... It is now more desirous than ever of establishing an alliance with another left of center faction, either Bhadase Maharaj's People's Democratic Party or the Butler group."[38]

The legislature in Trinidad and Tobago was dissolved, and general elections were to be held in September 1956. Whilst the colony did not have a legislature, Texas Oil Company offered to buy the Trinidad Oil Company. The Executive Council of the CNLP held a meeting at the Public Library in Port-of-Spain and passed a resolution condemning the oil deal.[39]

In July 1956, the public meetings of the CNLP were sparsely attended. On 26 July, the party held a meeting at Woodford Square in Port-of-Spain. Raymond Hamel-Smith and Quinton O'Connor, the two party leaders, were booed and heckled by the small crowd. The leader of the party, Rojas, who was also President General of OWTU, was absent. He faced serious opposition within the OWTU from members who did not want him in the political arena.

In 1955, the WIIP membership clearly expressed their views in the party's newsletter, *Freedom: The Whip*. The WIIP did not want any delays in the general elections. The party also rejected the recommendations of the Sinanan Constitution Reform Committee for a new Constitution.[40] The WIIP challenged Governor Beetham, accusing him of dismissing protests against his decision to implement a Constitution and proceed with elections.[41]

Industrial Stabilization Act

Williams began his political career amidst incessant labour unrest in the colony. From 1960–to 1964, there were at least 230 strikes involving 75,000 workers; a majority of strikes affected the island's two major industries: oil and sugar. Williams failed to assist the working class as problems from the colonial era persisted. Political independence meant little to the working class as economic oppression and injustice continued.

Williams' response to disturbances in the 1960s was met with uncompromising and calculated repression. The weapon employed was thus legislative, via instruments such as the Industrial Stabilization Act (ISA) enacted on 18 March 1965. This act cancelled the right of unions to take strike action. The trade unionists accused the Prime Minister of being dictatorial and the ISA of returning labour to the bygone colonial era when the administration cancelled the right of unions to take strike action. As was expected, similar to a previous era, labour leaders protested the government's violation of this right; however, Williams was on the warpath against the labour movement.

Undoubtedly, the ISA crippled the unions, and Williams threw caution to the wind and aggressively undermined the labour movement. He rode a dangerous trail. The power of unions to represent the working class was now placed in the hands of an Industrial Court. The OWTU's newspaper, *The Vanguard*, condemned the ISA for conducting a "bloodless takeover." Unfortunately, for the working class, sit-downs, go-slows and strikes were now criminal activities.

The OWTU constantly challenged the oppressive ISA. The Appeal Court, headed by Chief Justice Sir Hugh Wooding, determined that although unions had "freedom" to strike, they did not possess the "right" to strike. The union further appealed to the Privy Council but even there, they lost their case. The ISA was upheld. It prohibited strikes in the public service, prison, Pension and Fire services and the Defence Force. Also included were essential services such as electricity, health and water. The new Industrial Court was convened in 1965. Lennox Pierre, in an article in *We The People*, argued that "the government for their own lunatic reasons wanted among other things to stop strikes and interfere in free collective bargaining, so they passed the Industrial Stabilisation Act." He further noted that two British lawyers (Queen's Counsel) contended that the ISA was "constitutionally invalid" and should be "set aside."[42]

One of the first unions accused of violating the ISA was the Transport Industrial Workers Union (TIWU) which was fined $3,000. The issue, in 1967, involved the union's involvement in a work stoppage of a company that produced paint. The magistrate felt that the union was responsible, but the union claimed that the workers independently took their action. The embassy in Port-of-Spain analysed the impact of the decision by the Government of Trinidad and Tobago (GOTT):

> The action by the GOTT may serve as a deterrent to a rash of small work stoppages that have taken place over the past six months. The unions involved have been the leftist-led unions – the TIWU and the Hotel Workers Union, with full support from the Oilfields Workers Trade Union. It is obvious that the unions were pushing the GOTT to see just how far they could go before legal action was taken against them under the penalty provisions of the ISA. Now they know.[43]

In January 1969, in a secret report, the American Ambassador noted the implications of the legislation:

> There have been no strikes or lock-outs of any significance since the enactment of the Industrial Stabilization Act of 1965...While the new system has eliminated work stoppages due to strikes and lock-outs, it has greatly weakened collective bargaining... Government, industry and labor are agreed that revisions in the Industrial Stabilization Act are necessary, and labor's more militant wing would like to see the Act repealed altogether.[44]

The divided and uncertain nature of the opposition ensured Williams won the elections. For instance, after the issue of the ISA, the DLP suspended two of its members for supporting the government on the seemingly oppressive labour legislation.[45] On 20 February 1970, the first in a series of meetings of a Tripartite Conference was held. The focus was on the ISA. George Weekes, President General of the OWTU, was not part of these discussions because the OWTU was not affiliated with the Trinidad and Tobago Labour Congress (TTLC). The American Embassy noted the dissatisfaction of Weekes who described the conference as a "sell-out" by the Congress because they "begun by demanding outright appeal of the ISA, but then proceeded to negotiate amendments to it."[46] Weekes not only represented the oil workers but was one of the prominent working-class voices.

Trade unionists continued their opposition to the ISA and, in 1972, it was replaced by the Industrial Relations Act which made cosmetic changes to the ISA but returned to the unions a limited right to strike possibly where negotiations have broken down; the act, however, emphasized governmental intervention and arbitration of the Industrial Court.

Most of the trade unions now viewed Williams' regime as anti-labour. Williams would have certainly viewed these disruptive elements of labour as hostile and recalcitrant. Why was there agitation, protest and unrest among the working class? The reasons were familiar: low salaries, long hours of work, lack of health benefits, poor housing, need for better safety measures in the industries as well as unfair negotiations with multinationals whose interest came first and whose objective was profiteering through cheap labour and unfettered exploitation of natural resources.

It is obvious that the oppression of the working class, whether from externally driven investors or from local governmental policies, would meet with resistance from various labour unions, even if it meant protest against the Williams regime. Couldn't the doctor, the enlightened anti-colonialist and author of *Capitalism and Slavery*, be more appreciative of the suffering masses on the local labour front?

Williams successfully dealt with his political foes, both within the PNM and from the parliamentary opposition. As the country's highest leader, his political base was unshakeable for twenty-five years. However, he continued to face the forces that he perceived as the greatest nuisance and singular threat to him from the brave personalities in labour.

Workers and Farmers Party and Democratic Labour Party

In August 1965, C. L. R. James and Stephen Maharaj formed the Workers and Farmers Party (WFP) which was formally launched in October 1965. James was also the founder and editor of the Party's paper *We The People*. Among the Aims of the Draft Constitution of the WFP was to end "all traces of racial discrimination and racial superiority" and to better manage the country's economic and financial resources. The party also focused on developing the local trade and industry.[47] This new political party envisioned a government that was controlled by the working class "by establishing a sound and scientifically based farming community, and by making labor aware that not only its rights but its contributions to all aspects of social progress are the constant concern of a Workers and Farmers Government."[48] This thrust of the party was evident in a letter to the editor by Carl Pratt, who reported on a conversation with a dock worker: "the great weakness in P.N.M. and D.L.P. defences lay in their being unwilling or unable to re-organise the economy away from the old colonial base." Ivar Oxaal in an essay noted that the PNM had relied on "foreign-owned corporations."[49]

The WFP had a vision for the revitalization of the agricultural sector in Trinidad and Tobago. One of the party's prominent members was Dr J. M. Dube who condemned monoculture and advocated for an alternative programme, "Diversification is imperative for the full utilization of our land and human resources."[50] He saw diversification as contributing to a "prosperous peasantry" as well as a "large and ready market" to absorb an industrialized sector.[51] Dube felt that diversification would create "a more secure, more healthy economy."[52] His views reflected the party's main goal of focusing on the local and moving away from the reliance on foreign capital and resources.

In addition, Dube was adamant that milk and meat would produce handsome profits to the country.[53] However, he does not clearly explain how the government would encourage or train dairy farmers. He suggested the use of swamp land and contended thus: "All unused land must be brought into cultivation."[54] Dube believed the uniqueness of peasant farmers in Trinidad and Tobago and described them as "a most modern and scientific people."[55] In August 1965, there was an article by "Expert Analysis" that regarding land under sugar cane cultivation there should be a limit of 250 acres.[56]

The party placed emphasis on organizing the masses. The editorial of the *We The People* would remind its readers and supporters of the need to appoint an organizer for each constituency.[57] The party, in 1965, also hosted weekly Ibis lectures at its headquarters. Among the speakers were Stephen Maharaj, Jack Kelshall and C. L. R. James.

The WFP sought to appeal to the country's working class. An article in the OWTU's paper, *The Vanguard*, by George Bowrin, a trade unionist, made a bold statement that the PNM had "lost its magic," the DLP was "demoralised" and the Butler Party was "a name only." Bowrin was attempting to strengthen the claims of the WFP and he advised, "The W.F.P. must offer a programme which promises real change if it is to receive substantial support from the people."[58] Eugene Joseph in an article entitled "Workers Demand" advocated the need for national social security scheme, shorter working hours, better housing and progressive labour laws.[59] Such statements reflected the failure of the existing political framework.

James possessed the qualifications necessary to become a powerful asset to the colony's labour movement. However, he was branded a Communist and scorned. Ivar Oxaal noted that James had been neglected, treated with "indifference" and faced "persecution" in Trinidad and Tobago.

The WFP with its headquarters located in Ariapita Avenue, Woodbrook, in the city of Port-of-Spain had emerged from the bowels of the OWTU. Unfortunately, the grandiose plans of the WFP failed to materialize at the polls. The WFP received only 3 per cent of the popular vote and lost all their candidates' deposits. In Tunapuna, James, the defeated candidate, received 2.8 per cent of the vote.[60] Despite its idealistic ambitions and claims of being the representative of labour, the WFP never developed the comprehensive, and necessary, "organic links" with Trinidad's working class.[61] The government also sought to discourage this attempt at working-class unity and political reform.

In an article entitled "Human Rights Amidst Human Wrongs," Basdeo Panday, a member of the WFP, warned, "If you are employed 'with

Government' you had better not let it be known that you are a member of WFP. Worse still if you are unemployed and looking for work – … So much for your right to join political parties of your choice."[62] It was obvious that critics of the government were blacklisted, and this signalled the autocratic nature of Williams. In 1968, during the tripartite talks, the WFP was excluded, but others representing labour submitted proposals to "alleviate the sufferings of the masses." However, the government ignored these proposals and asked Clive Spencer whether he had "gone Red."[63]

The weakness of the opposition in the Legislative Council was obvious. One writer, using the pseudonym "Juvenile Secondary," in an article in *We The People*, entitled "Do We Have an Opposition," described the DLP as "dying" and "moribund." The writer also questioned the relationship between Capildeo and Williams:

> No leader – especially that of the opposition in a country – can be stooge and accomplice of the leader of the ruling party and still be a true leader. That's impossible. You cannot be here and there, and still be loyal, truthful, faithful and honest to your countrymen. That's a TRAITOR.[64]

Ronald Hoolasie of the WFP also realized that the opposition was "within the folds of the P.N.M." and made an observation, "In this setting one can see only the militant Trade Unions remain as the bulwark of Democracy and the only real opposition in the country today."[65]

1970s and the working class

Black Power of the late 1960s and early 1970s promised to positively transform crucial sectors of society. The National Joint Action Committee (NJAC), based in Port-of-Spain, in their first issue of *Black Messenger*, made the following claim:

> The young Black students in the Secondary Schools … are kicking the old colonial curriculum into the typhoid-breeding cesspits of the schools and demanding that

> the teachers re-orient their whole approach to education to make it relevant to the Third World peoples seeking to develop themselves.[66]

There were other newsletters and pamphlets such as *Liberation*, *East Dry River Speaks*, *Belmont United Front*, *Embryo* and *Revolutionary* that espoused similar messages.

The bulletin *B.I.L.T.* (Black Indigenous Liberated Thought) advocated Black consciousness and in one issue emphasized the need to "purge Blackness of the negative meanings given to it in our white-oriented education system" and the "cultural rape."[67]

By 1968, there was an obvious deterioration of the relationship between the government and the trade union movement. It was an era of massive demonstrations, public marches and elements of militancy. This certainly threatened national security. In one of the demonstrations, 20,000 persons marched from Port-of-Spain to San Juan. Black Power activists were further empowered when labour joined their bandwagon. Oil, sugar, transport and electrical workers were soon supporting militant Black Power groups.

William Riviere believed that the absence of mass support for the Black Power in Trinidad and Tobago was due to "an inability to effectively overcome physical and psychological obstacles to the communication of the ideology." He further contended that poorly paid Indo-Trinidadian sugar workers displayed a "generally indifferent attitude" to Black Power events of 1970, and this, "must be understood on the basis largely of a failure to accept a definition of black."[68]

After weeks of unrest, interspersed with fire-bombings of certain banks and shops, particularly in Port-of-Spain, the next weapon against the government was a general strike planned for 21 and 22 April 1970. Williams did not hesitate, and a State of Emergency was declared on 21 April 1970. On the morning of 21 April 1970, a section of the Trinidad Defence Force mutinied, but these mutineers were intercepted by the Coast Guard at Chaguaramas and arrested.[69] If the military dissidents had been allowed to unite with the Black Power demonstrations, their combined forces would have certainly precipitated a violent confrontation with the island's security forces.

Williams did not hesitate to crush and incarcerate all insurrectionists, regardless of whether they were trade unionists, soldiers, university students or lecturers. Whether the unrest was ideologically, socially or politically inspired, it was suppressed by military force or legislative instruments. The government was successful in neutralizing the Black Power movement because of the inherent weakness of NJAC. Riviere contended that NJAC "had not sufficiently considered the elementary distinction between support and commitment, that is, between a person sympathizing with a cause and one involved in struggle" and the People's Parliaments "did not constitute a forum for discussing problems and finding solutions."[70]

During this period of socio-political instability, Williams introduced the infamous Public Order Bill (1970). The bill was designed to give unlimited powers to the police: the power to enter premises as well as to seize and arrest offenders. In addition, the Defence Force was given powers similar to that of the police. Furthermore, public meetings, marches, demonstrations and the use of loudspeakers were permitted only with the authorization of the Commissioner of Police.

On 10 May 1970, Richard Ishmael, President of the Caribbean Congress of Labour (CCL), said the Congress "condemned the violent concept of Black Power advocated by Stokely Carmichael." Ishmael remarked that the Congress felt economic prosperity of the Afro-Caribbean "must be achieved through peaceful methods – not through violent revolution against imperialism, capitalism and the white power structure." On 31 August 1970, Eric Williams assured the public of the country's ideological goal, "We differ from the Socialist countries of the Third World in our decision not to proceed on the basis of the total rejection of foreign capital and the total control of the economy by the State."[71]

Some disenchanted OWTU workers petitioned the Minister of Labour and complained that the union was misallocating a sum of $71,000 from its Strike Fund. However, Verne Edwards, the First Vice President of the OWTU, said the names on the petition were not of union members. Edwards blamed agents of the PNM who sought "to embarrass the Executive and to enforce the detention of our union President."[72] As a result of the petition, on 14 May 1970, the police under the Emergency regulations, raided the OWTU's headquarters, its press and its Palm Club restaurant. The police seized negatives, literature, films, union records and documents. Two months later, five detainees were held under the Emergency Order

Act. Among them were Syl Lowhar, an economist employed at the Ministry of Agriculture, and also Chairman of Tapia, and the Dominica-born Dr William Riviere, who felt the "university campus in the West Indies have been regarded as hotbeds of Communism."[73]

Pressure was placed on the Attorney General who cancelled a Tripartite Conference planned for 20 April, which was supposed to finalize the legislation to restore the right to strike. On 25 May 1970, the General Council of the TTLC despatched a letter to the Attorney General. The correspondence protested the revision of the Emergency Powers Regulation which allowed the police the power to inspect and seize trade union documents. The TTLC requested the Attorney General to "take appropriate action to correct this discriminatory measure against the trade union movement."[74]

The anti-strike provisions of the ISA did not intimidate workers. In April 1970, the US Embassy noted the "growing militancy in wake of continuing Black Power protest."[75] This included walkouts among water workers and work stoppages involving 600 sugar workers at the Brechin Castle factory. The sugar workers wanted bonuses, fringe benefits and guaranteed employment. Interestingly, this protest action occurred despite Bhadase Maraj, President of ATSE+FWTU, demanding that workers return to work.

Williams instituted several changes, as evident in his message to the Caribbean Cane Farmers Association in August 1970 in Port-of-Spain. He claimed that the government "bought out" Orange Grove and obtained 51 per cent of the shares in Caroni. In addition, Williams boasted that Trinidad and Tobago was the first Commonwealth nation to have national control of the sugar industry.[76]

The Public Order Bill was considered draconian and repressive, and it was condemned particularly by trade unions and others in the society. Williams was accused of creating a police state to entrench his dictatorial governance. The bill was withdrawn in October 1970 when some measure of peace was restored with the incarceration of leaders, and when Black Power and labour demonstrations subsided. Two months later, in a message to the nation, Eric Williams advised young people not to mimic developed countries, "where the young people tend to regard dropouts as heroes, to pour scorn on people who have achieved high standards, and prefer to shout slogans and obscenities."[77] Amidst this tense environment, in January 1971, the American Ambassador, in a secret report to the Department of State, noted a weakening of the movement:

> Black radicals using "Black Power" slogans took advantage of indecision and complacency by the Prime Minister and his advisors to bring about a serious crisis in the Spring of 1970. Black nationalist sentiment still exists in varying intensity in a significant segment of the younger Negro population, and is encouraged by the high rate of unemployment and economic inequalities. The fire seems to have at least temporarily gone out of the movement.[78]

Undoubtedly, the protests and disputes reflected the strength of the labour movement and the oppressive working conditions. In 1971, there were seventy work stoppages involving 18,566 workers with a loss of 138,362 man-days.[79] In 1971, in a workforce of an estimated 350,000 persons, 97,733 workers were unionized and 82 per cent of these workers were in unions affiliated to the TTLC.[80] The unemployment rate was at 12.5 per cent.

Passage of labour legislation meant that the number of strikes would be reduced. This was because workers in essential services (such as water, telephone, military) were unable to strike. In 1975, the TTLC, had approximately 85,000 members. Among the thirteen affiliates of the TTLC were TTPU, the Public Services Association (PSA), the Union of Commercial and Industrial Workers as well as the National Union of Government and Federated Workers (NUGFW).

The American Embassy noted that the powers of the Industrial Court "have been expanded to provide for compulsory arbitration in many situations and for the award of compensation." The embassy also added that "despite high unemployment, local attitudes and perhaps climatic factors do not generally result in high worker productivity."[81]

The United States had also established cordial relations with union leaders. In 1970, Selwyn John (General Secretary of NUGFW) requested a "Labour Leader" grant allowing members to travel and study trade union operations in the United States for one month. The embassy endorsed his request and justified their decision, "In view of the growing strength of labor unions in this country and their increasing interest they are showing such activities as worker education and the establishment of cooperatives."[82] Similarly, in 1972, the US Embassy offered a grant to Ursula Gittens (President of PSA, third Vice President of T&T Labour Congress and employee of WASA) to visit the United States for one month to consult with US union officials and meet important people who deal with consumer and women's affairs.[83] In 1975, Peter Budd, Trustee and dock worker of the SWWTU, planned to visit New York and Washington. He asked the US Embassy for assistance to receive a briefing on the activities of the Department of Labour and American Federation of Labor and Congress of Industrial Organization (AFL-CIO).[84]

United Labour Front

Williams' final encounter with the hostile forces of labour came in 1975. On 18 February 1975, a rally of the United Labour Front (ULF) was held in San Fernando. A telegram from the American Embassy indicated that, during the event, speakers "re-stated the familiar anti-government, anti-multinational corporation, nationalistic ideas and charges."[85] Weekes claimed the United States was planning to "use Trinidad as a base to launch an invasion of Venezuela." This never materialized. Weekes also blamed fire bombings on "mafia agents working for the CIA." Basdeo Panday, President of ATSE+FWTU, revealed plans for the sugar workers to be owners of the sugar industry and "construction of integrated factories which could process food as well as sugar." Raffique Shah, President of the ICFTU, claimed that it was a victory for his union that most of the Cane Farmers Incorporation and Cess Act were unconstitutional. However, the American Embassy noted, "the ICFTU played no direct role in the legal proceedings."[86]

Also present on the platform was James Millette, leader of the United National Independence Party, who was also a founding member of the ICFTU. Some of the members of Tapia were also present at the meeting.

The rally sent clear signals to Williams that his most formidable foe had an unmistakable political objective, namely, to wrest political power from him. What did the unions demand? Sugar workers had recently been awarded a 100 per cent wage increase. Basdeo Panday, who was also one of the leaders of ULF, wanted year-round work for sugar workers and profit-sharing to enable workers to purchase interests of Tate and Lyle, a British sugar giant, ; but, instead, it was alleged that the government was negotiating to buy these shares for itself. Williams' government was therefore chastised for being against workers. The oil workers negotiated for an 80 per cent wage increase from Texaco oil company but received only 30 per cent.

With the threat of a widespread national strike, Williams was prepared for a showdown. Amidst a work-to-rule, labour disruptions and industrial unrest, the Trinidad and Tobago Regiment deployed soldiers in seven vehicles to camp in South Trinidad, at Naparima Bowl, under the guise of attending a seminar for the soldiers on career guidance. Labour condemned this as intimidating. On Tuesday 18 March 1975, a prayer rally was organized by oil workers. This crippled the oil belt, and refineries at Pointe-a-Pierre and Brighton were shut down.

Oil workers insisted that the rally was for "peace, bread and justice." The ULF was not only merely challenging Tate and Lyle, and the Texaco, but it was also questioning the Williams' administration for its alliance with the multinational corporations.

The planned rally snowballed into a religious march from San Fernando to Port-of-Spain with 25,000 oil and sugar workers. Through state intervention, the march in San Fernando was stopped as police used teargas to disperse the crowd. There was police brutality. Williams had stopped the unions, but he was severely reprimanded for these incidents – this day was remembered as "Bloody Tuesday."

Subsequently, labour contested the general elections. The political coalition of the ULF, despite being a powerful force, suffered a fatal blow in the 1976 elections when they secured only ten seats; the Democratic Action Congress in Tobago won two seats while Williams' PNM formed the government with twenty-four seats.

In December 1978, Williams sent a representative of the government, Errol Mahabir (Minister of Petroleum and Mines) to meet with Weekes at his office in the Paramount Building, San Fernando. The meeting was the outcome of a strong letter that Weekes wrote to the government regarding

Texaco. This encounter ensured Weekes would not be viewed as a mere pawn but a powerful chess piece. Weekes was not simply the President General of the OWTU; he was one of the major voices of the working class who argued for a revolutionary transformation of the economy.

Williams avoided political power-sharing with labour as this enabled his political party to extend its appeal to all sectors of society, inclusive of the growing middle class. With broad-based electoral support, he garnered his parliamentary majority in constituencies which were outside the influence of major trade unions. Indeed, it was obvious that membership in Williams' PNM, particularly for electoral purposes, transcended loyalty to any trade union.

In January 1969, the American Ambassador in Port-of-Spain had a confidential discussion with Prime Minister Williams, in which the latter provided reasons for nominating Hochoy for re-appointment as Governor General of Trinidad and Tobago. This was due to Williams' belief that Hochoy "enjoys wide personal popularity" and that "no other Chinese of stature is available." Not surprisingly, the ambassador also concluded from his meeting with Williams that "it would be hazardous for Williams to nominate either a Negro or an East Indian. Hochoy offers only feasible symbol of continued stability amid rival communal tensions."[87]

Williams, a disciplinarian and stern father, dealt harshly with any wayward children, be it a union or a political party that dared to invade his political turf. There was little room for compassion or compromise. Political expediency and the desire to preserve power were given priority even at the expense of the working class. Despite the ill-treatment of labour, Williams could still depend on the electoral support from Afro-based unions such as the Communication Workers Union, OWTU and the SWWTU, particularly in the cities of Port-of-Spain and San Fernando, which remained the stronghold of his political party.

Labour leaders were committed to improving the conditions of the working class, but with pressures from the government, they had no alternative but to challenge Williams on the political front. Fortunately for him, from the 1950s till his death, labour was severely fragmented (as it is today and evidence of this was seen last Friday in Fyzabad). From the 1950s to 1981, labour was disunited because of differing ethnic and ideological bases which polarized unions in the largest industries, namely, petroleum and sugar. This weakened any political response to the Williams regime.

Notes

1. Confidential despatch to Department of State, 20 September 1950.
2. Confidential despatch to Department of State, 20 September 1950.
3. *The Clarion* 11 July 1953.
4. Confidential Despatch from American Consul General to Department of State, 23 March 1956.
5. *Report of Constitution Reform Committee, 1955 and Despatches Exchanged with the Secretary of State* (Trinidad: Government Printing Office, 1956), 20.
6. Despatch from American Consul General to Department of State, 28 June 1956.
7. Confidential despatch from American Consul General to Department of State, 23 March 1956.
8. *The Clarion* 10 April 1954.
9. *The Clarion* 3 April 1954.
10. Confidential Despatch from American Consul General to Department of State, 14 May 1954.
11. Confidential despatch from American Consulate to Washington, 21 May 1947.
12. Confidential despatch from American Consulate to Washington, 21 May 1947.
13. *The Clarion* 29 January 1949.
14. Confidential Despatch to Department of State, 20 September 1950,.
15. *The Clarion* 17 February 1951.
16. *The Clarion* 21 April 1951.
17. *The Clarion* 21 April 1951.
18. *The Clarion* 21 April 1951.
19. *The Clarion* 28 April 1951.
20. Classified note from Robert F. Dale to Department of State, 4 May 1951.
21. Despatch from American Consul General to Department of State, 28 June 1956.
22. Telegram from American Embassy to Department of State, 28 November 1969.
23. Confidential despatch from American Consul General to Department of State, 14 May 1954.
24. Despatch from American Consul General to Department of State, 24 January 1955.
25. Despatch from American Consul General to Department of State, 26 November 1956.
26. Despatch from American Consul General to Department of State, 26 November 1956.

27. Ryan, *Eric Williams*, 119.
28. Despatch from American Consul General to Department of State, 5 June 1957.
29. *The Clarion* 18 February 1956.
30. *The Clarion* 24 March 1956.
31. *The Clarion* 24 March 1956.
32. Confidential despatch from American Consul General to Department of State, 23 March 1956.
33. Confidential despatch from American Consul General to Department of State, 23 March 1956.
34. *The Clarion* 31 March 1956.
35. *The Clarion* 2 June 1956.
36. *The Clarion* 2 June 1956.
37. *The Clarion* 16 June 1956.
38. Despatch from American Consul General to Department of State, 28 June 1956.
39. *The Clarion* 16 June 1956.
40. *Freedom* September 1955, 1.
41. *Freedom* September 1955, 1.
42. *We The People* 27 August 1965.
43. Despatch from American Embassy to Department of State, 28 November 1967.
44. Secret Telegram from American Embassy to Department of State, 28 January 1969.
45. *The Nation* 29 November 1968.
46. Telegram from American Embassy to Department of State, 27 February 1970.
47. *We The People* 8 October 1965.
48. *The Vanguard* 27 August 1965. The Party Chairman and officers included S. C. Maharaj (Chairman), George Bowrin (First Vice Chairman), A. S. A. Khan (Second Vice Chairman), C. L. R. James (General Secretary), Dr S. H. Goopeesingh (Assistant General Secretary), C. Phill (Treasurer), Dr J. M. Dube (Public Relations Officer) and Basdeo Panday (Youth Organizer). *We The People* 19 November 1965.
49. *We The People* 24 September 1965.
50. Dr J. M. Dube, *Why We Must Reorganise Our Agriculture*. Founding Convention Document no. 2, 7.
51. *Why We Must Reorganise Our Agriculture*, 7.
52. *We The People* 19 June 1966.
53. *Why We Must Reorganise Our Agriculture*, 8.
54. *Why We Must Reorganise Our Agriculture*, 9.
55. *Why We Must Reorganise Our Agriculture*, 11.
56. *We The People* 20 August 1965.
57. *We The People* 9 July 1965.
58. *The Vanguard* 20 August 1965.
59. *We The People* 3 September 1965.

60. Kent Worcester, *C.L.R. James – A Political Biography* (New York: SUNY Press, 1996), 171.
61. Walton Look Lai, "C.L.R. James and Trinidad Nationalism," in Paget Henry and Paul Buhle, eds, *C.L.R. James' Caribbean* (Durham: Duke University Press, 1992), 199.
62. *The Vanguard* 10 August 1968.
63. Telegram from American Embassy to Department of State, 3 June 1970.
64. *We The People* 27 August 1965.
65. *We The People* 6 August 1965.
66. *Black Messenger*, n.d, 5.
67. *B.I.L.T. (Black Indigenous Liberated Thought)*, 4 (n.d.), n.p.
68. William Riviere, "Black Power NJAC and the 1970 Confrontation in the Caribbean: An Historical Interpretation," paper presented at the University of Pittsburgh annual seminar on the Black Man in the Caribbean, 1972, 54.
69. See also Jerome Teelucksingh, "Black Power in Trinidad and Tobago," in *Foundation Readings on the History of Trinidad and Tobago*, 349.
70. Riviere, "Black Power NJAC and the 1970 Confrontation in the Caribbean."
71. Prime Minister's Independence Day Message, 31 August 1970. Eric Williams Memorial Collection, University of the West Indies, St Augustine (hereafter cited as EWMC).
72. Telegram from American Embassy to Department of State, 19 May 1970.
73. *TG* 4 July 1970.
74. Telegram from American Embassy to Department of State, 3 June 1970.
75. Telegram from American Embassy to Department of State, 20 April 1970.
76. Address by the Prime Minister to the Ninth Annual Conference of the Caribbean Cane Farmers Association, Queen's Hall, Port-of-Spain, 17 August 1970, EWMC.
77. Prime Minister Christmas Message, 1970, EWMC.
78. Secret Telegram from American Embassy to Department of State, 25 January 1971.
79. Telegram from American Embassy to Department of State, 27 September 1972.
80. Enclosure 1, Telegram from American Embassy, Port-of-Spain, to Department of State, 21 June 1972.
81. Enclosure 1, Telegram from American Embassy, Port-of-Spain to Department of State, 21 June 1972.
82. Telegram from American Embassy, Port-of-Spain to Department of State, 14 April 1970.
83. Telegram from American Embassy, Port-of-Spain to Department of State, 7 April 1972.
84. Telegram from American Embassy to Department of State, 7 August 1975.
85. Telegram from American Embassy to Secretary of State, 19 February 1975.
86. Telegram from American Embassy to Secretary of State, 19 February 1975.
87. Secret telegram from American Embassy to Department of State, 23 January 1969.

Bibliography

Ali, Saeeda. "Caught Between the Past and Present: Chaguanas's Crumbling Lion House," Central Beat Magazine, https://centralbeat442655923.wordpress.com/2020/05/26/caught-between-the-past-and-present-chaguanass-crumbling-lion-house/ (accessed 28 December 2020).

Lequay, Alloy. *Winning against the Tide: A Life devoted to Sports and* Politics (La Romaine: RPL, 2001).

Look Lai, Walton. "C.L.R. James and Trinidad Nationalism," in Paget Henry and Paul Buhle, eds, *C.L.R. James' Caribbean* (Durham: Duke University Press, 1992).

Matthews, Gelien. "Lyrics to Build a Nation," in Jerome Teelucksingh and Shane Pantin, eds, *Regional Discourses on Society and History: Shaping the Caribbean* (New York: Peter Lang, 2020), 159–173.

Oxaal, Ivar. *Black Intellectuals Come to Power: The Rise of Creole Nationalism in Trinidad and Tobago* (Massachusetts: Schenkman Publishing, 1968).

Ramchand, Ken, ed. *Mr. Speaker, Sir: An Autobiography of Lionel Frank Seukeran: The Silver Tongued Orator* (San Fernando: Chandrabose Publications, 2006).

Riviere, William. "Black Power NJAC and the 1970 Confrontation in the Caribbean: An Historical Interpretation," paper presented at the University of Pittsburgh annual seminar on The Black Man in the Caribbean, 1972.

Siewah, Samroo, ed. *Lotus and the Dagger: The Capildeo Speeches (1957–1994)* (Tunapuna: Chakra Publishing House, 1994).

H.P. Singh: The Indian Struggle for Justice and Equality against Black Racism in Trinidad & Tobago (1956–1962) (Couva: Indian Review Press, 1993).

Teelucksingh, Jerome, and Shane Pantin, *Regional Discourses on Society and History: Shaping the Caribbean* (New York: Peter Lang, 2020).

Teelucksingh, Jerome. "Black Power in Trinidad and Tobago," *Foundation Readings on the History of Trinidad and Tobago* (Government of the Republic of Trinidad and Tobago: Ministry of Education, 2017), 343–357.

Worcester, Kent. *C.L.R. James – A Political Biography* (New York: SUNY Press, 1996).

Conclusion

The major setback for labour leaders in the Legislative Council (later known as Parliament) and Municipal Council was the persistent autocracy of the Crown Colony system which continued after Trinidad and Tobago attained Independence in 1962. The Colonial Office, through its local representatives – the Governors – ensured that they held ultimate power in all matters. This continued in the post-colonial era as the Prime Minister and his government possessed a similar power.

On the contrary, labour, through its representatives, played a pivotal role in charting the political course of Trinidad and Tobago. During election campaigns, the "voices of labour" regularly championed the rights of the working class in a hostile political system that favoured the ruling white upper class.

The sacrifice and fearless representation emanating from the rudimentary workers' associations of the early twentieth century to the well-constituted trade unions of subsequent decades were undeniable factors in the constitutional evolution of Trinidad and Tobago and the Anglophone Caribbean. Undoubtedly, the legislative and social reforms grudgingly undertaken by the mother country stemmed from more than a century of persistent undermining of the Crown Colony system of administration of the British colonies, and, among the forces at work in this process of transformation, the contribution of labour cannot be overestimated.

The results of the colony's general elections, from 1925 to 1976, provided tangible evidence that the representatives of labour certainly played a pivotal role in shaping the party politics of the colony. Prior to 1946, these men were able to win the sympathy of a limited voting population in certain districts as well as project an image as the defenders of the working class. This was an alternative political position being formulated, struggling for expression, reaching out for support and pleading for understanding. The campaigns and results of municipal elections demonstrated the willingness of labour to address problems facing the citizenry. Cipriani's tenure as Mayor of Port-of-Spain certainly strengthened the voice of labour in the municipal elections and was an asset in the TWA's campaign in the national elections.

Undoubtedly, the absence of formal party structures and the existence of a relatively small electoral following accentuated the pivotal role that Arthur Cipriani, F. E. M. Hosein, Timothy Roodal, Sarran Teelucksingh, Adrian Rienzi and Tubal Uriah Butler played for labour. Divisions of race and class evident in the voting patterns of the colony's early elections gradually became entrenched in the political system and served to undermine the unity of labour and weaken its political foundation during the 1950s and 1960s.

The arrogant and apathetic responses of the colonial government to the advice and questions of the elected members from labour coupled with the voting pattern, overwhelmingly in favour of the government, demonstrated the administration's unquestionable majority comprising colonial officials and nominated members. The composition of the Legislative Council also reflected class divisions as the capitalists and conservatives tended to support the Governor, whilst the labour representatives stood for the interests of the working class.

In the post-Second World War era, working-class organizations continued to boldly enter the arena of electoral politics but with limited success. Lethargic efforts at unity, coupled with the haunting race and class dichotomy, and the determination of imperial powers to suppress any forms of political radicalism frustrated the efforts of labour to secure political control in Trinidad and Tobago.

Prior to the granting of universal adult suffrage in 1946, certain factors challenged the representatives of labour in the general elections. First, the limited voting rights meant that the working class was unable to vote at the polls. Second, apart from Cipriani and Rienzi, there was an absence of charismatic labour leaders to influence the electorate. Cipriani's association with the TWA and the establishment of ties with the Labour Party in England made him one of the most important voices in the early labour movement in the politics of Trinidad and Tobago.

The race and class divisions existing in the colony surfaced during the campaigns of the general elections from 1925 to 1976. This meant that the electoral victory of a candidate was largely determined by the class and race of the candidate and that of the electorate. Finally, and more importantly, the composition of the Legislative Council favoured the Governor. Indeed, after the 1933 and 1938 elections, the TWA/TLP could boast of having only two elected members (Roodal and Cipriani) in the twenty-six-member Legislative Council. Unfortunately, as in the two previous elections of 1925 and 1928, this was only token representation as labour remained politically impotent and unable to approve legislation and enact reforms.

During the 1946 and 1950 elections, labour continued to be part of the political landscape with such parties as the TLP, TTTUC and SPTT. Their voices represented the working class in the colony.

The emergence and victory of the PNM in 1956 in addition to the introduction of organized party politics created a new political culture which quickly sounded the death knell of labour's prominence in the electoral arena. Despite the fact that the struggles and organizational structure of unions served as an incubator for political parties, labour suffered humiliating electoral defeats in subsequent elections.

Undoubtedly, the gallant efforts of labour in its challenge to British colonial policy paved the way for future Caribbean leaders such as Alexander Bustamante, Norman Manley, Vere Bird, Grantley Adams, Cheddi Jagan and T. A. Marryshow. They responded to the call of forging a nation, fashioning a people and liberating these West Indian colonies. The efforts of labour-based parties proved to be the main pillars of the political evolution and social transformation of Trinidad and Tobago. Prior to 1960, the appeals for self-government, Caribbean integration, improved working conditions and social and economic justice laid unshakeable foundations for the critical restructuring process for most of the Caribbean colonies that were transitioning from colony to republic.

In the twenty-first century, trade unions must devise more effective strategies, adopt a more radical stance and be outspoken in dealing with issues such as racism, human trafficking, corruption, drug trafficking and crime. Empty threats and occasional media conferences are lip service and have proven to be ineffective. The labour movement must intensify its struggles against any institutions, multinational corporations and persons who are economic parasites that drain our economy and exploit the working class. The labour movement seems to lack a clear ideology. This could indicate a need to educate and enlighten their workers. Few working-class persons appreciate the fact that trade unions were the most powerful opponents of colonialism and imperialism. Caribbean citizens owe their independent status to the long struggle of labour leaders and members who undermined European colonialism.

Some workers have lost faith because they are not prepared to fight in the trenches or endure any delays in the collective bargaining process that will result in more protest actions. There is considerable tension and anger among some workers. For instance, workers are waiting for salary increases. This disenchantment from workers is largely a result of a new generation of union members who are more educated and less tolerant of myopic leadership. Spineless labour leaders who make empty threats and seek cheap media publicity only serve to contribute to the loss of faith in trade unions. Many workers are frustrated and no longer want to be political pawns. Some workers are beginning to realize that broken promises and hypocrisy are part of previous, current and future governments.

Trade unions could become marginalized and appear irrelevant to contract workers. The reason is that trade unions usually limit their membership to full-time workers, as only they can afford to pay membership fees. Hence, labour should create special unions, with low membership fees. This could ensure that low-skilled workers are protected from victimization and compensated when they are injured. Non-unionized workers do not feel part of the labour movement.

Trade unions must continue the fight, but it must be directed against institutions and persons who are economic parasites that drain the Caribbean economy and exploit the working class. Labour leaders need to be progressive in their thinking and their concerns must not be restricted to their membership.

Labour Day and May Day are invaluable days for the trade union movement to assess their shortcomings, achievements and future strategies. The Labour Day celebrations have displayed a strong anti-government stance. The celebrations should not be interpreted as politicized but as seeking to protect the interests and rights of the workers. The condemnation of the government by the trade union leaders reflects a working class that feels marginalized and alienated. Labour Day is another opportunity for the trade union movement to reflect on the level of working-class unity.

The immediate benefits of tripartite arrangements include fewer work stoppages and protests resulting in increased profits and growth in the economy. In addition, it would aid in empowering trade unions as leaders would be more aware of the demands of the government and employers. This could have the positive effect of increasing the productivity of the workforce.

In the twenty-first century and beyond, it is crucial that labour has a voice in the political realm. This is one of the strategies to ensure that trade unions are respected and do not become marginalized and alienated. This is not a recent phenomenon. Trade unions should be wary that once they are politically stereotyped and stigmatized, it is difficult to shed their political colours and appear independent. Trade unions need to adopt an ideological stance and not be fooled or conned into accepting political handouts in return for a guarantee of reduced or no protests. The future appears partially bleak and dim because political parties tend to use trade unions to gain political office and after winning or losing an election, the unions are discarded or treated with contempt.

Appendices

Appendix 1

Composition of the Legislative Council on 12 December 1924

Horace A. Byatt	Governor, *President*
T. A. Vans Best	Colonial Secretary
W. C. Huggard	Attorney General
H. B. Walcott	Treasurer
R. H. Furness	Solicitor General
G. H. May	Inspector General of Constabulary
M. A. Murphy	Director of Public Works
K. S. Wise	Surgeon General
A. De Boissiere	Protector of Immigrants
T. R. Cutler	Collector of Customs
W. G. Freeman	Director of Agriculture
H. A. Alcazar	
A. Fraser	
A. H. Wight	
C. D. Lalla	
A. H. McShine	
L. A. P. O'Reilly	
J. B. D. Sellier	
A. B. Carr	
A. A. Sobrian	
G. F. Huggins	

Appendix 2

Members of the Legislative Council on 20 February 1925

Horace A. Byatt	Governor, *President*
T. A. Vans Best	Colonial Secretary
R. H. Furness	Acting Colonial Secretary
H. B. Walcott	Treasurer
Walter Harragin	Acting Solicitor General
G. H. May	Inspector General of Constabulary
M. A. Murphy	Director of Public Works
K. S. Wise	Surgeon General
A. de Boissiere	Protector of Immigrants
T. R. Cutler	Collector of Customs
W. G. Freeman	Director of Agriculture
J. Powter	General Manager of Railways
H. A. Alcazar	
A. B. Carr	
G. F. Huggins	
A. H. McShine	
L. A. P. O'Reilly	
C. H. Pierre	St David, St Andrew, Nariva and Mayaro
T. M. Kelshall	Victoria
J. A. A. Biggart	Tobago
A. A. Cipriani	Port-of-Spain
E. R. Clarke	St Patrick
A. V. Stollmeyer	St George
S. Teelucksingh	Caroni

Appendix 3

Results of the 1925 elections

Port-of-Spain	
A. A. Cipriani*	2,557
R. T. Rust	910
G. Johnston	378
Total voters	4,004
Caroni	
S. Teelucksingh	491
E. A. Robinson	235
Total voters	726
St Patrick	
A. A. Sobrian	269
E. Radcliffe-Clarke	314
Total voters	583
St George	
A. V. Stollmeyer[a]	707
A. Cory-Davies	206
Total voters	913

Two candidates were unopposed:

Victoria

T. M. Kelshall

Eastern Counties

C. H. Pierre[a]

* Labour candidates

Appendix 4

Election Campaign Ad of Sarran Teelucksingh

VOTE FOR TEELUCKSINGH and Live

Why?

1. Because he is the man of the people.
2. Because your interests and his are identical.
3. Because the modicum of representation we have is intended for the Sons of Trinidad.
4. Because it is never good to change horses in mid-stream.
5. Because TEELUCKSINGH has served you faithfully and well for three years.
6. Because he has identified himself with the Labour and Socialist Movement.
7. Because he is the plain open shilling that you can meet at every turn and in every place.

Vote LABOUR
Vote Teelucksingh

and DOWN WITH ROBINSON.
VOTE FOR TEELUCKSINGH

And Down with Robinson
(The Land grabber).

Why?

1. Because he is a Capitalist and swears by Capitalism.
2. Because his interest can never be identical with yours.
3. Because he will be bound to oppose the 8-hour day and put you to grind under a 15-hour day if possible.
4. Because it is part of his business always to keep down wages at the lowest levels.
5. Because he will always be bent upon keeping the price of Cane down.

6. Because he is a great exponent of industrial slavery, and was opposed to the abolition of child labour.
7. Because he has never given and will never give a square deal to the underdog.

Source: *Labour Leader* 4 February 1928

Appendix 5

Voter's register list showing the number of voters in 1928

Port-of-Spain	7,550
County of St George	2,916
County of Caroni	2,190
County of Victoria	2,744
County of St Patrick	1,933
Eastern Electoral District	2,833
Ward of Tobago	1,661
Total number of electors	21,827

Source: *TG* 14 January 1928

Appendix 6

Results of the 1928 elections
(Four constituencies were uncontested as the candidates were uncontested)

Port-of-Spain
A. A. Cipriani*

St George
F. E. M. Hosein*

Victoria
T. M. Kelshall

Eastern Counties
C. H. Pierre

Caroni	
S. Teelucksingh*	623
E. A. Robinson	358
St Patrick	
T. Roodal*	691
A. A. Sobrian	251
Tobago	
J. A. A. Biggart	361
A. Bonnet*	55

* Labour candidates

Appendix 7

List of candidates, their affiliation and the electorate in the 1933 elections

Port-of-Spain (Electorate 8,835)

A.A. Cipriani (Socialist)*

Eastern Counties (Electorate 2,828)

C. H. Pierre

St George (Electorate 3,651)

Paul Bissessar (unknown)
A. C. B. Singh (Independent Socialist)
Aldwyn Maillard (Socialist)*
(F. E. M. Hosein returned unopposed last election)

Victoria (Electorate 3,436)

T. M. Kelshall (Independent)
Harold Mahabir (Socialist)*
Harold Piper (Independent Socialist)
(Kelshall returned unopposed in the last election)

St Patrick (electorate 3,031)

T. Roodal (Socialist)*
Premchand Bunsee (Independent Socialist)

Caroni (electorate 2,384)

E. A. Robinson (Independent)
S. Teelucksingh (Independent Socialist)

* Labour candidates

Tobago (electorate 1,657)

Isaac Hope (Independent)
George F. Samuel (unknown)
John Isaac King (Independent)
Source: *TG* 5 January 1933

Appendix 8

Results of the 1933 elections

Three constituencies were uncontested – Port-of-Spain, St Patrick and the Eastern Counties

Victoria

T. M. Kelshall	791
H. Piper	517
H. Mahabir*	764

St George

A. Maillard	750
A. C. B. Singh	159

Tobago

I. Hope	346
J. I. King	117

* Labour candidates

Appendix 9

Manifesto of Timothy Roodal

Mr Roodal's Manifesto

TO THE ELECTORS OF THE COUNTY OF ST. PATRICK

FELLOW ELECTORS

Some of your number have invited me to contest at the forthcoming election the seat in the Legislative Council for the County of St. Patrick as a Labour and Socialist Candidate.

It is with pleasure and a sense of pride that I accept the great honour you seek to do me. I can only assure you that if I am returned I shall always uphold, and be true and loyal to, the great traditions of Labour and Socialism, based as they are on the great fundament of "the Fatherhood of God and the brotherhood of man," a fair day's wage for a fair day's work and a square deal for the underdog.

As Labour is built on this firm and steady foundation, as she is advancing onward and upward, not destroying but constructing, adjusting and consolidating her position, – and as she is one the eve of returning into power to guide the destinies of this great and mighty Empire, of which we form an integral factor it is incumbent on you to return only those who could conform to the Labour and Socialist platform.

The following are the planks of my platform:- (1) Poor relief; (2) Better Housing Accommodation; (3) Reduction of Taxes; (4) The imposition of an Export Tax on Oil; (5) Competitive Examination for entry into the Civil Service; (6) Introduction of a Statutory Eight Hour Day; (7) A minimum wage Bill; (8) Labour Bureaus; (9) Repeal of the Seditious Publication Ordinance; (10) Control by Government of the price of gasolene (sic) (11) Retrenchment.

Again thanking you and assuring you of my desire to serve.

I am, & c.,

Sgd. TIMOTHY ROODAL.

Source: *Labour Leader* 7 January 1928

www.ingramcontent.com/pod-product-compliance
Ingram Content Group UK Ltd.
Pitfield, Milton Keynes, MK11 3LW, UK
UKHW021845100926
8556IPUK00019B/1057

9 781803 743721